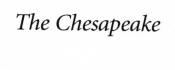

*The Chesapeake*

# The Chesapeake
## An Environmental Biography

## JOHN R. WENNERSTEN

*Maryland Historical Society*
**BALTIMORE**

Library of Congress Cataloging-in-Publication Data

Wennersten, John R., 1941–
    The Chesapeake : an environmental biography / John R. Wennersten.
        p.    cm.
    Includes bibliographical references and index.
    ISBN 0-938420-75-5 (ch. : alk. paper)
        1. Chesapeake Bay Region (Md. and Va.)—Environmental conditions—
    History. 2. Chesapeake Bay (Md. and Va.)—History. I. Title.

    GE155.C48 W46 2001
    333.73'09755'18—dc21                                   2001045251

Manufactured in the United States of America.
The paper used in this publication meets the minimum requirements of
the American National Standard for Information Sciences Permanence of
Paper for Printed Library Materials ANSI Z39.48-1984

The Maryland Historical Society extends special thanks to the Joseph Meyerhoff
Family Charitable Funds for generous support of this publication.

Cover photograph by David Prencipe

*To my wife, Ruth Ellen,*
*and my sons, Stewart and Matthew,*
*my most important Chesapeake resources*

# Contents

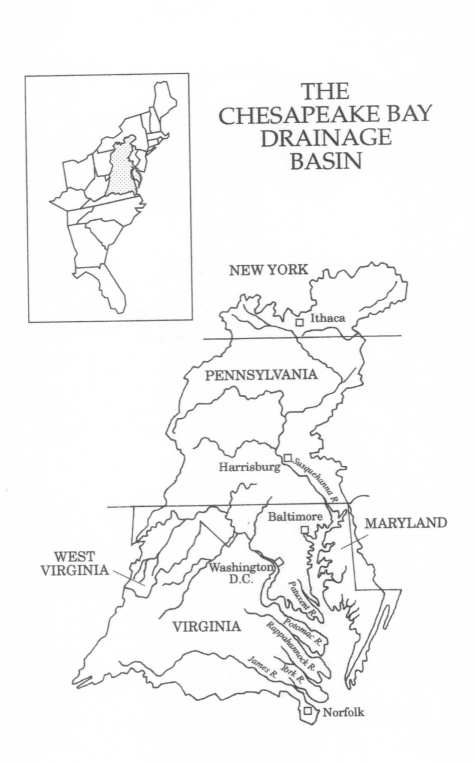

# THE CHESAPEAKE BAY DRAINAGE BASIN

NEW YORK

□ Ithaca

PENNSYLVANIA

Harrisburg □ *Susquehanna R.*

Baltimore □

MARYLAND

WEST
VIRGINIA

Washington
D.C.

*Patuxent R.*

VIRGINIA

*Potomac R.*

*Rappahannock R.*

*James R.*

*York R.*

□ Norfolk

# Introduction

"Environmental history seems always a narrative of pathos."
— Jack Temple Kirby, *Poquosin*

"Treading lightly on the land would restore a nature that was active, vital, and deeply sensual."
— Carolyn Merchant, *Ecological Revolutions*

Today the Chesapeake Bay of mid-Atlantic North America is an estuary in crisis. It is currently under assault by commercial and industrial development, population growth, agricultural pollution, resource mismanagement, and political ineptitude. At the heart of the crisis, from its declining oyster industry to the toxins found in its increasingly murky waters, are human— not aquatic—problems. Most of them begin far away from the bay itself, along the rivers that feed it. They begin with people who see little connection between themselves and the health and vitality of the Chesapeake. Most residents of the Chesapeake country today are metropolitan nomads. They do not react strongly to the destruction of the Chesapeake environment because their dependence on land and sea is not immediate to their feelings and livelihood.

People, as ecologists often point out, are the dynamic element in their own environment. Currently more than fifteen million live in the drainage area of Chesapeake Bay; most within a few hours' drive of the estuary. Population in the bay country is projected to grow 20 percent in the next thirty years, reports Saunders Hillyer, lands program director at the Chesapeake Bay Foundation. Population projections for the first years of the new twenty-first century indicate that another 2.5 million people will soon settle in the watershed, and their appetite will be voracious. Per capita consumption of land has more than doubled in the past thirty years. People in the Chesapeake are now using .66 acres of land per person.[1] Of the 2,700 swimming,

---

1. Howard Means, "The Great Outdoors," *Washingtonian Magazine,* April 1990.

floating, and flying species the bay supports, the most nettlesome by far is *Homo sapiens.*

A few facts on the pressures on the bay as an environmental resource are illuminating. In 1982 almost nine million pounds of pesticides were applied to the Chesapeake Bay country, an average of 1,148 pounds per square mile of cropland. Most of these toxins found their way to Chesapeake waters. In the same year approximately twenty-eight tons of phosphorus and one hundred thousand tons of nitrogen fertilizer flowed into the bay as "non-point" pollution. Over time Baltimore Harbor and its Patapsco River, and Norfolk Harbor and the Elizabeth River have become toxic industrial sinks where the concentration of poisonous metals in sediment is more than fifty times that in the middle of the bay. Toxins affect fish and oysters that feed on the bottom.[2] Add to this the treated and untreated sewage from thousands of Chesapeake communities, and sediment from real-estate development, and one can only wonder how the Chesapeake has been able to survive at all in modern times.[3] In his 1999 *State of the Bay Report,* Chesapeake Bay Foundation president William C. Baker noted that "water pollution from excessive nitrogen and phosphorus remains the Bay's most serious problem and it will continue to be until there is a long-term Baywide trend towards reduced levels of these polluting nutrients."[4]

The Chesapeake is the major waterway to Baltimore's busy harbor and serves twenty-four other ports in sixteen political subdivisions. It is a giant basin of salt, brackish, and fresh water fed by forty-eight tributaries. The world's most productive estuary, it yields annually some fifty to seventy million pounds a year in shellfish and finfish. As the late oceanographer Dr. Ian Morris observed, "we've almost got two Chesapeake Bays. One you can treat—formed by tributaries, the lakes and the rivers with a fragile nature that can go wrong. Then there's a big part of the Bay, the mainstem, that

2. United States Environmental Protection Agency, *Chesapeake Bay Program: Technical Studies, A Synthesis* (Washington, D.C., September, 1982], 22.

3. Tom Horton and William Eichbaum, *Turning the Tide: Saving the Chesapeake Bay* (Washington, D.C.: Island Press, 1991), 69. Tom Horton notes that by 1988 Virginia had the largest flow of sewage into the Bay (419 million gallons per day) followed by Maryland (356 million gallons per day), the District of Columbia and its Virginia and Maryland suburbs (300 million gallons per day), and Pennsylvania (280 million gallons per day).

4. Chesapeake Bay Foundation, *1999 State of the Bay Report,* September 17, 1999.

comes in contact with oceans. It might not be as free-flushing as you might like, but it's where man's influence is less."[5]

Chesapeake waters have been troubled since colonial times, and observers then and later commented on the despoliation of the Chesapeake landscape. As early as the Civil War, scientists were reporting the depletion of the Chesapeake fishery. The health of the bay and its tributaries was an important public issue by the end of the nineteenth century, and it would be erroneous to assume that environmental concern in the Chesapeake is a recent phenomenon. The only new development is the sheer magnitude of the bay's problems.

The Chesapeake is also known by its many rivers, both sluggish and powerful, possessed of romantic, strange-sounding Indian names like the Pocomoke, the Patuxent and the Rappahannock. Long before they were arteries of exploration, commerce, and development, these tributaries were natural arteries for spawning fish, home to shad and herring, and the source of fresh water for the bay's turbulent life cycle. Of these rivers, three have been especially notable for their impact on both nature and the human community: the James, the Potomac, and the Susquehanna. The James and the Potomac are long easily navigable rivers that have served historically as highways to the interior of the Chesapeake watershed. Along their banks, river towns and plantations grew. Later, canals enabled ambitious promoters and agriculturalists to transcend the limitations posed by the rapids of the fall line. The Susquehanna, last of the triad, is the most turbulent and unpredictable. Source of most of the fresh water that enters the bay, the Susquehanna in storm season boils and heaves its way south through the mountains and gorges of Pennsylvania to wreck havoc on Maryland's tidal waters. Too shallow for navigation and too strong ever to be completely tamed, the Susquehanna has always been the great variable in the environmental equation of Chesapeake history.

The Chesapeake Bay country was always a manipulated environment. Indians gave their name to the region, fired its forests, carved their agricultural systems, and harvested the fishery in ways reminiscent of most cultures in the throes of an environmentally transforming Neolithic revolution. Indians pursued their own selfish and material interests, often in part-

5. Interview with Dr. Ian Morris, Maryland Center for Environmental and Estuarine Studies, Horn Point, December 10, 1983.

nership with Europeans. To see Indians as sound ecologists and precursors of the modern environmental movement is too long for what never was.

As the colonial English emigrants spread up the river systems of the bay country, they attacked the forest to produce farms and plantations more in harmony with their own world view than in accommodation to the wilderness. Tobacco was the new profitable commodity of the English Chesapeake, and racial slavery provided the labor that the refuse of England's shore could no longer supply. An empire founded on smoke transformed the bay country. Gradually streams became polluted, the landscape eroded, the water quality began to deteriorate, and flash floods and spring freshets poured into the Chesapeake carrying debris and sediment of the tidewater regions and beyond.

Particularly in the nineteenth century, the development of towns and cities like Norfolk, Baltimore, Annapolis, and Washington, D.C., added an urban dimension to the problems of the Chesapeake. Factories, tanneries, and a burgeoning population tended to use the bay as a sinkhole. Cholera epidemics were common, forcing community leaders to pay greater attention to public health problems. Public sanitation in the nation's capital was especially appalling, and by the 1880s the pollution of the Potomac River with untreated sewage began to have calamitous consequences for shellfishing in the western regions of Chesapeake Bay. By 1889 Baltimore Harbor was known as "one of the great stenches of the world."

Further compounding the bay's problems were the immense logging operations in Pennsylvania along the Susquehanna River, which removed forest cover and intensified the floods of an historically dangerous river. The lumber barons of Williamsport, Pennsylvania, knew not and cared not for the consequences of the huge rafts of timber that they sent down river to be milled into lumber at Port Deposit, Maryland, and other sites. In an age when most Americans believed that land and water were unlimited it was easy to plunder an environment and move on.

It is more than a little ironic to note that, as the bay began to undergo some of the most severe ecological stresses in its history, the Chesapeake entered its golden age. From 1865 to about 1917 the Chesapeake fishery provided thousands of tons of fresh fish, crabs, and oysters and the estuary became world renowned for its seafood. Similarly, wealthy yachtsmen and sportsmen who deplored the loss of game from Delaware Bay and hated the pollution of the New Jersey shore turned increasingly to the Chesapeake Bay for recreation and leisure. Yacht builders for the corporate barons of America flocked to Annapolis, making the town a major ship-building metropolis.

By the turn of the century, the Chesapeake Bay increasingly came under the watchful eye of federal and state agencies who attempted to conserve the estuary's rapidly diminishing resources and improve the water quality. Unfortunately, regulatory squabbles, interstate rivalries, and government ineptitude limited conservation efforts in that region until well after World War II.

Significantly, most of the bay country remained primarily a stable agricultural region until the 1940s, despite the pressures of economic and population growth. Even an area like the Patuxent River watershed, which is within the shadow of our nation's capitol, retained two-thirds of its agricultural land base. After World War II the Patuxent began to hemorrhage its woods and farmland to development, and since the 1980s the amount of agricultural land in the Patuxent watershed is only about a third of what it was in the late nineteenth century.[6] The loss of much of Maryland's landscape to commercial and residential development and its attendant environmental impact on the bay has occurred in the life span of a single generation. Economic and demographic pressure on the environment came with such overwhelming intensity that, unlike the far West, the mid-Atlantic never had the luxury of time to debate the proper and efficient use of its lands and waters. Urbanization in Maryland came to dominate land use patterns in the Chesapeake long before it began to affect the West. Furthermore, in the Chesapeake region growth has often meant that some state or community gained material benefits while others suffered environmental damage. Environmental externalities such as mutual resource sharing have often brought Maryland, Virginia, and Pennsylvania into the federal courts, and arguments over access to natural resources and estuarine rights have wound their way ever upward until they were adjudicated by the United States Supreme Court.

Since the 1940s, enormous sums have been spent doctoring the Chesapeake Bay. In the last decade probably $100 million has been spent on water quality and conservation efforts. The monolithic study of the health of

---

6. "Agricultural Database Patuxent River Watershed," United States Geological Survey, National Mapping Division, August, 1999.

Chesapeake Bay commissioned by the Environmental Protection Agency in 1975 by itself cost $27 million by 1982.[7] Yet the patient has not improved and continues to do badly; largely in part due to the enormous quantity of sewage and municipal waste that continues to flow into the bay. Today reclamation, the misguided process of dredging and filling wetlands, has powerful supporters. The first commercial dredger of Chesapeake marshland came from Holland in 1766 to build the Chesapeake and Delaware Canal.[8] Even though reclamation of our marshes is legally proscribed, we have yet to see the last assault on our wetlands.

Historically, the Chesapeake never captured the public imagination in America as powerfully as did Yellowstone, Yosemite, or even the Hudson River Valley. The land around the bay is exceedingly flat, and during the early years of the Republic the bay was used principally as a traffic lane for the penetration of commerce in land on the James, Potomac, and other rivers. In his *Notes on the State of Virginia*, Thomas Jefferson gave scant mention of the Chesapeake. His attention focused on the mountains and the development of an American inland empire in the West. And although George Washington made a good deal of money harvesting shad on the Potomac, he was preoccupied with real-estate ventures in the upper reaches of the tidewater and the Ohio Valley beyond.

Although the Chesapeake is an inland sea, it does not have the sharp contrasts and rugged beauty of the Hudson Valley, which since colonial times has been a magnet on the east coast for tourists and travel writers. The Chesapeake does not promise a rough continent behind it as does the Hudson. The Chesapeake had no great novelist like James Fenimore Cooper, who in such stirring novels as *The Last of the Mohicans* painted a region rich in history and adventure. (In a small irony, Cooper was born and raised near Lake Otsego, New York, the wellspring of the Chesapeake.) The bay's perception problem began to change by the 1870s when prominent writers like Bayard Taylor of *Harper's Monthly Magazine* and others wrote romantic tributes to the Chesapeake country. Taylor was smitten by what he called

7. Steven G. Davison, Jay G. Merwin, John Capper, Garrett Power and Frank R. Shivers, Jr., *Chesapeake Waters: Four Centuries of Controversy, Concern and Legislation* (Centreville, Md.: Tidewater Publishers, 1997), 160.

8. Ralph H. Brown, *Historical Geography of the United States* (New York: Harcourt Brace, 1948), 103–7.

a quiet and tranquil land "with its Italianate climate and fruitfulness of Normandy." For these writers the Chesapeake tidewater was an enchanted region of colorful manor houses, genteel traditions, and pleasant living.[9] Such themes echo today in the pages of the *Washington Post* and *National Geographic,* heralding the region as an idyllic place of independent farmers, duck hunters, and watermen. Even those unfamiliar with the region are still able to make an association with Chesapeake crabs and oysters. James A. Michener's novel *Chesapeake* romanticized the bay and added fuel to an already explosive boom in real-estate development.

The subject of changes in the land has been examined by historians like William Cronon, Joseph Petulla, Roderick Nash, Albert Cowdrey, and others in the field of environmental history.[10] They have shown how changes in the environment unleashed great forces for social transformation in America. In this book I hope to extend the work of these pioneering scholars and in my own small way contribute to rewriting the traditional narrative of American social and economic history by looking at the impact of human agency on a regional environment. I am interested in showing how historical events surrounding the exploitation of the Chesapeake Bay country's natural resources have led to its contemporary environmental problems. Too often scholars have functioned as if environment, politics, economy, and public values were separate spheres. I hope to generate some fresh insight on the relationship of agriculture, maritime industries, urbanization, politics, and public opinion in the mid-Atlantic. This study focuses not just on the Chesapeake Bay itself but on the entire watershed from the Appalachians to New York to Pennsylvania to tidewater Maryland and Virginia. As writer Tom Horton has recently remarked to public audiences, the more the bay declines and its way of life vanishes, the more "Save

9. Bayard Taylor. "A Peninsular Canaan," *Harper's Monthly Magazine,* 57 (May, 1879): 802; "Down the Eastern Shore," *Harper's Monthly,* 50 (October 1871): 702–8. See also, "The Chesapeake Peninsula," *Scribner's Monthly,* 3 (March, 1872): 513–23.

10. William Cronon, *Changes in the Land: Indians, Colonists and the Ecology of New England* (New York: Hill and Wang, 1983); Joseph Petulla, *American Environmentalism, Values, Tactics, Priorities* (College Station: Texas A&M University Press, 1980);Roderick Nash, *Wilderness and the American Mind* (New Haven: Yale University Press, 1967); and Albert E. Cowdrey, *This Land, This South: An Environmental History* (Lexington: University Press of Kentucky, 1983).

the Bay!" bumper stickers one sees on automobiles and the more books are written about life and leisure in the Chesapeake Bay country. Perhaps the trend illustrates how we don't appreciate something until we are well along the way to losing it.

Over the course of time our modes of knowing about the environment and our treatment of nature as a social, economic, and scientific construct have changed remarkably. In her pioneering work, *Ecological Revolutions,* Carolyn Merchant points out that New England underwent two major ecological revolutions that powerfully influenced the development of human consciousness in the space of little more than two centuries. These revolutions, the pre-industrial subsistence and commodity agricultural revolution and the industrial revolution, set the stage for the transformation of that region. They introduced new forms of thinking and profoundly altered the ways in which humans valued themselves and related that "self" to the larger external world. The Chesapeake Bay country in its first two and a half centuries underwent similar revolutions, though on a somewhat different scale. Today changes in the global economy and the rise of ecological consciousness offer a chance for us to develop an ethic that is "oriented toward establishing sustainable relations with nature."[11]

Central to understanding Chesapeake Bay is a concept developed by the great ecologist, Garrett Hardin—"the tragedy of the commons." Like all commons in history, the Chesapeake Bay has been exploited because it was accessible and belonged to no one. When nothing is valued for what it is, everything is destined to be wasted. As Hardin and others have noted, the problem has no practical solution, for when private property supplants "the commons" it is difficult outside of coercion to prevent the satisfaction of human wants. Sometimes the tragedy of the commons has been more the "tragedy of the commoners," as those with most to lose in a declining fishery were the very instruments of that decline. Political control over the bay has always been bifurcated, and until recently no state or regional authority has had either the tools or the power to prevent environmental abuse. "Private property" continues to be the totem of the American social system.[12]

---

11. Carolyn Merchant, *Ecological Revolutions, Nature, Gender and Science in New England* (Chapel Hill: University of North Carolina Press, 1989), 267.

12. Garrett Hardin. "The Tragedy of the Commons," *Science,* 162 (December, 1968): 1243–48. See also Hardin, "Living on a Lifeboat," *Bioscience,* 24 (1974): 561–68.

Environments to a great extent are cultural constructs. They exist in the eye of the beholder, and over time the Chesapeake has meant many different things. Early settlers trying to survive in a difficult pestilential environment had neither the leisure nor the luxury to view landscape and seascape with thoughts of conservation. Until recently popular attitudes toward the environment focused on nature as an exploitable commodity. Different times beheld different ethics, and it would be wrong to see only malice in the behavior of previous generations. Today rationales for preserving threatened natural environments involve contentious economic, societal, and political factors. Analyzing environments in terms of wise use or cost-benefit analysis is not always fruitful or rational because the environment is not a ledger book. Arguments that environments or ecosystems contribute to our stability and survival often are dismissed by critics who argue that it is quite difficult to determine what "survival" means. One anti-ecology critic has gone so far as to assert that "if we want undisturbed natural areas, it might be best to develop some of them in other countries."[13] We are only just beginning to grapple with issues about nature's long-term costs and benefits—the value of open space or the worth of clean water.

The environmental history of the Chesapeake is full of odd conjunctions, of symbiosis and survival, of neglect and despoliation. This book, therefore, is about both the changing Chesapeake Bay and the transformation of environmental values. If we can learn anything from the history of Chesapeake Bay we can at least see how our environment and its attendant public policy problems have evolved and how the region has been transformed both for good and ill.

When it comes to environmental transformation and disaster, the Chesapeake is hardly unique. Great Plains cattlemen, for example, built their industry upon the open range, a basis that became more and more insecure. Following severe winter losses in the 1880s, the range cattlemen disappeared. A catastrophe similar to that which befell the American Indians is now being visited upon the bay country's farmers, watermen, and independent craftsmen. As Wendell Berry has pointed out, "sooner or later all of us who live on the land become redskins—that is we become designated victims of

---

13. Martin H. Krieger, "What's Wrong with Plastic Trees?" *Science,* 179 (February, 1973): 447.

an entirely ruthless, officially sanctioned and subsidized exploitation."[14] The Chesapeake Bay country faces serious challenges in the years to come. In part this is a consequence of its near-colonial status relative to the rest of the mid-Atlantic, because it produces so many raw materials like seafood, timber, and poultry.[15]

This book is not a scientific study of Chesapeake biota. Scholars seeking such information should turn to specialized works like *Chesapeake Bay:An Introduction to an Ecosystem* published in 1982 by the U.S. Environmental Protection Agency. Rather, this book focuses on ideas about the value of an estuarine environment over time and traces the evolution and problems of public stewardship of the bay. The eighteenth and nineteenth centuries are disproportionately represented here because during these years that the principal human decisions on the bay's fate were made. Those early conflicts and contention set in motion precedents that determined the course of the bay in modern times.

As a cultural and ecological model for the Atlantic coast, the Chesapeake is probably indispensable. We thrive best when both man and wild environments like the bay survive. Thus this book ultimately deals with that most difficult question, the question of propriety. What is the appropriate culture and technology for the Chesapeake Bay region? We as a nation are much defined by our waters, and estuaries like the Chesapeake are cradles of life that ultimately help to define and shape the human experience.

Until recently, wrote cultural historian Leo Marx, the ideological counterpart of the nation's physical expansion has been its "celebration of quantity. What has been valued most in American popular culture is growth, development, size and by extension, change in wealth and power." As long as people operate on the assumption that economic considerations override the preservation of anything there can never be an environmental ethic of any sort, and the environment can never be given any permanent protec-

14. See Ernest Staples Osgood, *The Day of the Cattleman* (Chicago: University of Chicago Press, 1929), 216. Wendell Berry, *The Unsettling of America: Culture and Agriculture* (San Francisco: Sierra Club Books, 1977), 4.

15. For another perspective on the colonial dependency of a bioregion see Herbert Fite, "The Great Plains: Promises, Problems and Prospects," in Brian W. Blouet and Frederick C. Luebke, eds., *The Great Plains, Environment and Culture* (Lincoln: University of Nebraska Press, 1977), 200.

tion. Fortunately a powerful trend in "green thinking" is calling into question a society dominated by mechanistic and commercial systems of value. "Green thinking" holds that it is time for nature to reestablish its dominion. Diversification in nature results in greater biological control and stabilization of the environment.[16]

Occasionally environments are rescued and stabilized by what can only be referred to as a change in public perception. This can be as simple as changing from knowing a place and living in it to cherishing a place and living responsibly in it. If our Chesapeake region is to be saved and cherished it will require ceaseless watchfulness and care because the contrary values of the so-called "affluent society" threaten to obliterate the region. What action we take and how quickly we take it, argued Leo Marx, "depend in large measure upon the credibility of the alarmists."[17] Before we succumb to the shibboleths of growth and progress we must ask where progress is taking us, whether we consent to the ride, and if the destination is worth the price of the ticket. As we enter the new century with anticipation and concern we would do well to recall the lament of William K. Brooks, the Johns Hopkins scientist, who looked at the Chesapeake's future in 1891 and wrote: "We have wasted our inheritance by improvidence and mismanagement, and blind confidence."[18]

16. For an extended discussion of whether the new "green thinking" is incompatible with Western traditions and Western civilization see Eugene C. Hargrove, "The Historical Foundation of American Environmental Attitudes," *Environmental Ethics,* 1 (Fall 1979): 209–40.

17. Leo Marx, "American Institutions and Ecological Ideals," *Science,* 170 (November, 1970): 947–48, 951.

18. W. K. Brooks, *The Oyster: A Popular Summary of Scientific Study* (Baltimore: Johns Hopkins University Press, 1891), 3.

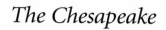

*The Chesapeake*

## CHAPTER ONE

# The New World Environment
# of Chesapeake Bay

"There is also hope of finding gold, for the neighboring people
wear bracelets of gold and long strings of pearls."
— *Instructions to the Colonists*, Lord Baltimore, 1633

"Heaven and Earth never agreed to frame a better place for man's
habitation."
— Captain John Smith, *True Relation of
Occurrences and Accidents in Virginia*

## Early Geologic History

In terms of its geologic history, Chesapeake Bay is a relatively young environment. About twenty thousand years ago, according to geologists, an ice sheet extended from the Arctic Circle to the headwaters of the Susquehanna River in New York and Pennsylvania. In some places this sheet was a mile in thickness. Although the region that was to become the Chesapeake Bay country was free of ice, it would not be free of its long-term effects. The great ice sheet would carve out the mountains and valleys of the Chesapeake watershed. Also during this period the level of the sea was much lower than its current position, having retreated beyond a dry Atlantic continental shelf.

The Blue Ridge mountains five hundred million years ago were a volcanic island chain, and the hills and valleys of the western Chesapeake Bay country still give evidence of the lava flow that created them. In the mid-Cretaceous period of one hundred million years ago, the region that became the Chesapeake was a wet, tropical place, the habitat of meat-eating and herbivore dinosaurs. Over the vast ranges of time mastodons, saber-toothed tigers, and crocodiles inhabited the Chesapeake. The vertebrae of long extinct and strange animals have been dug out of the sandy soil of Charles County's Calvert Cliffs. Paleo-Indians hunted elephants in the Chesapeake region.[1] Evidence of a mysterious environmental past haunted

1. C. Vance Haynes Jr., "Elephant Hunting in North America," *Scientific American*, 224 (1966): 104–12.

the first European settlers of the Chesapeake. In his 1724 book, *The Present State of Virginia,* the ever-curious parson Hugh Jones remarked that "in most places at a great depth, and far distant from the sea, are many great beds of strange shells, and bones, and teeth of beasts vastly different from any land or water animals now found."[2]

The large coastal plain left by retreating glaciers some fifteen thousand years ago was subsequently carved into a low valley by the powerful waters of the Susquehanna River. A subarctic climate prevailed in what is now the bay country. Scientists estimate that the mean annual temperature was probably twenty degrees Fahrenheit colder than it is now. The freshwater streams of the present Potomac, York, and James Rivers flowed into the Susquehanna, which discharged its waters into the Atlantic Ocean at what is now the Virginia Capes. Over time the sea pushed two hundred miles inland, engulfing this low valley. The ocean flooded all but the large beds of resistant deposits of land called necks (small peninsulas) so characteristic of the Chesapeake today. Geologists use a curious word to describe the process of engulfment. They refer to it as a "transgression"—a strong word for such an impersonal natural process. The rising waters of the bay, quips Chesapeake scientist J. R. Schubel, made waterfront property just as perilous an investment in the prehistoric period as it is today. "For most of the past 15,000 years man has been fleeing from the sea. He still is." From fifteen thousand years ago until five thousand years ago, the most dramatic environmental impact in the region was the sea, which rose three feet each century. To dramatize the impact of this rise in sea levels, imagine this: a rise of only thirty feet in sea level would inundate Baltimore, Washington, Norfolk, Annapolis and the Eastern Shore. Compared to the dominion of rivers and seas in the region, human control over the Chesapeake has been remarkably slight.[3] Roughly three thousand years ago the bay as we know it was complete. Dense forests covered the shorelines and the bay's rivers and tributaries flowed into a clear and fecund estuary.

An important result of the early geologic history of the bay was the development of the "piedmont rivers" of the western Chesapeake. Rivers like

2. Hugh Jones, *The Present State of Virginia* (1724, repr., Chapel Hill: University of North Carolina Press, 1956), 51.

3. J. R. Schubel, *The Living Chesapeake* (Baltimore: The Johns Hopkins University Press, 1981), 5, 8.

the Potomac and James have their origin in the rolling Appalachian pied-mont, and at their fall lines or rapids these rivers are not navigable. In the early colonial history of Maryland and Virginia this fall line would limit the expansion of plantation society and constitute a cultural dividing line in the Chesapeake between upcountry farmers and the tidewater gentry. As early as the seventeenth century, European artists like Theodore de Bry sketched Indians panning for gold in the piedmont rivers using hollow reeds to extract the metal from the sand. Indians used gold for ornamental and ceremonial purposes. Well into the twentieth century prospectors flocked to Great Falls on the Potomac to pan gold and find a rich nugget.[4]

## Chesapeake Waters

The Chesapeake Bay is the largest estuary on the East Coast of North America. As a mixing zone of fresh and salt water, the balance between the two is vital for plant and animal life in the bay. The fresh waters from the Susquehanna and other tributaries enable the Chesapeake to renew itself from the ocean's saline onslaught. The Susquehanna alone discharges forty thousand cubic feet per second of fresh water into the bay. This hydraulic or "flushing" capacity allows the Chesapeake to renew itself. The estuary is home to more than 2,700 species of plants and animals. Since prehistoric times man has harvested fish, crabs, and oysters from the Chesapeake. The presence of large oyster middens (refuse heaps) along the rivers of the Chesapeake's Eastern Shore are testimony of the bay's magnificent bounty long before Europeans and Africans came to the region. The Nanticoke In-dians, for example, were fond of raking up large piles of oysters from creek bottoms with forked sticks and indulging in feasts that sometimes lasted several days. The largest oyster midden left by the Indians in the Chesa-peake Bay region covered nearly thirty acres of land near Pope's Creek on the Potomac River.[5]

Although there are more than 850 bays and estuaries along the coasts of the United States, the Chesapeake Bay is considered by many scientists to

4. Karen R. Kuff, "Gold in Maryland," Occasional Papers, Maryland Geological Society, 1987.

5. John R. Wennersten, *The Oyster Wars of Chesapeake Bay* (Centreville, Md.: Tidewater Publishers, 1981), 5.

be the crown jewel. In the words of Dr. Eugene Cronin of the University of Maryland, it is "more valuable for human uses than any other estuary and vulnerable to destruction from human use and abuse."[6]Because large and varying amounts of fresh water enter the bay, the salinity of the Chesapeake constantly changes, creating a rare and difficult environment to which organisms from fresh or salt water must adapt.

Estuaries like the Chesapeake are dynamic environments where physical and chemical changes can be abrupt over short distances. The word estuary itself is derived from the Latin *Aestuarium,* which means boiling or heaving sea tide. Following the rhythm of the tides the salinity of bay waters can change from 8 percent to 10 percent as water makes its transition from the rivers to the estuary. Circulating waters trap sediments with nutrients that sustain plant life that in turn serves as the base of the Chesapeake food chain. The muck and mire of Chesapeake wetlands are rich soils fed by rivers and enriched with oxygen by tidal action. The estuary's brackish water provides a nursery for a variety of organisms and fish that eventually move out to sea. The bay's wetlands, to which large carnivorous fish are not adapted, are also a haven for much small marine life. Aquatic plants, marsh grasses and microscopic plants called phytoplankton provide a food mass upon which all other life in the bay depends. Clams and oysters filter the water and grow fat from nutrients. Fish graze in the floating meadows of plankton as well as in sea grass and become the food of crabs and other carnivores like the osprey. Over the past three centuries the Chesapeake has been one of the best fishing grounds in the world, often producing as much as twelve tons of fish per square mile. In recent times, however, the fishery has been less able to withstand man-made changes. Estuarine marshlands have figured largely in human history as both refuge and quagmire. "Since Biblical times, the transformation of wetlands astride principal river mouths has been part of the ancient western dream of conquest over nature's physical forces," notes ecologist Joseph Siry.[7]

The Chesapeake lies north and south, 195 miles in length, and curves only two points of the compass from the Capes to Swan Point. The bay's

6. Cited in Arthur Sherwood, *Understanding the Chesapeake* (Centreville, Md.: Tidewater Publishers, 1973), 39.

7. Joseph V. Siry, *Marshes of the Ocean Shore, Development of an Ecological Ethic* (College Station: Texas A&M University Press, 1984), 4.

depth varies considerably from 156 feet to about nineteen feet in the channel at the entrance to the Susquehanna River. With a mean depth of only twenty-one feet, the bay is a shallow pan easily disturbed by winds and storms. More than 150 rivers, creeks, and branches empty into the bay, and the Chesapeake has nearly five thousand miles of shoreline. The Chesapeake Bay watershed covers 64,900 square miles, including parts of New York and Pennsylvania as well as Maryland, Virginia, and West Virginia. Its drainage area equals the geography of six New England states.

The Chesapeake's main tributaries are equally impressive. These navigable rivers influenced settlement patterns in the region and facilitated direct trade between plantation wharves and London merchants. Given the utility of the Chesapeake waterways, colonists in the region built few roads. This reliance on the Chesapeake as an artery of commerce and cultural and political exchange was the principal factor in the development of Maryland and Virginia. The bay obviated the necessity for the development of towns as commercial centers because Chesapeake planters could ship directly to the merchants of Bristol and London.

On the western shore of Virginia are four navigable rivers: the Potomac, Rappahannock, York, and James. Of these the most easily traveled was the James River, a tributary that extended 160 miles to the fall line. During the colonial period, vessels of 150 tons could sail up the James to within five miles of Richmond. The Potomac also offered a long navigable admittance of 110 miles from its mouth to the falls above Georgetown. On Maryland's western shore the Patuxent was an exceptionally deep river that admitted very large ocean craft for twenty miles. The Choptank and the Miles on the Eastern Shore were navigable for more than ten miles, as was the Patapsco River at the north end of the bay. Despite its mighty presence, the Susquehanna was navigable for only five miles, and shoals blocked the rivers of the Eastern Shore of Virginia.

The direction of wind largely influences the climate of the Chesapeake Bay. North and northwest wind brings clear and cold air, while winds from the south bring warm temperatures even in mid-winter. One of the well-known characteristics of the Chesapeake is the variableness of its winds, and because of them temperatures in the region can suddenly change from extremely cold to uncomfortably hot. Southwest winds bring dangerous squalls and electrical storms that hasten mariners to safe anchorages. While on a Quaker mission in Maryland in the winter of 1672, George Fox noted that in the midst of fierce cold "the wind turning into the South, it grew so hot that we could hardly bear the heat and the next day, the wind changing back into the North, we could scarcely endure the cold."[8]

While it has no dangerous rocks or reefs, the shallow Chesapeake is encumbered with numerous shoals that are a hindrance to navigation. Rivers deposit sand and gravel in offshore bars, causing many a hapless mariner to unexpectedly run aground while sailing on the bay. The geography of the bay remains remarkably unchanged even though the waters of the Chesapeake have eroded some islands and indented the coastline. A comparison of Captain John Smith's seventeenth-century map with a current map of the area finds the old drawing still fairly accurate. Even the names that Smith gave to the islands and rivers remain. It should also be mentioned that for a century after the original settlement at Jamestown, Smith's chart remained the standard map of the colonial Chesapeake. As late as 1873 this map was used as a reference to solve a heated boundary dispute between Maryland and Virginia.[9]

## Indians and Chesapeake Ecology

The Indian presence in the Chesapeake Bay country goes back as far as ten thousand years. While little remains of Paleo-Indian culture, it is possible today to find fluted projectile points in farm fields that were fashioned by the Indians of this period. Our first significant glimpse of the aboriginal population of the Chesapeake Bay comes during the Archaic Period (8,000 to 1,000 B.C.) By that time Indians were living in well-defined geographic area in bands of twenty-five to fifty people. From their chopping and scraping tools of polished stone, we can surmise that they were deer hunters. Writes Chesapeake Indian historian Frank W. Porter: "Because they did not know how to grow their own food and did not have any domestic animals, the Archaic Indians had to travel with the changes of the season to find food." The Archaic Indians of the Chesapeake killed animals with javelins or short spears ejected by hand-held spear throwers. Chesapeake Indians at

8. George Fox, *Journal & Autobiography: Two Years in America, 1671–1673,* cited in Aubrey C. Land, *Colonial Maryland: A History* (Milwood, N.Y.: KTO Press, 1981), 64.

9. Richard Morton, *Colonial Virginia: The Tidewater Period, 1607–1710,* 2 vols. (Chapel Hill: University of North Carolina Press, 1960), 1:24.

this time were also inadvertent ecologists. Deer have such a high reproductive capacity that had they not been hunted, they would have overgrazed their habitat.[10]

The Indians were the products of a bay and river environment and the influence of their habitat bound them tightly to their way of life. The rivers also served as channels of communication that enabled the Indians of the early Chesapeake to maintain contact with tribal cultures far up the Susquehanna River and into the Appalachians via the Potomac.

By the dawn of English settlement the Indians of the Chesapeake comprised a number of small, semi-nomadic tribes that congregated in villages, usually along river banks. These villages varied in size and permanence. Archeologist Wayne E. Clark has found subsistence remains in the area of the Potomac that indicate "horticultural base camps that were occupied throughout the year by part of the populace. Their economy was based on slash and burn agriculture with extensive deer hunting for the procurement of meat." Besides meat, deer provided an "elaborate bone industry" of tools and decorative items.[11]

Long before the contact period, corn production had been an Indian staple in the region. Corn, which is derived from the wild grass of southern Mexico known as teosinte, had spread over several thousand years from Chile to the mouth of the St. Lawrence River.[12] By the time of Captain John Smith aboriginal corn or maize culture in the Chesapeake was quite sophisticated. Corn was basic to the aboriginal diet, and English visitors to the Chesapeake noted that Indian warehouses brimmed with it. Captain John Smith during his exploration of Chesapeake Bay reported extensive Indian cornfields, and in 1620 William Stratchey, who had spent time in Jamestown as lieutenant governor of the colony, observed that Indian communities in tidewater Virginia had between two and three thousand acres of land planted in vineyards and corn. In his narrative on the Virginia plan-

10. Frank W. Porter III, *Maryland Indians, Yesterday and Today* (Baltimore: Maryland Historical Society, 1983), 5. See also Charles Hudson, *The Southeastern Indians* (Knoxville: University of Tennessee Press, 1976), 44–55.

11. Wayne E. Clark, "The Origin of the Piscataway and Related Indian Cultures," *Maryland Historical Magazine*, 75 (1980): 15.

12. George M. Beadle, "The Ancestry of Corn," *Scientific American*, 242 (1980): 112. Beadle argues that the development of corn by Indians "remains man's most remarkable plant-breeding achievement."

tation Thomas Harriot noted that "mayze is a graine of marvelous great increase; of thousand, fifteen hundred and some two thousand fold." Harriot noted that in addition to baking corn bread, the Indians boiled and parched corn to make hominy."[13] Indians were versatile farmers and grew a number of crops—melons, cucumber, gourds, peas, and beans. They also grew large crops of sunflowers and made soup from the seeds. The Indians grew several crops together in their gardens, usually squash with corn. Until recently Indians of the Chesapeake have been depicted as migratory hunters devoid of any ability to clear the forest and cultivate the land. The actual historical record, however, shows the Indians to be cultivators of the soil and keepers of a rich biological store. When the first settlers arrived, they enountered indigenous people who were well along the route to a successful Neolithic revolution and hardly savages inhabiting a dense impenetrable wilderness.[14] Historian Timothy Silver writes that despite an extensive Indian agriculture, there was little soil erosion. "Many of the first Europeans," he writes, "were amazed at the clarity of the various streams and rivers which seemed to carry little sediment even during high water."[15]

When the athletic and well-fed Princess Pocahantas visited the half-starved colonists at Jamestown she could not have failed to recognize the

13. According to Helen Rountree and Thomas Davidson, it was maize agriculture that gave such a distinctive character to Indian culture in the Chesapeake. See Helen Rountree and Thomas E. Davidson, *Eastern Shore Indians of Virginia and Maryland* (Charlottesville: University Press of Virginia, 1997), 21. See also William Strachey, "Historiae of Travaile Into Virginica Britanica, 1610–1612," in David B. Quinn, ed., *New American World: A Documentary History of North America to 1612,* 5 vols. (New York: Arno Press, 1979– ), 5:352; and Thomas Harriot, *Narrative of the First Plantation of Virginia* (1590) in Wayne Rasmusen, ed. *Readings in the History of American Agriculture* (Urbana: University of Illinois Press, 1960), 14. The significance of corn exchange in the personal and economic relations of whites and Indians in the early Chesapeake is summarized in Stephen R. Potter, "Early English Effects on Virginia Algonquian Exchange and Tribute in the Tidewater Potomac," in Peter H. Wood et al., eds., *Powhatan's Mantle, Indians in the Colonial Southeast* (Lincoln: University of Nebraska Press, 1989), 151–72.

14. For elaboration on this theme see Michael Williams, *Americans and Their Forests* (Cambridge: Cambridge University Press, 1992), 33.

15. Timothy Silver, *A New Face on the Countryside: Indians, Colonists, and Slaves in the South Atlantic Forests, 1500–1800* (Cambridge: Cambridge University Press, 1990), 49.

superiority of Indian agriculture over the miserable and incompetent attempts of the English newcomers. Ironically for the latter, Carl Sauer has noted, "food was at hand for man, beast, and fowl in diversity and abundance unknown to Europe."[16] The Indians also had a keen interest in wild plants and were astute botanical observers. They gathered acorns, harvested wild grapes, and collected several species of roots and tubers. Indians of the Chesapeake followed four basic types of subsistence: they hunted game animals, gathered wild fruits and nuts, fished the bay and rivers, and harvested crops.

The richness of the aboriginal food base indicates a complex tribal system based on shared values and an appreciation of nature that enabled them to live well in a generous land without spoiling it. Indian women also played a major role in aboriginal agriculture, indicating significant gender differentiation in the local Indian economy. As agriculturalists, women had significant political authority in the warrior dominant tribal culture. Historian Gary B. Nash has observed that women even played an important role in Indian military affairs "for it was the women who supplied the moccasins and food for military expeditions, and a decision to withhold those supplies was tantamount to vetoing a military foray."[17] Hugh Jones, an Episcopal cleric and historian, described Indian women in less flattering tones. "The women," Jones wrote, "do all the hard labor such as cutting down the trees, planting corn etc., carrying burthens, and all other work; the men only hunting, fishing, and fowling, and drinking, dancing, and sleeping."[18] Jones also had little good to say of the Indians he encountered from the province of Maryland. The cause of their "diminishing" proceeded from "warrs among themselves." Although he thought the Indians were cowards in battle, "yett when taken prisoner and condemned, they'll dye like heroes braving the most exquisite tortures that cann be invented, and singing all the time they are upon the racke."[19]

16. Carl Ortwin Sauer, *Sixteenth Century North America* (Berkeley: University of California Press, 1971), 295.

17. Gary B. Nash, *Red, White, and Black: The Peoples of Early America* (Englewood Cliffs: Prentice-Hall, 1974), 21.

18. Hugh Jones, *The Present State of Virginia* (Chapel Hill: University of North Carolina Press, 1956), 55.

19. Michael G. Kammen, ed., "Maryland in 1699: A Letter from the Reverend Hugh Jones," *Journal of Southern History*, 29 (1963): 372.

In tilling their plots, the Indians used mattocks or hoes with long handles. They grew tobacco in separate fields away from their beans and corn. The tobacco was the harsh-tasting but potent *nicotana rustica* which was used for tribal political and religious ceremonies. Much like medieval peasants, the Indians lived in villages and small towns, usually consisting of ten to twelve quonset huts of log and bark whose roofs and walls formed an inverted U. These villages also contained "sweating houses," primitive saunas out of which, said one observer, "when they are almost smothered with heat, they run into a river." They used sweathouses to cure physical ailments and "distempers."[20]

The Indians were the first Chesapeake watermen. They were skilled at harvesting oysters with wooden rakes from the shallow bay waters and shooting large fish with wooden arrows. At night they built torch fires in their canoes and paddled to shoal waters to attract fish. Usually the Indians gigged them with sharpened sticks. They were especially skilled in the use of weirs and traps to harvest large amounts of fish and grilled their huge catches over open fires. The most detailed study of Indian fishing is provided by Robert Beverly, a Virginia planter and historian who described a sturgeon hunt in 1705.

> The Indian way of Catching Sturgeon, when they came into the narrow part of the Rivers, was by a Man's clapping a Noose over their Tail, and by keeping fast his hold. Thus a Fish finding itself entangled, wou'd flounce, and often pull him under Water. and then that Man was counted a Cockarouse or brave Fellow, that woul'd not let go; till with Swimming, Wading, and Diving, he had tired the Sturgeon and brought it ashore.[21]

For Thomas Harriot, the perceptive reporter of the first Virginia settlement at Roanoke Island, the Indians were a remarkable water-borne culture. "Doubtless it is a pleasant sight," Harriot wrote, "to see the people,

20. Ibid. 55.
21. Robert Beverly, *History and Present State of Virginia, 1705,* quoted in John C. Pearson, "The Fish and Fisheries of Colonial Virginia," *William and Mary Quarterly,* series 2, vol. 22 (1942): 357. Pearson notes that even though the first colonists were aware of the record fish harvests along the shores of New England and Carolina, they brought no fishing gear with them to Jamestown in 1607.

sometimes wading and going, sometimes sailing in those rivers, which are shallow and not deep, free from all care of heaping up riches for their posterity, content with their state, and living friendly together of those things which God of his bounty hath given unto them." Additionally, he noted that the Indians were very sober in their eating and drinking and subsequently very long lived because they did not oppress nature."[22] In *Keepers of the Game*, Calvin Martin suggests that need and not technology was the overwhelming factor in the Indian's relationship with nature and was regulated by "cultural considerations" that respected the religious significance of man's relationship with game as well as the agricultural world. Hunting taboos, for example, regulated how much game would be taken in the forest and "the overkill of wildlife would have been resented by the animal kingdom as an act comparable to genocide." From an Indian spiritual viewpoint, the prey had as much right to the forest as the hunter.[23] Also, as Carolyn Merchant has noted, "patterns of production were integrated with their cosmologies and forms of consciousness on the eve of European colonization."[24] Europeans did not understand the formative powers of nature, nor did they understand the interdependence of flora, fauna, and seascape. The Europeans would undertake an ecological revolution in the Chesapeake that had as its main thrust the extermination of wild animal life and the commodification of nature. Nature was something to be bought, sold, traded, and developed—ideas that would remain in force in the bay country long after the English colonists had vanished into history.

English colonists in the Chesapeake found that it was nearly impossible for the Indians to starve at the hand of nature. Therefore, in conflicts with the Indians, the colonists waged environmental warfare by burning their corn fields and pulling up their fishing weirs. During the Indian wars of 1622 in Virginia, for example, a colonial militia sailed up the Potomac River and put a vast acreage of Indian corn to the torch. Throughout the period,

---

22. Thomas Harriot, "A briefe and true report of the new found land of Virginia" (1588), in Michael Alexander, ed., *Discovering the New World Based on the Books of Theodore DeBry* (New York: Harper and Row, 1976), 77, 79.

23. Calvin Martin, *Keepers of the Game, Indian-Animal Relationships and the Fur Trade* (Berkeley: University of California Press, 1978), 39.

24. Carolyn Merchant, *Ecological Revolutions, Nature Gender and Science in New England* (Chapel Hill: University of North Carolina Press,1989), 23.

Indians and Europeans had what anthropologist Helen Rountree has called "multiple conflicting agendas."[25]

According to historical demographers, the Indian population in coastal Maryland and Virginia at the time of the first English settlement can be estimated at about 33,000, with some 11,000 of these resident in Maryland in 1630. Forest scholar Michael Williams has argued that the population density of most areas of the Atlantic forest was "probably even greater than that of densely settled parts of western Europe."[26] Using figures provided by Douglas Ubelaker, one can estimate that over 30 percent of all Indians living in the south Atlantic region lived in the Chesapeake area.[27] Further, Hu Maxwell estimated Indian population density in Virginia to be about one Indian per 1,600 acres at a time when the American average was more like one Indian per 8,000 acres. The aboriginal population density can probably be explained by the rich Chesapeake Bay fishery and the successes of local maize agriculture.[28] This was a thickly settled area which may have gone into a demographic crisis even without contact with European culture and disease.

Indian tribes of the Delmarva Peninsula [Delaware, Maryland and Virginia] during the seventeenth and eighteenth centuries have recently been studied by historical anthropologists Helen Rountree and Thomas Davidson. They have artfully reconstructed the lost world of tribes like the Accomacs, Choptanks, Wicomiss, Pocomokes and Nanticokes whose names continue to identify the rivers, marshes and forests of the region.

Delmarva Indians were farmers and foragers who had a keen knowledge of the edible foods of Chesapeake waters and marshlands that ranged from oysters and fish to *tuckahoe* [a marsh tuber] and wild rice. Unlike other

25. Helen C. Rountree, "The Powhatans and the English: A Case of Multiple Conflicting Agendas," in *Powhatan Foreign Relations, 1500–1722* (Charlottesville: University Press of Virginia, 1993), 173–205.

26. Williams, *Americans and Their Forests*, 33.

27. Silver, *New Face on the Countryside*, 38; Reamor R. DeLaBarre, "Chesapeake Indian Population" (Unpublished M.A. thesis, Johns Hopkins University, 1958); Douglas H. Ubelaker, "Prehistoric New World Population Size: Historical Review and Current Appraisal of North American Estimates," *American Journal of Physical Anthropology*, 45 (1976): 664.

28. Hu Maxwell, "Use and Abuse of Forests by the Virginia Indians," *William and Mary Quarterly*, 19 (1910): 73–76.

areas of the Chesapeake watershed like New York, tribal populations were small, rarely exceeding five hundred members, a fact that partially explains why the demographic onslaught of the English marginalized and eventually overwhelmed the tribes of the Eastern Shore of Maryland and Virginia. Life was always more difficult for Indians on the Virginia Eastern Shore than in Maryland, where lush oak forests provided ample supplies of nuts and deer. What emerges from studies like this is a portrait of self-sustaining Indian populations who understood their environment and were aware that it could treat them harshly at times.[29] However, the bay's bounty in nut-bearing trees, deer, fish, and wetland tuber plants exempted Chesapeake Indians from harsh considerations of population control such as infanticide practiced elsewhere in aboriginal North America.

Thus, while the Indians lived satisfactorily, theirs was certainly no Edenic existence. Long before the coming of the Europeans, the Indians experienced wars, famine, and pestilence. As Alfred Crosby and others have pointed out, Indians originally came from Asia and were but the first invaders of the American environment. It is difficult to know how much change the Indian initiated in the Chesapeake ecosystem. The factors that precipitate environmental change are complex. As William Cronon has argued in a recent study, it is "increasingly difficult to know which ecosystem is interacting with which culture."[30]

The opinion that the Chesapeake Bay country at the time of the initial European settlement was covered with a vigorous unbroken forest primeval is erroneous. Respected forest historian Hu Maxwell has noted that while woods covered a great deal of the Chesapeake landscape, Indians had made serious inroads on them. According to Maxwell, at the time of the first English explorations, "Indians had succeeded in deforesting thirty or forty acres for every individual in their tribes."[31] Furthermore, Gordon M. Days's research also suggests that the forests of the mid-Atlantic had been

29. For an extensive study of Eastern Shore Indian tribes of Virginia and Maryland from the seventeenth century to the breakup of the last reservation during the War of 1812, see Helen C. Rountree and Thomas E. Davidson, *Eastern Shore Indians of Virginia and Maryland*. Pages 203–15 on Indian ecology are very useful.

30. William Cronon, *Changes in the Land, Indians, Colonists, and the Ecology of New England* (New York: McGraw Hill, 1983), 14.

31. Hu Maxwell, "Use and Abuse of Forests," 73.

significantly disturbed by the Indians well before the first arrival of the white man. The Indians, Day writes, "commonly set fire to the forests in order to drive game, improve visibility for travel, drive away reptiles, increase the supply of grass seeds and berries and for offense and defense in war."[32] In many localities of the Chesapeake only mature trees remained, and they were so thinned and depleted that the forest resembled more a park than a wilderness. Captain John Smith observed that the trees of the Chesapeake had been so pruned by fire "that man may gallop a horse through these woods." Indians, adds agricultural historian E. L Jones, were so adept at firing the woodlands for cornfields and growing browse for deer that they "inadvertently created ecological conditions favorable to the entry of white farmers." Jones argues that "it would have taken a generation of English settlers to produce the extent of the ready-made Indian clearings that they found in the Chesapeake and elsewhere."[33] As the Indians depended upon a large amount of firewood, the forests of the Chesapeake were systematically cut; the use of firewood by the Iroquois and Delaware tribes in the region has been described by historical ecologists as prodigious. Indians needed about 16,000 poles for longhouses in villages that contained a thousand people and thousands of stakes for their palisades. Indian clearings in woodlands often ranged from 150 to six hundred acres. These fields for obvious reasons would subsequently become the first tobacco plantations of the English. The Indians usually felled trees with stone axes, and in the harvesting of firewood women worked side by side with the men. When the distance between available timber and the village became inconvenient, Indians moved to a new forest locale.[34]

In 1625 an expedition of English colonists saw at a great distance fires set by the Indians on the southwest side of Chesapeake Bay, and sightings of smoke and the haze of forest fires set by Indians were common in the early colonial period. William Byrd recorded in his diary the discomfort he suffered while surveying the dividing line between Virginia and the Carolinas "from firings of the woods by the Indians."[35] The fires tended to modify the

32. Gordon M. Day, "The Indian as an Ecological Factor in the Northeastern Forest," *Ecology*, 34 (1953): 334.

33. Cited in Maxwell, "Use and Abuse of Forests," 88; E. L. Jones, "Creative Disruptions in American Agriculture, 1620–1820," *Agricultural History,* 48 (1974): 515.

34. Williams, *Americans and Their Forests,* 37.

35. Quoted in Maxwell, "Use and Abuse of Forests," 93.

species composition of Chesapeake forests and create large treeless areas. The nitrogen-rich ash of forest fires may have increased soil fertility. One forestry expert who has studied the impact of Indian fires suggests that Indians were careful users of fire as a tool to manage the land and to promote their welfare.[36] What is truly remarkable, however, is how well the forest and its underlying vegetation were able to regenerate themselves even after fires of massive proportions. The first English colonists reported an abundance of wild strawberries, which could only thrive in open spaces or thinned woods. Also wild fruit trees like the plum and persimmon are sun-loving, and colonists found them plentiful in the Chesapeake country.

Despite Indian incendiarism, the seventeenth-century forest of the Chesapeake had a distinctive cathedral-like quality. Honeysuckle, laurel, and sumac rose from the water's edge to form a green perimeter to large stands of woods. The vast forest of the early Chesapeake was a world of mighty first growth trees, and soaring walnut, oak, and cypress trees eighteen feet in circumference darkened large parts of the forest floor. One early English visitor to the Chesapeake was profoundly impressed by the woodlands, remarking that the forest "seemed like the retreat of some Ancient Druids."[37]

The first contacts between Indian and white European in the bay country were hardly friendly. History records that in 1561 a party of Spanish navigators entered the Chesapeake Bay, kidnapped an important Powhatan Indian, and carried him off to Mexico. The Spanish, in search of gold and silver, believed that the natives would help them locate a Chesapeake El Dorado. While the Indian was of little help in this regard, the colonial viceroy, Don Luis Velasco, was most impressed by his aristocratic bearing. The Indian was subsequently named "Don Luis" after the viceroy and transferred to Cuba. Later this proud citizen of the Chesapeake traveled to Spain, lived at the king's expense, and fooled Dominican monks into believing that the Chesapeake country was a worthless disease-ridden place.

In August 1570, "Don Luis" returned to the New World, this time under the command of one Captain Vincent Gonzales, whose mission was to plant

---

36. Stephen J. Pyne, *Fire in America: A Cultural History of Wild Land and Rural Fire* (Princeton: Princeton University Press, 1982), 74.

37. Quoted in Arthur Pierce Middleton, *Tobacco Coast: A Maritime History of the Chesapeake Bay in the Colonial Era* (1953 repr. Baltimore: Johns Hopkins University Press, 1989), 60.

Jesuit missionaries in the bay country. Gonzales located the mouth of the Chesapeake on September 10, 1570, and landed "Don Luis" and a party of Jesuits led by Juan Bautista Segura. The Indians they encountered seemed destitute. They had suffered a poor corn harvest, and the previous winter had been particularly harsh, killing off the game. With the onset of winter "Don Luis" and the Indians deserted the Jesuits, leaving the priests to subsist on roots and herbs from the forest. "Don Luis" and his confederates subsequently attacked the Jesuits when they were in a weakened state and clubbed them to death. Only a small boy named Alonso survived to tell the tale the following summer when a Spanish relief expedition arrived at the mouth of the Chesapeake. Sailors spotted the Indians wearing the Jesuits' robes. One Indian who came aboard was imprisoned by the sailors and taken back to Havana in chains.[38] Long before the coming of the English colonists, the waters of the Chesapeake would be troubled by racial conflicts. Red and white stood face to face in the bay country, and the Indians often regarded the latter as an audacious intruder and deadly enemy. As the European invasion of the Chesapeake intensified, Indian native culture deteriorated. Hostilities over the possession of the landscape grew accordingly.

## Arcadian Myth and Environmental Reality

While it is now generally accepted that Giovanni da Verrazano missed the Chesapeake during his epic voyage of exploration along the Atlantic coast in 1524, the mariner did establish contact with the coastal Indians. Verrazano noted in his log that he and his crew did not find a single stone on the land for a distance of two hundred leagues. The Indians, he also observed, were adept at using fire to make dugout canoes. While Verrazano named the region Arcadia, the mariner's treatment of the Indians was hardly "Arcadian." Verrazano's men kidnapped an old woman and snatched a child from her mother's arms.[39]

38. Woodberry Lowery, *The Spanish Settlements Within the Present Limits of the United States: Florida, 1562–1574*, Volume 2 (New York: Russell and Russell, 1959), 359–66.

39. Samuel Eliot Morison, *The European Discovery of America, The Northern Voyages, A.D. 500–1600* (New York: Oxford University Press, 1971), 298.

The first significant European exploration of the Chesapeake Bay was probably that of Captain Vincent Gonzales in 1588, eighteen years after he had brought "Don Luis" and the Spanish Jesuits. In that very decisive year in the imperial contest between England and Spain, Gonzales sailed a packet boat, the *San Lucar,* with thirty soldiers northward from St Augustine toward the Virginia coast with a mission of gathering intelligence on the extent of English settlement in that area. His vessel arrived at the mouth of the Chesapeake in June 1588. Entering the bay, Gonzales was impressed by the ease of navigation on the main body of water and its tributaries and commented on the fertility of the soil, the plenitude of the chestnut and walnut trees, and the abundance of deer and fish.[40]

The first English account of the environment of the Chesapeake Bay country is probably that of Sir Ralph Lane in the late sixteenth century. Lane was an experienced soldier of England's Irish wars who accompanied Sir Richard Grenville on a military expedition to Sir Walter Raleigh's ill-fated Virginia colony in 1585. During a scouting expedition in the Chesapeake, he reported that the natives were amiable and curious and that the land seemed good. The region, he wrote, was pleasant "for fertility of the soil and for the commodity of the sea, besides multitudes of bears [being excellent victual] with great woods of sassafras and walnut."[41] He also observed that the Indians smeared themselves with bear grease, which may have been designed to ward off pestilential Chesapeake salt marsh mosquitoes and green head flies.

Sir Walter Raleigh's colonists heard about the bay from Indians who visited Pamlico Sound, the region of the lost colony, in 1586. From their descriptions, John White sketched the Chesapeake on his crude map of Virginia. This vague reference excited Richard Hakluyt, the geographer, who urged Raleigh to occupy the new territory. Flemish historian and geographer Theodore De Bry identified the bay in his book, calling it *Chesepiocc*

---

40. Morison, *European Discovery of America,* 296–99; Lawrence C. Wroth, ed., *The Voyages of Giovanni Da Verrazano, 1524–1528* (New Haven: Yale University Press, 1970), 136; Juan Menendez Marques, "The Voyages of Vincente Gonzales to Chesapeake Bay in 1588," in David B. Quinn, ed., *New American World: A Documentary History of North America to 1612,* Volume 5 (New York: Arno Press, 1979), 60–63.

41. Cited in Michael Fox, *Undreamed Shores, England's Wasted Empire in America* (New York: Scribner's, 1974), 155.

*Sinus*, a name derived from the Indian word *Tschiswapeki* or great water.[42] The earliest known chart of the Chesapeake Bay from a navigational standpoint was that of Robert Tindall, who accompanied Christopher Newport on the first voyage of the Jamestown settlement in 1607. Tindall sailed up the James River to King Powhatan's village at the fall line. His map, however, deals mostly with the James and York rivers.[43] Maps like his of the Chesapeake Bay country are more useful as pieces of art than as instruments for seafaring. A general lack of detailed charts of the bay during the early years gave employment to local pilots who knew the channels, shoals, sandbanks, and occasional "oyster reefs" in the Chesapeake.

Midst all the promotional drivel of the late sixteenth and early seventeenth centuries, one work stands out: Thomas Harriot's *A Brief and True Report of the New Found Land of Virginia* (1590). Harriot combined his narrative with the drawings John White made of aborigines in the Carolinas during their stint on the Raleigh expedition to Roanoke Island. The work contains descriptions of birds, trees, fish, and animal life in general as well as some of the best cartography of the Atlantic coastline at that time. Harriot's was a down-to-earth New World that contained everything from the behavior of skunks to the eating habits of Indians. His book was a worthy product of an Oxford-educated Renaissance man.[44] Although Harriot's work was a generally up-beat account of the new found land, he had a healthy appreciation of the Indian as a cultural and military adversary. For Harriot, the New World was both fecund and problematic, a judgment that few could gainsay. Unfortunately the promotional tracts of the Virginia Company reached an audience far wider than Harriot's and promised a land that by "careful wisdomes" would produce gold and "Flowe with milk and honey." Captain John Smith's reports of the Virginia settlement at Jamestown added to the promotional fog of greed and optimism that surrounded the early Chesapeake.

As a front line dispatch from Virginia in 1608, Smith's *True Relation of*

---

42. Alexander, ed., *Discovering the New World* , 60–64.

43. William B. Cumming, "Early maps of the Chesapeake Bay Area: Their Relation to Settlement and Society," in David B. Quinn, ed., *Early Maryland in a Wider World* (Detroit: Wayne State University Press, 1982), 279.

44. Richard Beale Davis, *Intellectual Life in the Colonial South, 1585–1763* (Knoxville: University of Tennessee Press, 1978), 10–13.

*Occurrences and Accidents in Virginia* is a masterpiece of epic narrative that downplayed the problems with the Indians as well as the difficulties of seasoning in a perilous new environment. While Captain Smith wrote of his problems with Chief Powhatan and his fellow colonists, he nonetheless described the Chesapeake as a potential paradise. Smith wrote in felicitous phrases that have been widely quoted over the centuries in Maryland and Virginia: "Heaven and Earth never agreed to frame a better place for man's habitation. Here are mountains, hills, plains, valleys, rivers, and brooks all running into a fair bay, compassed but for the mouth with a fruitful and delightsome land."

The future of the Chesapeake and its inhabitants would change profoundly in the summer of 1608 when Captain Smith made his epic voyage of exploration up the bay. When Smith set sail from Virginia in an open barge of "three tonnes burthen," with a frightened and muddled crew of fourteen, the struggling English settlement of Jamestown was a year old. In addition to the thrill of adventure, Smith hoped to find economic opportunities in the region that would help defray the expenses of New World colonization for the Royal Virginia Company. The crew consisted of six inexperienced gentlemen, seven soldiers, and Smith's friend Walter Russell, a "doctor of Physicke." They carried bread and water and were well supplied with munitions. Captain Smith had no real authority over the men and had to lead them by exhortation and the force of his character. His voyage of discovery lasted about two months and covered more than three thousand nautical miles.

At great risk to himself and his crew and with exhausting labor, Smith visited many inlets, rivers, and bays on both sides of the Chesapeake from Cape Charles to the head of the bay. On the Maryland side he missed several rivers like the Severn and Magothy.[45] Smith sailed up the Patapsco and may have entered the harbor of present-day Baltimore. From his writings we know that Smith ascended the Potomac River as far as the falls above Georgetown and brought back with him valuable ethnographic information on the Indian tribes of the region. His writings also reveal that he had a sharp eye for environmental detail. Of the *Patawomeke* [Potomac] River

45. See Steven G. Davidson, Jay G. Merwin Jr., John Capper, Garrett Power, and Frank R. Shivers Jr., *Chesapeake Waters:Four Centuries of Controversy, Concern and Legislation* (Centreville, Md.: Tidewater Publishers, 1997), 23.

Smith wrote: "It is navigable 140 miles, and fed as the rest with many sweet rivers and springs, which fall from the bordering hils. . . . . many of them are planted and yeelede no less plenty and variety of fruit that the river exceedeth the abundance of fish." Smith also noted that the region was rich in otter and beaver."[46] For possible Indian trade, Captain Smith and his men carried an assortment of beads, bells, looking glasses, and copper jewelry. If Smith could not win by entreaty, he would buy Indian friendship. Part farce and part odyssey, Smith's Chesapeake journey constitutes an important account of the bay at the dawn of settlement. When Smith subsequently published his account, it would electrify the English imagination and provide a storehouse of information [true and erroneous] on the environment of Chesapeake Bay.

On entering the Chesapeake from the James, Smith was carried by strong winds across the water to the vicinity of Cape Charles. Near the present site of Cheriton, Virginia, Smith discovered a village of Indians he called Accohannocks. Ever the skilled ethnologist, he counted forty Indians who spoke the Powhatan language. Having acquired a small vocabulary of Indian words in this dialect during his short tenure at Jamestown, Smith was able to communicate with them. These Indians, he found, were part of a vast confederation that had been put together by the great chief Powhatan who ruled from his capital near the present site of Richmond.

In retrospect it seems odd that Smith sailed with such an incompetent crew. Few, including Smith, knew much about seamanship, and the bay soon proved a formidable match for them. While sailing northward along the Eastern Shore, Smith wrote, "we discovered the winde and waters so much increased with thunder, lightening and raine, that our mast and sayle blew overboard and such mighty waves overracked us in that small barge that with great labor we kept her from sinking by freeing out the water."[47] The crew ultimately repaired the sail with its shirts but lost their food, leaving them to subsist on oatmeal, water, roots, and fish. Apparently the "gentlemen" on board got more than they bargained for from a springtime Chesapeake squall.

Years of scholarly controversy has determined that Smith sailed up the

46. Philip Barber, ed., *The Complete Works of Captain John Smith,* 3 vols. (Chapel Hill: University of North Carolina Press, 1972),1:148, 228.
47. Ibid., 2:163–65.

Pocomoke River in search of fresh water. In the process he discovered what ship captains ultimately put to advantage on long voyages—that tannin from tree roots and vegetable matter gave the water a dark brown color and kept it "sweet" or drinkable. The islands off Pocomoke Sound still bear Smith's name. After storms, thirst, and several misadventures with hostile Indians in the area of the Nanticoke River, Captain Smith sailed his barque into the Sassafras River. Fish were everywhere so plentiful that Smith and his men jokingly attempted to catch them with frying pans. Ever the gallant soldier, Smith even speared a sting ray with his sword and received a wound from the ray's tail that caused him considerable pain.

From a commercial standpoint, the voyage was a bungled affair and Smith found neither gold nor lasting peace with the Indians. His voyage did provide, however, valuable information as to the extent of the Chesapeake and the nature of its aboriginal inhabitants.[48] Captain Smith managed to draw a crude but accurate map of the Chesapeake shoreline, but his notions of the hinterland dissolved into drawings of nude Indians and trees. For this explorer, the great interior of the Chesapeake Bay country remained *terra incognita*. While Smith followed the Indian term in calling the estuary the Chesapeake, it is doubtful that the Indian word *Chisapeack* conforms to Smith's translation of it as "Mother of Waters." The closest translation from Algonquian is probably "great salt oyster bay," but this conundrum is better left to etymology than to history.

Taken together, the most interesting and accurate parts of the early Chesapeake country narratives deal with the bay itself. From a maritime point of view, the bay's fishery was simply astonishing and prompted excited comment throughout the colonial era. The variety, size, and abundance of fish in the Chesapeake easily surpassed that of European waters. The bay was the domain of the porpoise, giant sea turtle, pike, carp, mullet, shad, sturgeon, blue crab, eel, and oyster. Looking beyond the bay, Sir George Percy, a member of Captain John Smith's settlement, in 1607 observed that the land around it was "good and fruitful, with excellent timber. We did see many Squirrels, Conies, and diverse other Fowles and we found store of Turkie

48. Robert L. Swain Jr., "The Chesapeake Bay: Origin of the Name and First Explorers," in Charles Branch Clark, ed., *History of the Eastern Shore of Maryland and Virginia,* 2 vols. (New York: Lewis Historical Publishing Company, 1950), 1:1–14.

nests and many eggs."[49] Such an environment prompted exclamation and surprise from Reverend Andrew White, the Maryland Jesuit, who came to the bay on *The Ark* in 1634. Wrote Father White: "I will end therefore with the soyle, which is excellent, so that we cannot sett downe a foot, but tred on strawberries, raspaires, fallen mulberry vines acchorns, walnutts, saxafras." The woods abounded with "infinite bird life — swans, eagles, geese, ducks and partridge," Father White exulted, "by which all appear, the place abounds not alone with profit, but also with pleasure."[50] Father White was also one of the first in the region to note vast stores of white and blue marl which could serve a number of uses as a fertilizer and soil conditioner. The exuberant Jesuit envisioned an English system of general husbandry based on corn, vegetables, and imported silk production. He also sensed the possibilities of a local wine industry based on the vast expanses of wild grapes flourishing in the Chesapeake.

All of the Chesapeake's early explorers noted that the Indians were well-acquainted with oysters and valued them highly. While at Cape Henry, Captain Smith and his men discovered an Indian campfire in a forest clearing and found several baskets heaped with oysters. The Englishmen ate some raw and roasted the others and Captain Smith found them "large and delicate in taste." Oysters were so plentiful that ships would run aground on oyster beds like the huge "oyster reef" at the mouth of King's Creek on the Virginia shore. When George Percy served as commander of the early Jamestown settlement in 1607, he confiscated large mounds of freshly roasted oysters from the terrified Indians.[51]

Interestingly, the first settlers in the Chesapeake identified bay oysters as hardship food. Colonists on Kent Island, for example, often complained during economic and political crises that they "were reduced to eating oysters." Also, during the so-called "starving time" in Jamestown, a number of colonists repaired to the oyster banks of the lower James River and subsisted on nothing but oysters and a pint of Indian corn apiece per week. Much later in 1705 Francis Makemie, the famous Presbyterian preacher,

49. "Observations of Sir George Percy," in Lyon Gardiner Tyler, ed., *Narratives of Early Virginia, 1606–1625* (New York: Charles Scribner's Sons, 1907), 10.

50. "Father White's Relation, 1634," in Clayton Colman Hall, ed., *Narratives of Early Maryland, 1633–1684* (New York: Charles Scribner's Sons, 1910), 46.

51. Tyler, *Narratives of Early Virginia*, 10.

encouraged the reluctant colonists to exploit the Chesapeake's resources and formulated an elaborate plan for transoceanic trade in pickled oysters. His dream of turning the Chesapeake into a seafood empire was not realized during the colonial period.[52]

From a literary standpoint, the most interesting environmental narrative of the early Chesapeake was that of George Alsop. When he published his *A Character of the Province of Maryland* in 1666, Alsop wrote that he was so excited about Maryland "that I am almost out of breath." Alsop had served as an indentured servant at Patuxent on the western shore of the bay colony in exchange for his £6 passage to the New World. His account of the richness of the Chesapeake excited London readers. "Deer are as common as London cuckholds," he wrote, and the wild life so ample that no man starved in Maryland. "Dwell here and be rich," Alsop advised. "For every man lives quietly and follows his labor. Here's no Newgates for pilfering felons nor any Bridewell to lash the soul of Concupiscence into chaste repentance."[53] The popularity of Alsop's work in England helped to weaken the reliability of other reports from indentured servants that Maryland was more like Hell than a deer park. But settlers of that time believed the environmental information that they wanted to believe. Reality seldom intruded.

English settlers were both fascinated and troubled by the Chesapeake climate. It was far different from that which they had experienced in England. As Carville Earle has written, the English were possessed of a notion that latitude determined climate. Thus the English reasoned that the Chesapeake would be the same in climate and environment as the temperate Mediterranean. "Here," Earle writes, "was a premise for uproarious comedy and, at times, tragedy." The early environmental history of the Chesapeake would be a chronicle of failed attempts at vineyards and wine making and silk making. Also, the English were unaccustomed to the storms and torrential rains of the Chesapeake as well as the tropical summers of the region.[54] The English could not comprehend the powerful environmental

52. Wennersten, *Oyster Wars of Chesapeake Bay*, 5–6.
53. George Alsop, *A Character of the Province of Maryland* (1666, repr., Baltimore: Johns Hopkins University Press, 1980), 36. See also Darin E. Fields, "George Alsop's Indentured Servant in *A Character of the Province of Maryland*," *Maryland Historical Magazine*, 85 (1990): 221–35.
54. Carville Earle, "Environment, Disease, and Mortality in Early Virginia," *Journal of Historical Geography*, 5 (1979): 365–66.

forces that were at work in the Chesapeake Bay country, and it took them a long time to learn new ways. Environmental adaptation, at times, was painful indeed.

Even in the context of disease and war-ravaged seventeenth-century Europe, the mortality rate of white Englishmen in the Chesapeake during the first settlement of Virginia was astonishingly high. Of 7,549 persons who came to Virginia between 1607 and 1624, only 1,095 survived. Disease made the early Chesapeake a grave for 6,454 Englishmen. War and natural causes probably claimed upwards of only 1,500.[55]

The English arrived at Jamestown in May 1607, and experienced enervating heat and subsequent death-dealing autumnal fevers. Problems of adjustment to climate as well as personal health and diet probably help to explain why the original 105 colonists were reduced to thirty-two by the spring of 1608. Sir George Percy remarked in his journal that the cold winter of 1607 had decimated the colony. The next two winters, fortunately, were mild. William Strachey, who spent three years in Virginia, reported "fayre and summery weather." Although the Virginia settlers were not as meticulous in their observations of the weather as the Puritans of Massachusetts Bay, we do know that the Chesapeake was spared hard winters and heavy snowfalls until the winters of 1641–42 and 1645–46.[56] Given the unpredictability of winter weather in the region, colonists never knew what to expect. The characteristic feature of Chesapeake weather, as we have seen, was the variability of its winds, which in turn greatly influenced temperatures. When the wind began to blow out of the northwest, temperatures could plummet. And much to the surprise of colonists, winter blizzards could come out of the south with lightning swiftness. Winter squalls and bay storms were violent and made navigation on the Chesapeake a harrowing experience.

One of the major flaws of the Jamestown enterprise was that investors of

55. Wyndon B. Blanton, "Epidemics, Real and Imaginary, and Other Factors Influencing Seventeenth-Century Virginia's Population," *Bulletin of the History of Medicine,* 31 (1957): 454.

56. See David M. Ludlum, *Early American Winters* (Boston: American Meteorological Society, 1966), 1:32–35. See also Robert I. Rotberg and Theodore K. Rabb,. eds., *Climate and History: Studies in Interdisciplinary History* (Princeton: Princeton University Press, 1981), 3.

the Virginia Company badly miscalculated the Chesapeake environment. Staunch mercantilists that they were, they believed that the English colonies should be a source of valuable commodities and expected Jamestown to produce large amounts of gold, silver, copper, salt, and gemstones. Precious time was wasted on attempts at silk production and the raising of exotic plants. As we have seen earlier, the English believed their own propaganda about the region rather than seeking to understand the environmental realities of the bay country. The colonists thought the natives would prove to be faithful servants and believed they would easily discover precious metals. Neither hope proved true. Worse, the so-called "starving time" of the Jamestown colony in its early years ironically took place in an environment rich in agriculture and local fisheries. Simply put, cultural misperceptions and political factionalism nearly devastated the colony when the means of survival were everywhere at hand. Small wonder that Captain John Smith, who in his travels up the bay delighted in trying to catch fish in a frying pan, was so exasperated by the colonists' laziness and incompetence. Too many were merchant adventurers who abhorred any type of manual labor. In the Chesapeake region that gave sustenance, shelter, wealth, and leisure to nearly 30,000 Indians, the English fought each other over scraps of bread and may have resorted to cannibalism to survive. During his tenure as commander of the Jamestown colony, Smith finally brought a measure of prosperity and order to the contentious settlement. But when he sailed to England, famine ensued.

Throughout this trying period, the James River teemed with Atlantic sturgeon. In 1609 John Rolfe and others reported that two men could easily wade in the water and ax forty sizeable sturgeon weighing one hundred pounds each. Such an amount was enough to furnish each "starving" colonist with two pounds of fish daily and sufficient thiamine to ward off beriberi. Most colonists simply did not want to become fishermen and died as a result of their beliefs.[57] The only way the colony could survive was through constant reprovisioning from England and the hard dictatorial rule of colonial officers like Sir Thomas Dale and Sir Thomas Gates. When Gates became governor of Virginia in 1609, he removed many of the colonists from Jamestown upriver to a better environment within fifteen miles of the

57. See Pearson, "Fish and Fisheries of Colonial Virginia," 357.

falls. Called Henrico, this settlement had a fort, well-framed houses, and a hospital for the sick. This marked a new era of adaptation to the Chesapeake environment. Yet as late as 1616 the colony was a precarious enterprise whose 350 settlers hung on but grimly. The colony's fortunes improved when the Virginia Company decided to send farmers rather than gentlemen to the plantations of the Chesapeake. After 1630 concessions of free land brought more than 4,500 settlers to Virginia.

The Chesapeake Bay of this period also needs to be understood as a disease environment as much as a wilderness environment. Colonists brought many of their health problems with them. Ocean voyages were a long ordeal fraught with storms and other perils. The passage of the *Susan Constant, Goodspeed,* and *Discovery*, for example, lasted over four months, and the colonists arrived in such a dysentery-weakened and starved condition that few could work even if they wanted to do so. It took a long time for the settlers in Maryland and Virginia to "season" in the Chesapeake. Sir George Percy best summed up the early afflictions of Englishmen in the Chesapeake when he wrote that "our men were destroyed with cruell diseases such as Swellings, Flixes, Burning Fevers, and by warres, and some departed suddenly, but for the most part they died of mere famine." Those that survived were reduced to "most feeble wretches" surviving on "a small can of Barley sod in water to five men a day, our drink cold water taken out of the River, which was a floud verie salt, and at low tide of slime and silt, which was the destruction of many of our men."[58] Percy ends this part of his account with a reflection on the health and vigor of the local Indians who washed themselves in the river each morning. An important question to ask at this point is why was there such a dissimilarity of health between the two cultures? Gordon Jones, a medical researcher who has studied public health at colonial Jamestown during the initial period, has concluded that typhoid fever brought aboard ship to Virginia was responsible for many of the deaths at Jamestown.[59]

The first European settlers in the Chesapeake brought other virulent diseases with them as well. Among the worst was smallpox, a disease in histo-

---

58. "Observations by George Percy," in Gardner, *Narratives of Early Virginia*, 21–23.

59. Gordon Jones, "The First Epidemic in Colonial America," *Virginia Magazine of History and Biography*, 71 (1963): 3–10.

rian Alfred Crosby's phrase, "with seven league boots" as it was easily transported by boat, canoe, or horse. The pustules of the disease destroyed the skin and reduced the body to a horrible condition after an incubation period of ten to fifteen days. Algonquian Indians picked up smallpox from the Puritans of New England, and by the 1640s it was ravaging the aboriginal populations of the Chesapeake. In this case the disease traveled by Indian canoe down the Susquehanna as healthy Indians who fled the sick took the disease with them. Crosby found that the disease decimated the Indian populations by as much as 50 percent. Smallpox leapt the continent, reaching Indian populations in Puget Sound by 1783.

The Indians had no immunity to the diseases of the Old World. And disease probably had more to do with English success in pushing back the Indian on the Chesapeake frontier than military success or political accommodation. In addition to smallpox, the Indians had to contend with measles, diptheria, chicken pox, bubonic plague, yellow fever, whooping cough, dysentery, and influenza. In the holds of English vessels moored in the Chesapeake were a host of pathogens which could decimate tribes and destroy aboriginal culture. Alfred Crosby adds that in "virgin soil epidemics no one is immune so nearly everyone gets sick at once. Whether the Europeans or Africans came to Native Americans in war or peace, they always brought death with them."[60] For their part in the new disease environment created by Indian-European interaction in the Chesapeake, the Indians transferred intestinal parasites, yaws, syphilis, polio, and hepatitis to unsuspecting colonists.

English life spans were short in the early Chesapeake. Women in their childbearing years ran a much greater risk of dying from some disease, and childhood deaths were commonplace. In practically every respect, disease left its mark on those who survived the New World seasoning process. Historians Darrett and Anita Rutman have found that malaria, a European import, was rife in the Chesapeake by the late seventeenth century. No Chesapeake colonist was immune from this disease, and it was "more of a debilitator than a killer." Yet malaria disrupted the nascent agricultural system of the Chesapeake by "hampering productivity." The Rutmans also

---

60. Alfred Crosby, *Ecological Imperialism: The Biological Expansion of Europe* (Cambridge: Cambridge University Press, 1986), 210–13. See also Crosby, "Virgin Soil Epidemics as a Factor in the Aboriginal Depopulation in America," *William and Mary Quarterly*, 3rd series, vol. 33 (1976): 295.

found sharp geographical differences in health in various counties of the Virginia colony. Communities far removed from mosquito-infested swamps and salt marshes fared better in health than those that did. Further, English communities that penned their cattle and horses instead of allowing them to range in the forest fared better in health as the insects preferred animal to human blood. Concluded the Rutmans: "Economy, social structure, culture—all conceivably bore the imprint of malaria in the early Chesapeake."[61]

Finally, access to uncontaminated drinking water was probably the most important factor in the disease environment of the Chesapeake. For if the colonists drank contaminated water, they inevitably came down with dysentery, which reduced their ability to ward off pathogens. Carville Earle found a "marked improvement in mortality rates following the redistribution of the population into healthier freshwater environments." The demographic history of early Virginia is all the more tragic because the leaders of the colony were aware that contaminated water spawned epidemics. Political considerations as well as the fear of the Indian menace made them reluctant to disperse their people. "From a demographic standpoint," writes Earle, "the best thing that happened in early Virginia was the dissolution of the company with its fixation on Jamestown."[62]

## Enviro-Racial Dynamics and the Fur Trade

From an enviro-racial standpoint, Indian problems intensified the problems of colonists in Virginia. Chief Powhatan had a good grasp of the demographic implications of the European invasion of the bay country and was so belligerent that the Virginia Company began a ruthless campaign against the aborigines. Soldiers killed Indian children and put an Indian queen to the sword. Indian hostility to the foreigner did not extend to the African slave, however. During the uprising of 1622 in which Powhatan's warriors massacred many of the English, no African was killed. Historian

61. Darrett B. Rutman and Anita H. Rutman, "Of Agues and Fevers: Malaria in the Early Chesapeake," *William and Mary Quarterly*, 3rd series, vol. 33 (1976): 41–44, 60.

62. Carville Earle, "Environment, Disease, and Mortality in Early Virginia," in Thad W. Tate and David Ammerman, eds., *The Chesapeake in the Seventeenth Century, Essays on Anglo-American Society and Politics* (New York: W. W. Norton Co., 1979), 113, 125.

Philip Bruce believed that "their color had been influential in saving them from the ferocity of the savages."[63]

When Maryland colonists came to the Chesapeake in 1634, they suffered fewer environmental problems because they had better water supplies. The Indians they encountered had also been trading with the English and French for the better part of two generations. From his stronghold on Kent Island, William Claiborne had a prosperous trade in beaver pelts with the Susquehanna Indians. There were even a few Englishmen who had gone "native" and lived with the Patuxent Indians on the western Chesapeake shore. Captain Henry Fleet, a Potomac River fur trader in the 1630s had undertaken expeditions into the mountains beyond the fall line to obtain a rich store of beaver pelts. Like the rest of the small band of English traders who acquired furs for London firms such as William Cloberry and Company, Captain Fleet was far from pleased by Lord Baltimore's Chesapeake intrusion. Settlement, Fleet feared, would only make game scarce and stir up the natives. His fears, though, were unwarranted. The plentiful supply of beaver on Maryland's Eastern Shore, for example, gave rise to a protected trading culture between Indians and whites that prevented massive settlement of whites for nearly a century. Maryland's Calvert proprietors preferred Indians and the profits of fur trading to land-hungry and contentious settlers in their domain.[64] The commerce in deer skins was also important and Indians readily exchanged hides for manufactured goods. Deer skin gloves were so popular in London that in the 1630s the deerskin trade became a public mania in Virginia. Colonial authorities were forced to outlaw the commerce in 1631 out of fear that the deerskin trade would divert the settlers' attention away from agriculture.[65]

Until recently historians have downplayed the role of the fur trade in the colonial Chesapeake economy. Scholars like Margaret Morriss characterized the fur trade as a local industry that never became an appreciable part of Chesapeake commerce. Maryland, she wrote, "never exported to England

63. Philip Alexander Bruce, *Economic History of Virginia in the Seventeenth Century,* 2 vols. (New York: Peter Smith, 1935), 2:71.

64. Rountree and Davidson, *Eastern Shore Indians of Maryland and Virginia,* 87–88.

65. Silver, *A New Face on the Countryside,* 72.

furs of sufficient value to tempt people into the trade."[66] Beaver, muskrat, and raccoon, however, were valued staples, and their role in the early Chesapeake enviro-economy is just now beginning to be understood. Hunters plundered beaver ponds and used beaver dams as sites for water grist mills. Even today in the Chesapeake many of the local highways bear the name "Beaver Grade Road" or "Beaver Dam Road." The most significant regional fur trade, however, was conducted by Virginia planters with Indians in the Carolinas. Financed largely by planters in the tidewater like William Byrd, the fur industry was a trade diaspora that spread from the Chickasaw Indians westward to the Great Plains and beyond.[67]

During the 1630s an increasing economic dynamic arose in the Maryland Chesapeake based on the fur trade of the upper bay. While Claiborne's fort on Kent Island was occasionally attacked by warriors from the south, the Susquehannocks left it undisturbed. According to Frederick Fausz, the Susquehannocks and Claiborne's men "formed an intercultural interest group based on a mutually beneficial trade and enjoyed the most positive Anglo-Indian relationship in the early seventeenth century. This trade created a network of commerce that stretched from beaver dams of the piedmont and Appalachia to the warehouses of London." In 1638 Claiborne's elaborate trading operation with the Indians brought in 7,488 pounds of beaver pelts worth £4,493 at twelve shillings a pound.[68] That was more than enough wealth to tempt people to enter the trade. As late as 1728 William Byrd of Westover complained that his surveying party had great difficulty in Virginia and North Carolina climbing beaver dams. "These industrious animals," Byrd wrote in his *History of the Dividing Line*, "had dammed up the water so high that we had much adversity to get over."[69] When the tidewater fur trade died out it was due more to intertribal rivalries and the problems of colonial administration than to the availability of beaver.[70] From

66. Margaret Shove Morriss, *The Colonial Trade of Maryland* (Baltimore: The Johns Hopkins University Press, 1927), 14.

67. For the business interests of the Byrd family, see Pierre Marabaud, *William Byrd of Westover, 1674-1744* (Charlottesville: University Press of Virginia, 1971).

68. J. Frederick Fausz, "Present at the Creation: The Chesapeake World that Greeted Maryland Colonists," *Maryland Historical Magazine*, 79 (1984): 12.

69. Louis B. Wright, ed., *The Prose Works of William Byrd of Westover* (Cambridge: Harvard University Press, 1966), 233.

70. J. Frederick Fausz, "Merging and Emerging Worlds, Anglo-Indian Interest

an ecological standpoint the fur trade marks the beginning of the transformation of the Chesapeake from region to resource. Beaver became a resource the colonists could exploit for profit and sustenance.

Early colonists had an ambivalent attitude toward the forest itself. While it provided the Englishmen with furs, shelter, food, warmth, and other essential materials, they at the same time destroyed it as if it were an enemy. Like most Europeans, colonists were not at home in a forest environment. Fear of the forest is part of western culture and seems a deeply ingrained aspect of human nature. The word *panic* traces back to the fear that many Europeans had of the rites of the god Pan in deep dark woods. As ecologist Lynn White has shown, people have often been a dynamic negative part of their environment. Adaptation to and survival in harmony with the woodlands of North America was not part of the European cultural outlook. To the European a tree was nothing more than "a physical fact," notes White. "Christendom gave no credibility to woodlands as sacred groves of nature. Furthermore, to assume, as the Indians did, that there was a spiritual focus to nature was frankly idolatrous."[71] The early colonists approached the forests much in the same manner that Europeans had since the Neolithic period. They cleared the original forests with axes, burned the cut material, and then planted small fields of cereals and other crops and used areas for pasturing grazing animals. The deforestation was carried out with slash and burn techniques. Colonists girdled trees of their bark to kill them, later felling them with an axe and burning them. Land no longer capable of growing useful crops was abandoned. Words like "place," "landscape," or "setting" were foreign to the English moral imagination in the early Chesapeake. Unlike the hunting and gathering cultures they displaced, the English lived in an environment and did not reflect on it.[72] As Paul Shepard and others have observed, the celebration of the wilderness would occur

---

Groups and the Development of the Seventeenth-Century Chesapeake," in Lois Green Carr, Philip D. Morgan, and Jean B. Russo eds., *Colonial Chesapeake Society* (Williamsburg: The Institute of Early American History and Culture, 1988), 87–91.

71. Lynn White Jr., "The Historical Roots of Our Ecological Crisis, *Science,* 155 (March 10, 1967): 1206–7.

72. The Indians of the Atlantic Coast had an elaborate series of control mechanisms in their culture that instilled respect for the land and its wildlife. European technological attitudes were largely "incompatible" with Indian spiritual beliefs and economic practice. See Martin, *Keepers of the Game,* 35, 59.

only when nostalgia and the yearning for landscape and the primitive became the prerogative of the privileged few.[73]

## The Tobacco Revolution

The agricultural system of the colonial Chesapeake did not have a smooth
evolution. The introduction of cattle and goats as meat and dairy supply
proved less successful than the English had hoped. By 1661, for example,
only 144 head of cattle, 216 goats, and six horses were left in the Virginia
colony. Pigs, however, flourished in the Chesapeake, and colonists reported
"infinite hogges in heards all over the woods."[74] Livestock ran wild in the
forest, much to the vexation of the colonists, and deer so damaged crops
that Indians were hired to kill them off. Most of the grain supply during
peaceful times was gotten through trade with the Indians. By the 1620s the
grain dependence shifted, and Indians bought large amounts of corn from
English plantations.

Although John Rolfe is known chiefly for making the first interracial
marriage in British North America, his primary claim to fame resides in his
introduction of tobacco as a staple crop to the English colonies. Tobacco,
which eventually became one of Europe's most widely used narcotics, was
not indigenous to the Chesapeake. It probably came to the region as a trade
and ceremonial article from the Indians to the south. Indians considered it
a special gift from the Great Spirit.

Tobacco first became known to the Europeans following the voyage of
Christopher Columbus in 1492. Columbus and his men found tobacco being cultivated by the Indians of the West Indies but Europeans showed little
interest in the plant until the middle of the sixteenth century. By the 1560s
the Portuguese were smoking tobacco brought aboard their ships from
Florida. John Rolfe began his experiments with native tobacco weed in
Jamestown in 1612. The historical record is unclear as to whether Rolfe
used the seeds of local tobacco or a West Indian variety, but the product
was declared to be of excellent quality. Tobacco use is recorded in England

73. Paul Shepard, "Place in American Culture," *The North American Review,*
262 (1977): 22.

74. Cited in Lewis C. Gray, *History of Agriculture in the Southern United States to
1860,* 2 vols. (Gloucester, Mass.: Peter Smith, 1958), 1:20.

during the reign of Queen Elizabeth I, but it was not until Sir Francis Drake brought a boatload of the weed to England from the West Indies that smoking became a popular social custom. The first significant cargo of 105 pounds of Chesapeake tobacco arrived in England in 1615 from Rolfe's plantation aboard *The Flying Horse of Flushing.*

Sir Walter Raleigh, whose original colony at Roanoke Island went up in smoke, became England's patron of tobacco and did more to introduce the art of smoking in Europe than any man. Tobacco smoking at this time must be seen as one of the many trends made fashionable by the dandies of the court of King James I. The king was not amused. Writing in his anonymously published *Counterblast to Tobacco,* James noted that smoking was "a custom loathsome to the eye, hateful to the nose, harmful to the brain, dangerous to the lungs, and in the black stinking fumes thereof, nearest resembling the horrible stygian smoke of the pit that is bottomless."[75]

With John Rolfe cultivating tobacco and Sir Walter Raleigh popularizing it, the Chesapeake weed became enormously successful. Virginia tobacco exports skyrocketed from 2,300 pounds in 1616 to three million pounds by 1638. The loamy soil of the Chesapeake was ideally suited to the cultivation of tobacco, and indentured servants to work the land were plentiful. The latter had been most willing to leave the prisons, pestholes, and declining English countryside for a chance in the New World and signed themselves into harsh servitude for terms lasting from four to seven years. Brought to the Chesapeake by the shipload, these indentured servants would transform the wilderness into booming tobacco plantations. The race for land, men, and wealth was on, and the Chesapeake Bay country would be profoundly changed by the new monoculture. Neither the great Virginia massacre of 1622, in which Indians led by Chief Opechancanough killed more than 350 English settlers nor the dread plague of 1622–23 diminished the colonial dream of a tobacco empire.

When a census was taken in the Virginia colony in 1669 only eleven of the twenty-eight tribes described by John Smith in 1608 remained, and only about two thousand Indians were left in tidewater Virginia. The Indians had been literally overwhelmed by a tidal wave of English migrants. European culture sapped the vitality of Indian life, and disease and liquor took

75. Quoted in Nash, *Red, White and Black,* 52.

their toll. In Maryland, Father Andrew White urged the colonists to treat the Indians with "Prudence" and "Charity" and make to them Christians instead of "hunting them from place to place as you would doe a wolf."[76] White's admonition went unheeded. Only those Indians of the Appalachian Mountains and Susquehanna River valley who remained outside of tobacco's imperial sway prevailed. Carolyn Merchant's appraisal of the fate of Indians in New England applies equally well to the Chesapeake: "The devastating changes in biological reproduction were soon followed by equally momentous changes in social reproduction that altered land tenure. In place of the Indian view of the habitat as a tribal home, the English imposed a legal concept of private property that would convert Indian lands to trapping territories."[77]

By the 1630s the great expeditions of exploration and map-making in the region had been concluded. The colonies had been established, if somewhat tenuously, in areas of the Chesapeake called Maryland and Virginia. The Indians and the English had each taken the other's measure as well as goods and diseases, and the process of English adaptation to the Chesapeake Bay environment was well under way. Englishmen did not accept the randomness of nature but sought to impose system and regular pattern on the wilderness. Cleared land rather than the forest became a symbol of order and civilization. Most Englishmen shared Richard Hakluyt's view that large-scale agriculture with the Indians as a plantation work force was the Chesapeake's destiny. Both land and Indians were passive objects upon which European culture would imprint its design.[78] With the expansion of tobacco culture, beaver dams and channels and ponds that had done so much to preserve watersheds and equalize stream flows vanished as well. An integrated ecosystem that had been able to resist for centuries the hand of the Indian now began to deconstruct.

If anything, the early experience of Europeans in the Chesapeake demonstrated how powerful cultural considerations were in dealing with environmental phenomena. They viewed the environment as a dead or inert

---

76. "Father White's Relation," in Hall, *Narratives of Early Maryland*, 90.

77. Merchant, *Ecological Revolutions*, 57.

78. Richard Hakluyt, "Discourse of Western Planting," quoted in Jack P. Greene, *The Intellectual Construction of America* (Chapel Hill: University of North Carolina Press, 1993), 36.

thing rather than an active force in human adaptation and survival. Economy, social structure, and culture profoundly conditioned the Chesapeake Bay environment. Almost by accident tobacco became the first cash crop of the Chesapeake, and the development of commodity agriculture intensified changes at work in the region in ways that Captain John Smith and Father Andrew White would never have imagined.

## CHAPTER TWO

# Tobacco Culture and Deforestation

"The common planters of the Chesapeake were slovens
in agriculture."
— Rhys Isaac, *The Transformation of Virginia, 1740–1790*

"As a way of relating to Nature, agriculture is something of a loose
cannon."
— Colin A. Duncan, *Environmental History Review,* 1991

"Heaven and Earth never agreed to frame a better place for man's
habitation."
— Captain John Smith, *True Relation of Occurrences
and Accidents in Virginia*

## "Damn your souls, raise tobacco!"

All forms of life modify their contexts, and the colonial transformation of
the Chesapeake country from a backwoods economy to a tobacco empire is
an important episode in the transformation of the mid-Atlantic region to
1800. Throughout this period profound changes took place in the landscape that affected patterns of climate, water quality, settlement, and economic opportunity. In the seventeenth century an English colonial official
surprised a Virginia parson with the admonition, "Damn your souls, raise
tobacco!" By 1800, however, it was apparent that the Chesapeake environment, not English souls, had been damned by agricultural practice.

Tobacco culture expanded rapidly in the seventeenth-century Chesapeake
because it was the only commodity not regulated or controlled by the English government that the colonists could easily turn into money. Grain in
the seventeenth century brought two shillings, six pence a bushel, while
tobacco brought three shillings a hundred weight. Colonial wheat had to
compete against English wheat, and Chesapeake planters had only one other
outlet for surplus grain—Holland. As Holland was both a grain-importing
nation and a great trading enemy of the English, the mother country prohibited this kind of trade. Also, wrote economic historian Philip A. Bruce,

the rich mould of virgin forest soil tended to be not the best type of soil for growing wheat as the stalk grew prodigiously at the expense of the actual cereal. As early as 1649, Virginia colonists in the Norfolk area farmed several hundred acres of wheat—on old Indian fields and mostly for local consumption. In the main, the process of opening new grounds was so difficult that large acreages for wheat production were impracticable.[1] For most of the seventeenth century, wheat farming in the Chesapeake was dependent upon the hoe. Primitive wooden ploughs available after 1640 could not break the tough root systems of virgin soils. Wheat, therefore, was usually planted on land already weakened by successive plantings of tobacco.

Although lumber and naval stores were profitable in this initial period, they were expensive to transport in terms of their after cost yield. As Avery Craven, a pioneering scholar of the Chesapeake, noted, tobacco "alone seemed capable of lifting the colonist quickly from the severe conditions of frontier life into the comforts of former days." Prices were sufficiently high that a man's labor in tobacco brought him six times the financial yield he might get by cultivating other crops. Even during periods of exceptionally low prices, tobacco had an assured market in England. A planter needed only a small acreage for a profitable crop, an important consideration when he faced an intractable wilderness that had to be cleared with crude tools. Tobacco could easily be shipped in thousand-pound hogsheads and could withstand a long and frequently stormy voyage to London and other tobacco ports.[2]

Tobacco was an intensive crop that required unceasing labor. George Alsop, a former indentured servant turned Maryland publicist, offered a well-informed view of tobacco planting as he saw it in the seventeenth century. The tobacco season, Alsop reported, began in March or April with the sowing of thousands of tiny tobacco seeds in special beds that were protected from the elements. In June the small tobacco plants were transported and set in hillocks created by hoeing dirt about a man's leg as high as the knee. During the summer, planters pruned excessive leaves from the tobacco stalks and by mid-September the crop was cut down and hung in

1. Philip A. Bruce, *Economic History of Virginia in the Seventeenth Century*, 2 vols. (New York: Peter Smith, 1935), 1:257.

2. Avery Odelle Craven, *Soil Exhaustion as a Factor in the Agricultural History of Virginia and Maryland, 1606–1860* (Gloucester, Mass.: Peter Smith, 1965), 30.

sheds to dry. Once dried, the tobacco was tied into bundles and packed into hogsheads. The tobacco fleet arrived between November and January to transport the crop to London and Bristol. Winter time was reserved for clearing new land; and planters and servants and slaves attacked the woods by girdling trees and burning underbrush to meet tobacco's voracious appetite for new fertile soil. The best soils were relatively rich and brownish in color. Nineteenth-century planters would call them "mulatto lands."

Tobacco planting in the Chesapeake was a crude form of agriculture compared to English practices of harrowing, cross-plowing, and ditching. A single farmer with one hoe could easily tend a three-acre plot and clear a crop of 1,200 pounds of tobacco. Planting patterns differed somewhat in the region. Maryland planters sought to produce large quantities of cheap oronocco tobacco because there was a steady market for it while Virginians preferred to grow more delicate, expensive, sweet-smelling varieties.

The tobacco mentality affected all aspects of Chesapeake life. The quality and quantity of a planter's tobacco crop determined his moral worth. With tobacco he could purchase servants and slaves; Anglican churches like St. Luke's in Queen Anne's County, Maryland, were built by tobacco. Taxes, public levies, and aid to the indigent were all figured in tobacco equivalents. Historian G. K. Davies records that in 1621 even English brides sold in Bermuda for a hundred pounds of tobacco apiece.[3] Given the shortage of hard currency in the Chesapeake, tobacco itself became a kind of money. "Tobacco is the current Coyn of Maryland," observed George Alsop, "and will sooner purchase commodities from merchants than money."[4] Tobacco, adds T. H. Breen, "added a dimension to the colonists perception of time and place" and transformed the language of agriculture. Growing good tobacco gave a planter a sense of pride in what was essentially a *parvenu* society. It became the one respectable form of agriculture and conveyed "a source of meaningful social identity as well as a means to maintain a high standard of living."[5]

3. G. K. Davies, *The North Atlantic World in the Seventeenth Century* (Minneapolis: University of Minnesota Press, 1974), 144.

4. George Alsop, *A Character of the Province of Maryland,* (1666, repr. Baltimore: The Johns Hopkins University Press, 1880), 68–69.

5. T. H. Breen, *Tobacco Culture: The Mentality of the Great Tidewater Planters on the Eve of the Revolution* (Princeton: Princeton University Press, 1985), 22, 71.

Given the primitive nature of the Chesapeake environment in the colonial period, the statistics on tobacco production in the region are truly remarkable. In 1668–69 London received nine million pounds of tobacco, and another sixteen million pounds headed for the European market. This left enough tobacco on the English market, quips G. K. Davies, to give one and one-half pounds of tobacco to every man, woman and child in England and Wales.[6]

The plantation was the first attempt at commodity agriculture in the New World and must be viewed as a kind of industrial and agricultural process that was not in harmony with the landscape. It is ironic to add at this juncture that the colonial assault on the Chesapeake environment took place during the time that the English began to protect their countryside. Between 1570 and 1640 farmsteads were preserved, woodlands and heaths restored, and maple and sycamore trees celebrated by poets and agriculturalists alike. In the words of landscape historian W. G. Hoskins, this period saw the "Flowering of Rural England."[7]

During the seventeenth century and well into the eighteenth, Maryland and Virginia planters followed a unique form of agriculture—what recent scholars have termed "the Chesapeake system of husbandry." Using simple tools like hoes and axes to exploit local resources, planters grew tobacco on recently cleared plots of twenty acres and put less fertile acreage into long fallow. The main problem with this tobacco system, argue Lois Green Carr and Russell R. Menard, was that so much attention was given to tobacco production that planters did not grow enough grain to feed livestock. "The inability to feed livestock and hence use manure, trapped planters into long rotations that limited their options to expand." Colonists in the seventeenth-century Chesapeake were well known for their lack of interest in the production of foodstuffs. As late as 1676, and despite large harvests of Indian corn and fruit, Maryland imported peas, mackerel, codfish, biscuit and malt from New England. Given the enormous Chesapeake fishery that was at hand, it seems incredible that Chesapeake planters would import fish products. It was not until the late eighteenth century that Chesapeake planta-

6. Davies, *North Atlantic World*, 146.
7. W. G. Hoskins, *The Making of the English Landscape* (London: Penguin Books, 1985), 154–63.

tions would grow sufficient corn to feed livestock and serve as an export crop.[8] Also, after 1651 the British mercantile system taxed colonial grain heavily as a means of protecting English domestic agriculture. The colonial grain trade with England was not significant until 1760.

The tobacco pricing system also helped to create a problematic agricultural base in the Chesapeake Bay country. Until the 1680s the price of tobacco had been satisfactory, encouraging the development of numerous plantations throughout the Maryland and Virginia tidewater. Even though the actual price of tobacco declined during this period, planters were able to pursue economies of scale by planting more tobacco on fresh lands. Thus with the increase of productivity, tobacco cultivation continued its rule of the tidewater.

The first major depression in the tobacco economy occurred between 1680 and 1720, when foreign wars and very low prices decimated the industry. Larger planters, who could use African slave labor and the economies of scale to withstand periods of tobacco depression, squeezed out planters on small holdings or on marginal lands. This development occurred at a time when land prices in the Chesapeake increased significantly, making it still more difficult for poor white families to form households and grow tobacco on small freeholds. Moreover, only the larger planters had the wealth and the land to develop alternative crops for export, enabling them to withstand hard times. As Allan Kulikoff and others have noted, between 1690 and 1770 more than 100,000 black slaves were imported to the Chesapeake, and slave labor tended to drive white freeholders off uncompetitive farms. After 1750, when European demand for tobacco increased, the tidewater gentry took its profits. In Kulikoff's words, "white families for the first time had to leave the Chesapeake in order to make a living."[9]

The consequences of internal migration coupled with changing economics had disastrous environmental consequences in the Chesapeake. In the

8. Lois Green Carr and Russell R. Menard, "Land, Labor, and the Economics of Scale in Early Maryland: Some Limits to Growth in the System of Chesapeake Husbandry," *Journal of Economic History,* 49 (1989): 413, 417. See also Margaret Shove Morris, *Colonial Trade of Maryland, 1689–1715* (Baltimore: The Johns Hopkins University Press, 1914), 15.

9. Allan Kulikoff, *Tobacco and Slaves: The Development of Southern Cultures in the Chesapeake, 1680–1800* (Chapel Hill: University of North Carolina Press, 1986), 77.

piedmont of western Maryland and Virginia, these small farmers would start the same ruinous system of tobacco culture—the only money crop they could grow. By 1800 practically all of the piedmont had been planted at least once in tobacco. As scholars like Russell Menard have observed, tobacco dominated the export sector of the Chesapeake. The industry's growth reflects a monolith "that reverberated through the entire society" and conditioned "the level of material well-being in the colonies."[10] Never again in the environmental history of the Chesapeake would a single agricultural staple have such power to transform a region and mobilize a population. The Chesapeake was called "the Tobacco Coast" for good reason.

Small freeholders were caught up in a land-greedy tobacco culture that expanded ever westward until the mountains of Appalachia presented geographic obstacles to the transport and marketing of the royal weed. It is worth noting that planters, both rich and poor, had little patience with geographic obstacles. As early as 1749 planters on the James and Appomattox rivers in Virginia demanded that the colonial government provide funds to clear the rivers of falls and rapids so that tobacco hogsheads could be brought to the royal warehouses by canoe and small boat.[11] There is no doubt that tobacco was one of the driving forces behind land exploitation in the Chesapeake, and land hunger made the gentry of this region different from their English counterparts. The Chesapeake planter was part land speculator, part merchant, and part farmer, a man who made his living more as an entrepreneur than as the head of an inherited estate. Land, like the tobacco it produced, was a commodity. It held little of the symbolic significance that it did for the English gentry.

By 1732 tobacco culture had become a costly way of life. Planters had great investments in land, servants, and slaves, and only the wealthy could deal with the uncertainties of the tobacco pricing system. Although many small farmers remained in the Chesapeake by the mid-eighteenth century, an aristocratic tidewater oligarchy had also arisen. Historian Paul Clemens wrote that tobacco eventually produced an elite in the Chesapeake that "rivaled the landlords of New York's Hudson Valley, the great sugar planters of

10. Russell R. Menard, "The Tobacco Industry in the Chesapeake Colonies, 1617–1730: An Interpretation," *Research in Economic History,* 5 (1980): 156.

11. Richard Morton, *Colonial Virginia,* Vol. 2 (Chapel Hill: University of North Carolina Press, 1960), 558.

the West Indies, and the gentry of England."[12] On Virginia's Eastern Shore the Jenifer family owned more than eight thousand acres. In 1732, the year of his death, Robert Carter, the richest planter in Virginia, had left some 330,000 acres to his heirs. The Beverley, Fitzhugh, Byrd, and Thoroughgood families owned impressive estates as well. The greatest of the land grants in colonial Virginia was that owned by Lord Culpepper, comprising six million acres of the northern neck between the Potomac and Rappahannock rivers.[13] Large tracts encompassing thousands of acres of Chesapeake tobacco land were also owned by Maryland gentry like the Carrolls, Pacas, Lloyds, and Tilghmans. On both sides of the Chesapeake a rich and powerful society of cousins played marital ring-around-rosey and built an entrenched class system and a plantation society that had a decidedly feudal overtone. The gentry also bought up large tracts of land in the western piedmont and experimented with vineyards, flax, and hemp industries in the valleys of the Blue Ridge. For the poorer classes in the region before the American Revolution, there was no escaping the grasp of the Chesapeake gentry.

Tobacco's dominance extended deeply into the economic behavior of small freehold farmers. In his research historian Aubrey Land discovered that in the Chesapeake area in the eighteenth century both small producers and great were bound to the tobacco market. For example, wrote Land, "forty percent of the growers in four prime tobacco-producing counties in southern Maryland in the decade 1750–1759 marketed crops of less than 2,000 pounds, amounting to four hogsheads or less." Tobacco prices were never consistently low enough to threaten the Chesapeake with ruin, and the habits and skills of Chesapeake farmers could not easily adapt to radical changes in husbandry. In the end freeholders were just as committed to a ruinous system of agriculture as slaveholders.[14]

12. Paul Clemens, *The Atlantic Economy and Colonial Maryland's Eastern Shore: From Tobacco to Grain* (Ithaca: Cornell University Press, 1980), 121.

13. Paul W. Gates, *History of Public Land Law Development* (Washington, D.C.: Public Law Review Commission, 1968), 37.

14. Aubrey C. Land, "Economic Behavior in a Planting Society: The Eighteenth-Century Chesapeake," *Journal of Southern History,* 33 (1967): 473.

## The Assault on the Forest

Despite the rapid expansion of tobacco culture in its southern region, much of the seventeenth-century Chesapeake watershed remained heavily forested. Though planters were eager to knock down the forest for their cash crop, clearing land was not easy given the available technologies of that era. Clearing new land was often so difficult and time-consuming that it was left to the sweat labor of indentured servants and black slaves. Furthermore, settlers believed that harmful illnesses lurking in the dark mould of decayed leaves and wood caused epidemics and that clearing the forest released them. As late as 1724 the Reverend Hugh Jones would write of Virginia that the "whole country is a perfect forest, except where the woods are cleared for plantations."[15] Jones's "perfect forest" would not last; and by the time of the American Revolution the timber resources of the Chesapeake Bay country had been seriously depleted. Deforestation would have serious consequences for the rivers of the Chesapeake basin and ultimately for the estuary itself.

The assault on the forest was inextricably tied to economic developments in the bay country and in the Atlantic community of the British empire. In the seventeenth century the long timber shortage in England had reached a point where even the price of firewood had trebled. Since Elizabethan times England had relied on the northern countries of the Baltic for its supply of ship masts and lumber. But recurrent wars, international politics, and English mercantile policy made the Baltic an unreliable source of supply by 1700. Population increase with its attendant demand for wood and wood products and the inefficient administration of royal forests in England contributed to the timber crisis. In England brewers, bakers, glassblowers, and limeburners needed vast quantities of wood. Further, the demand for timbers for mine shafts and buildings was insatiable.[16]

England's timber shortage worried the English navy. A warship could require as many as two thousand oak trees in its construction, and by 1700 England's coal fleet of 1,600 vessels required the lumber of thousands of

15. Hugh Jones, *The Present State of Virginia* (1724, repr., Chapel Hill: University of North Carolina Press, 1956), 74.

16. For background on England's timber crisis see Charles F. Carroll, *The Timber Economy of Puritan New England* (Providence: Brown University Press, 1973), 13.

trees. Thus did England look to New England and the Chesapeake colonies as a source of timber. While Puritan New England supplied the bulk of the lumber used by the English during the period, a not inconsiderable amount of timber flowed out of the Chesapeake to the mother country, Ireland, and the Caribbean. A good portion of it went to the islands of Barbados and Antigua, whose land had been deforested to permit the operation of financially lucrative sugar plantations. Most exported lumber was in the form of rough planking and barrel staves. In return Marylanders received rum, sugar, and cash. The woodsman and his ox-drawn timbercart was as much a part of the Chesapeake landscape as the indentured servant and black slave in the tobacco field.

Timber was a popular and valuable commodity in Maryland, and the county courts contain an ample number of suits over wood lots and timber theft. One such case is illustrative. In Charles County in 1665, John Chaireman sued Robert Downes, charging that Downes had pirated lumber from his forest tract equivalent to the value of two thousand pounds of tobacco. Such a sum represented a good year's work for a farmhand on a Chesapeake tobacco plantation. During squabbles over timber, ownership of valuable tools like broadaxes and cross-cut saws also became items of litigation.[17]

Even after tobacco came to dominate the Chesapeake economy, lumber exports from the region remained important. By 1768–69, for example, Virginia and Maryland exported over three million barrel staves to England, Ireland, and Europe and cut almost a million boards for the Atlantic coastal trade.[18] From Maryland to Georgia the timber economy produced a quarter million casks annually to be used as tobacco hogsheads and molasses barrels. A recent study of the Atlantic timber economy points out that "cooperage employed more craftsmen than any other activity in the South."[19] In Talbot County on Maryland's Eastern Shore, for example, coopers did a thriving business supplying planters and ship captains with kegs, barrels,

---

17. William Hand Browne, et al., eds., *Archives of Maryland*, 73 vols. (Baltimore: Maryland Historical Society, 1883–1972), Court Series, 40:214–15, 49:106.

18. Lewis C. Gray, *History of Agriculture in the Southern United States to 1860*, 2 vols. (1933 repr. Gloucester, Mass.: Peter Smith, 1968), 2:1019.

19. Thomas R. Cox, et al., *This Well-Wooded Land: Americans and Their Forests from Colonial Times to the Present* (Lincoln: University of Nebraska Press, 1985), 19.

pails, tuns, and a variety of other containers.[20] The trade of cooper was so profitable in colonial Virginia that many craftsmen became large landowners within a short period of time, and it was common for coopers in the lower Norfolk area to amass plantations of five hundred acres or more.[21]

Recently it has been estimated that by the eve of the American Revolution the value of wood products exported from the Chesapeake to England was third after tobacco and grain. Certainly after 1680 forest products played an important role in the Chesapeake economy. Economic historians John McCusker and Russell Menard have pointed out that by the 1760s "the region resembled a horseshoe, with a plantation district raising tobacco for export to Europe in the center and a farming area yielding foodstuffs, forest products, hemp and flax for a variety of markets around the periphery."[22]

The lumber trade in the Chesapeake began as early as 1607 at Jamestown when the colonists shipped hand-sawn clapboards to England. History records the establishment of a water-powered sawmill at the falls of the James River as early as 1611. Tobacco planters like William Fitzhugh and William Byrd owned sawmills and imported milling equipment to the Chesapeake from Germany. In fact, William Byrd of Westover was such a lumber enthusiast that he boasted his sawmill could rip two thousand feet of board in five hours.[23] From 1632 onward the lands of the Eastern Shore of Virginia known as Accomac Plantation were an important source of timber and ship masts, and most of the proud oaks of the region were reserved for the English navy. Although planters on the James River looked down upon their cousins across the bay as crude woodsmen and herders, they nonetheless eagerly bought their timber. The forests of the Eastern Shore of Virginia also provided ample firewood for numerous small tanneries near Cape Charles that manufactured fine leather products for the James River and Northern Neck aristocracy.[24]

20. Jean B. Russo, *Free Workers in a Plantation Economy: Talbot County, Maryland 1690–1759* (New York: Garland Publishing, Inc., 1989), 225–26.

21. Bruce, *Economic History of Virginia in the Seventeenth Century,* 2:421.

22. John J. McCusker and Russell R. Menard, *The Economy of British America, 1607–1789* (Chapel Hill: University of North Carolina Press, 1985), 120.

23. Cox, *This Well-Wooded Land,* 14.

24. Nora Miller Turman, *The Eastern Shore of Virginia, 1603–1694* (Onancock, Va.: Eastern Shore News, Inc., 1955), 25.

Colonial trade records for the Chesapeake indicate a healthy regional trade in pitch, tar, turpentine, plank, and hogsheads. This trade was carried on mostly from the James River area of Virginia and the Eastern Shore of Maryland. Chesapeake lumbermen also had a small trade with the Madeira Islands, sending them pipe staves and ship timbers. So lucrative was the Chesapeake lumber trade that in 1742 Andrew Tonnard of Deptford, England, proposed to bring twenty sawyers to the colony to embark on an ambitious lumber and building scheme. Nothing came of this proposal but Maryland's government envisioned a thriving pitch and lumber products industry in the Chesapeake for England's merchant fleet.[25]

Under the Navigation Acts of 1660 timber came under the enumeration clause and in the eighteenth century could only be shipped to England. Inasmuch as timber was a ready resource of cash and internal trade, Chesapeake lumbermen were bitter over the restrictions and quietly evaded the law. Some historians believe that the colonial resentment over English timber policy after 1760 may have contributed to growing revolutionary consciousness. Suffice to say that the colonists in the Chesapeake felt little guilt in selling lumber and naval stores to England's old trading enemy, the Dutch.

Of course, the colonial assault on the forests of the Chesapeake was not a new phenomenon. As we have already seen, the Indians had been burning the forests and cutting firewood long before the first white man arrived in the region. What was new was the English belief that the extermination of the forest was a necessary preliminary to the economic development of the Chesapeake. Tobacco did well on freshly cleared land. The native soil was deep and loamy and the rewards to be gotten from tobacco so great that a tobacco imperialism emerged in the Chesapeake. Tobacco controlled everything from what was to be cultivated to the organization of the trade system and labor supply to the cultural life of the region. For an aspiring planter the model was six hundred acres of tobacco land surrounded by 2,400 acres of woods. While such plantations of three thousand acres were few in number, they set the tone for Chesapeake attitudes towards land and forest. As land wore out, the forest would be cleared using slash and burn

---

25. See "Description of Virginia Commerce," *William and Mary Quarterly,* series 1, vol. 14 (1905): 87–93; Margaret Shove Moriss, *Colonial Trade of Maryland, 1689–1715* (Baltimore: The Johns Hopkins University Press, 1914), 54–55.

methods that had not been seen in Europe for centuries. Unlike more primitive economies where such land use was a means of survival for individuals, this practice became a source of monetary profit for whomever owned the property. As Paul Sears, a renowned ecologist, has noted, the forest, though "a welcome source of fuel and timber, as well as game, was regarded principally as an obstacle to agriculture."[26]

The development of the Virginia "worm" fence illustrates the lavish consumption of wood in the colonial Chesapeake. Today the colonial rail zigzag worm fence seems a quaint reminder of our colonial heritage. Farmers needed to protect their corn and tobacco from the depredations of wild horses, cattle, and hogs. These fences, however, used six to ten rails at alternating angles. One mile of worm fence required 6,500 rails of timber. The use of this type of fence was unknown in timber-poor England and illustrates how wood was a central factor in the agricultural development of the Chesapeake.

Pressure on the Chesapeake woods intensified in the eighteenth century when it became increasingly difficult for small farmers to acquire land for tobacco farms. As previously mentioned, most good land after 1700 in the Chesapeake was in the hands of a planter elite that chose to hold on to land as a family investment. Thus many landless colonials migrated to the pine barrens, swamps, and piedmont areas of Maryland and Virginia and developed a backwoods economy of trapping, subsistence agriculture, and lumbering. "Live-oakers" cut ship timbers in the oak groves of piedmont Virginia, and lumberjacks felled cypress in the Pocomoke Swamp of Maryland's Eastern Shore. Often felling trees twelve to eighteen feet in girth, Chesapeake woodsmen transformed the forest into lumber, potash, and naval stores for England.[27] Loggers especially prized the cypress trees of the swampy Chesapeake. Their wood made excellent roofing material and was the source of a small but significant shingle industry. Most shingles were cut by slaves during the winter season and sold in bulk to the Caribbean. Cypress logs withstood rot and were valued in all forms of construction. From the late seventeenth century on, huge quantities of cedar and cypress were taken

26. Paul Sears, *Deserts on the March* (4th edition; Norman: University of Oklahoma Press, 1980), 46.

27. Richard G. Lillard, *The Great Forest* (New York: Da Capo Press, 1973), 114–15.

out of the Pocomoke Swamp of Maryland and the Dismal Swamp of Virginia.[28] Even on the Northern Neck of Virginia and on the upper Eastern Shore of Maryland, planters viewed themselves as part-time loggers and exploited their wood lots for profit during periods of low tobacco prices. For the colonists the forests of the Chesapeake were a boundless resource.

Clearing timber was part of the westward movement in the Chesapeake. Farmers in this region saw forests not as natural preserves but as soil gauges. As forest historian Richard Lillard puts it, the denser the shrubbery and trees, the faster their rate of growth and the better the soil. "In Virginia, land bearing oak trees, huge timber trees and two foot black mould" was best for tobacco planting. Pine lands wore out easily and corn grew best on land cleared of white oak.[29]

Chesapeake farmers and planters had little use for the forest as an aesthetic end in itself. Trees on the horizon irritated their eyes; they wanted to see bare ground. This crude materialism was amply documented by Isaac Weld, an Englishman who visited the Chesapeake from 1795 to 1797. As Weld saw it, "the generality of Americans stare with astonishment at a person who can feel delight in passing through such a country as this. They have an unconquerable aversion to trees; not one is spared. It appears strange that in a country where the rays of the sun act with such prodigious power, some few trees near the habitations should not be spared, whose foliage might afford a cooling during the parching heats of summer."[30]

The assault on Maryland's forest by 1720 was especially evident in All Hallows Parish on the western shore in what is now Anne Arundel County. All Hallows had an exceptionally large stand of oak trees, including the prized white and red oaks. Given the scarcity of building stone and imported brick, the forest provided the materials for everything from tobacco drying sheds to the mansions that the tidewater elite constructed in the parish. Tobacco culture placed heavy pressure on the woodlands of All Hallows as well, and thousands of young trees were girdled so that young tobacco seedlings could

28. Timothy Silver, *A New Face on the Countryside: Indians, Colonists, and Slaves in the South Atlantic Forest, 1500–1800* (New York: Cambridge University Press, 1990), 119.

29. Lillard, *Great Forest*, 67.

30. Isaac Weld Jr., *Travels Through the States of North America and the Provinces of Upper and Lower Canada During the Years 1795, 1796, 1797* (1807, repr., New York: Augustus M. Kelly, 1970), 39–40.

be planted in the midst of dead trees. As geographer Carville Earle has written about the region, the "thick forest, which usually separated near neighbors in 1699, had given way to a new panorama. In 1767, 49 percent of Anne Arundel Manor [All Hallows Area] was lacking or scarce of timber."[31] Similarly, in Somerset County on Maryland's Eastern Shore, planters mined the forests for timber and ship masts and turned their woodlands into charcoal, firewood, and barrel staves. Somerset's lumberjacks, fueled by prodigious amounts of alcoholic cider made from local orchards, had long quit tobacco farming because of the low quality of their product and directed their energies toward extracting wealth from the forest.[32]

Removing the forest canopy meant that rainwater ran off more quickly and the soil dried out and hardened faster. With the elimination of shade trees, temperatures rose higher in summer and increased the rate of evaporation. The intense summer heat made people feel lazy and ill. Seasoned veterans of the Chesapeake referred to them as "climate struck." Although the forest canopy thins in winter, it still restricts the sun's heat from rising off the soil. According to Timothy Silver, agricultural clearing "creates more severe temperature fluctuations. Without forest canopy to moderate extremes, summer temperatures become hotter and winter readings colder."[33]

George Washington, a devoted agriculturalist and keen observer of the weather, noted in his diaries that after 1760 the winters grew exceptionally cold in the Chesapeake. Between 1767 and 1797 Washington recorded a number of harsh winters. His diary for January 26–29, 1772, contains the comment that he had difficulty moving about his Mount Vernon plantation, "the snow being up to the breast of a Tall Horse everywhere." Later that February, Washington complained of being shut up for ten or twelve days by the deepest snow which I suppose the oldest living ever remembers to have seen in this country." He also noted that in older settlements where

31. Carville V. Earle, *The Evolution of a Tidewater Settlement System, All Hallows Parish, 1650–1783* (Chicago: University of Chicago Department of Geography, Research Paper no. 170, 1970), 34.

32. Lois Green Carr, "Diversification in the Colonial Chesapeake, Somerset County, Maryland, in Comparative Perspective," in Lois Green Carr, Philip D. Morgan, and Jean B. Russo, eds., *Colonial Chesapeake Society* (Chapel Hill: University of North Carolina Press, 1988), 342–82.

33. See Jones, *Present State of Virginia*, 84; Silver, *New Face on the Countryside*, 13.

the woods had been seriously depleted, severe winters killed a large number of farm animals that had been allowed to range freely and taught the planters the necessity of housing and feeding their stock in winter.[34]

From the time of the English arrival, the forests of the Chesapeake Bay country had nothing like the stability of their European counterparts. In England and other parts of Europe, woodlands had high social and economic value. Only infrequently were they grubbed out by individual owners of forest property. Craftsmen often protected woodlands out of economic self-interest. Even in the process of iron-making, workers used mainly scrap timber and underwood and protected their supplies. Such was not the case in Maryland and Virginia. The Chesapeake forest existed to be exploited. The Americans made no distinction between harvesting trees and destroying woodland.[35]

By the eve of the American Revolution Benjamin Franklin and other public figures complained of the scarcity of wood, which had formerly been "at any man's door" in the mid-Atlantic, and William Strickland, a keen-eyed English traveler noted in his journal how the woods had been ravaged in New England and the Chesapeake. Because of the paucity of statistics it is difficult to gauge the extent of the destruction of the Chesapeake woods. Forest historian Michael Williams estimates that about 265 billion board feet of lumber was cut on the Atlantic coast during the colonial period. Of that, he writes, close to 100 billion board feet came out of the Chesapeake and Carolinas. "Like the land cleared for agriculture during these centuries, wood used for fuel was as plentiful as air—and who wrote about that or recorded statistics about it?"[36]

One other important product of the Chesapeake forest should not be overlooked—sassafras. Widely used in Europe for treating a host of human ailments from gout to liver complaints to venereal diseases, sassafras was a

34. Quoted in David M. Ludlum, *Early American Winters,* Vol. 1 (Boston: American Meteorlogical Society, 1966), 145.

35. See Oliver Rackham, *The History of the Countryside* (London: J. M.Dent, 1986), 90–91.

36. William Strickland, *Journal of a Tour in the United States of America, 1794–1795* (London: Bulmer Publishers, 1801, repr., New York Historical Society, 1971), 75, 169, 203; Michael Williams, *Americans and Their Forests* (Cambridge: Cambridge University Press, 1992), 81.

popular Chesapeake export in the seventeenth and eighteenth centuries. Sassafras chips and roots from the Chesapeake were sold abroad where they were boiled into teas thought to be good for "purifying the blood." Whenever there was room on board a ship bound for London or Bristol, captains stored a hogshead of sassafras. Roots of sassafras harvested from the peninsula between the York and James rivers of Virginia were especially prized, and the Sassafras River on the Eastern Shore of Maryland owes its name to colonial root grubbers who believed they had found the magic cure-all for disease.[37]

## The Process of Environmental Change

The Chesapeake Bay country is subject to heavy rainfall. During the summer, storms can deluge the region with as much as fifteen inches in a three-day period. The Potomac and Susquehanna Rivers carry the bulk of the heavy runoff from the land. Scientists have estimated that almost 53 percent of the rainfall in the Potomac Basin reaches the sea, and at flood tide the Potomac can discharge 219,000 feet per second. Historical studies of the hydrology of the region indicate that in the late seventeenth century great storms whipped the rivers into flood tide. In 1667 and 1685, the major rivers of eastern Virginia rose between thirty and forty feet in a short time, causing widespread and severe destruction in the tobacco colony. In 1724 and 1738 violent rains and floods along the James River and the Rappahannock destroyed most of the tobacco. In the late eighteenth century destructive freshets raised the waters of the James, Rappahannock, and Roanoke over forty feet above the average. Floods swept away wharves, tobacco houses, barns, and manor houses and created obstacles to navigation on the rivers. News of disastrous floods during the colonial period was regularly carried in the pages of the *Virginia Gazette*. The worst flood occurred in 1771, when the James River rose twenty feet higher than its previous flood stage, destroyed numerous buildings, and swept away three thousand

---

37. Louis B. Wright, *The Dream of Prosperity in Colonial America* (New York: New York University Press, 1965), 46–47. If the English crown had spent as much money developing the rich pharmacopea of the Chesapeake as it did on its delusions of fostering silk production in the region, both colonies and king would have been more prosperous.

hogsheads of tobacco. According to one study of this flooding, "many trees driven by the rapidity of the current imperiled even the largest ships, driving them from their moorings and carrying several ashore and drowning a number of mariners." Ship channels in the Chesapeake rivers were clogged with sand, and good soil from many plantations along the James was carried off in the deluge. To historian Arthur Middleton, the reason for such intense flooding was clear: "a result of the rapid settlement and deforestation of the piedmont upcountry during the eighteenth century.[38] Finally a violent flood in Virginia in 1790 prompted Thomas Jefferson to rant against "such rains as never came since Noah's flood" and lament that "clear profits will not repay the damage done to the land."[39]

Even under moderate rainfall the Chesapeake country is subject to destructive washing. Tobacco farming and slash and burn deforestation intensified the process. Because much of the Chesapeake region is composed of sandy and clay loam soils, rainfall runoff can cause serious erosion to the landscape. Constant planting of tobacco and corn loosens the soil and weakens its binding capacity. The topsoil can be carried away in a single heavy rainfall. The James River at flood crest can carry almost 300,000 cubic yards of soil during a single span of twenty-four hours. Historically the Potomac River carries in suspension nearly four hundred pounds of soil for every acre in its drainage basin.[40] Such freshets in the seventeenth century did serious damage to the lands of William Byrd along the James and ruined several planters in the Northern Neck. Without forest cover the land cannot absorb the heavy rains of the Chesapeake's summer and winter months.

Accumulated silt in the river beds made waterways shallower. The Manokin River in Somerset County, Maryland, for example, at one time admitted large ships all the way to the town of Princess Anne. By 1800 a three-ton vessel could scarcely navigate the increasingly shallow waterway. Colonists further compounded this problem by dumping large amounts of debris, soil, and ballast into the harbors and rivers. As early as 1680 the Virginia Assembly passed a law prohibiting the felling of trees into the rivers for crude docking facilities and in 1691 forbade the dumping of ship

38. Middleton, *Tobacco Coast,* 58.

39. Quoted in Craven, *Soil Exhaustion,* 28.

40. For historical estimates of Potomac River sedimentation see C. C. Babb, "The Sediment of the Potomac River," *Science,* 21 (1893): 342–43.

ballast such as stone, gravel, and chalk into Virginia waters. In both instances the law was honored more in the breach than in the observance. In Maryland colonists dumped ballast with impunity. The Maryland Assembly in 1735 was forced to enact legislation forbidding the practice and established a fine of fifty pounds sterling per case. By the mid-eighteenth century, Chesapeake inhabitants were complaining of numerous obstructions in their rivers that hindered navigation and commerce.[41]

The process of environmental change in the Chesapeake at this time is reflected in the increasing sedimentation rates of Chesapeake rivers. Roughly speaking, it took about fifty years before erosion runoff converted open water ports at river heads into mudflats. Using the data provided by L. G. Gottschalk, it is safe to assume that the cycle of sedimentation in the Chesapeake was well under way before 1750 and the introduction of grain farming and plow agriculture that scholars like Carville Earle claim was destructive to the region.[42] Erosion, wrote Gottschalk, "sets off a vast chain of secondary consequences: it reduces filtration, thereby causing a lowering of water tables and the drying up of streams and springs."[43] From the seventeenth century onward the clearing of land in the watershed started a cycle of erosion that rapidly filled many Chesapeake rivers. Environmental geographer Grace Brush has stated that her research on the upper bay indicates "a twofold increase in the amount of sediment accumulation when the amount of land cleared changes from 20% to 40% to 50%." Rates of sedimentation in Chesapeake waters "are always higher after European settlement than before."[44] For example, in the area of Joppa Town in what is now Baltimore County, Maryland, the Gunpowder River was silting in long before changes in agricultural practice were manifest in the region. Joppa Town went into decline in 1768 as its waters were no longer navigable. The plow

41. Middleton, *Tobacco Coast,* 99–100.

42. L. G. Gottschalk, "Effects of Soil Erosion on Navigation in the Upper Chesapeake Bay," *Geographical Review,* 35 (1945): 219–38; Carville Earle, "The Myth of the Southern Soil Miner: Macrohistory, Agricultural Innovation and Environmental Change," in Donald Worster, ed., *The Ends of the Earth: Perspectives On Modern Environmental History* (Cambridge: Cambridge University Press, 1988), 175–215.

43. Gottschalk, "Effects of Erosion in Chesapeake Bay," 222.

44. Grace S. Brush, "Geology and Paleoecology of Chesapeake Bay: A Long Term Monitoring Tool for Management," *Journal of the Washington Academy of Sciences,* 76 (1986): 153.

and grain agriculture were not in extensive use in this area prior to 1750. The Patuxent River afforded a good waterway for planters in 1705, but by 1759 the prosperous tobacco port of Upper Marlboro was a large swamp overgrown with marsh grass, reeds, rushes, and shrubs.[45] Much of the silt that entered Chesapeake Bay was high in nitrogen and phosphorus. Analysis of sediment samples taken by Grace Brush indicates that the increased siltation and nutrient content of these waters must have had a profound impact upon the bay's ecosystem. According to one scientist, "the demersal eggs of some fish, for example, would have been more frequently covered by sediment. There is a strong possibility that the reduction in the populations of some species began in the late eighteenth and early nineteenth centuries."[46] Sedimentation, on the other hand, had no effect on ports such as Annapolis that were located near the entrances to the estuary. In the case of Annapolis, the watershed of the Severn River was rather small in comparison with the size of the estuary.

The development of local manufacturing in the Chesapeake also contributed to the growing environmental problems. The discovery of iron in the Virginia and Maryland piedmont was a boon to colonists who needed iron tools and implements, and iron furnaces became part of the regional economy. While the Chesapeake fell below New England in wood products, its iron works developed by planter-capitalists were superior to others in the colonies. The Principio Iron Furnace, Nottingham Furnace, and Lancashire Works in Maryland were exceptionally productive. Further, the Accakeek Iron Mines and Furnace in Stafford County, Virginia, were widely known for quality pig iron. In iron the Chesapeake capitalists, wrote historian Aubrey Land, "developed works that measured up to European standards for pig and bar production."[47] Iron furnaces used charcoal to heat the

45. Gottschalk, "Effects of Erosion in Chesapeake Bay," 233.

46. Brush notes that there is preserved in sediments deposited in the Chesapeake Bay and its tributaries a continuous historical record of the last several thousand years which can serve as a "surrogate of environmental conditions." See Brush, "Geology and Paleoecology of Chesapeake Bay," 147. See also Henry M. Miller, "Transforming a Splendid and Delightsome Land: Colonists and Ecological Change in the Chesapeake, 1607–1820," *Journal of the Washington Academy of Sciences,* 76 (1986): 184.

47. Aubrey C. Land, "Economic Behavior in a Planting Society: The Eighteenth-Century Chesapeake," *Journal of Southern History,* 33 (1967): 480.

iron ore, in many cases bog iron, to a molten state. This necessitated an army of lumberjacks and charcoal burners at the furnace sites. Most iron furnaces produced a thousand tons or more of iron per year. According to forest historian Douglas MacCleery "the impact on the forest locally was significant. A 1,000-ton ironworks required between 20,000 and 30,000 acres of forest to sustain itself."[48] So rural iron manufacture and environmental desolation went hand in hand. By 1779, for example, the lands that surrounded Accakeek Iron Mines and Furnace were so broken and denuded that the land could not be sold. Even though iron had not been mined there in twenty years, the ugliness of the region left an indelible impression on visitors.[49]

The Chesapeake's growing potash industry took its toll as well. Potash or potassium carbonate was a convenient by-product of burnt forests. England's business community used potash in glass-making and other industrial processes, and farmers used it as fertilizer. Potash-making was just as timber-intensive as iron manufacture; three to five acres of timber land had to be burned to yield a ton of potash. Despite its excellence as a fertilizer, Chesapeake planters seldom used potash. The increasing demand for potash in European manufacturing made it too important an export to be used locally.

## Chesapeake Waters

It is appropriate to ask what impact changes in the regional environment during the colonial period had on the Chesapeake Bay itself. So much of what later happened to the bay was dependent upon rapid population growth, but at this point, population pressures on the landscape do not seem to have had a corresponding deleterious impact on the bay. Chesapeake waters seem to have been more resilient than Chesapeake soils. However, some tendencies in the maritime environment of the Chesapeake are worthy of mention. First, the construction of mill dams and other obstructions on Chesapeake rivers may have worked to deplete fish populations because they made it more difficult for migrating fish like shad and herring to swim upstream to spawn. The first areas to feel the effects of this prob-

---

48. Douglass W. MacCleery, *American Forests: A History of Resiliency and Recovery* (Durham, North Carolina: Forest History Society, 1994), 13.

49. Cox, *Well-Wooded Land*, 15.

lem, writes ecology historian David Hardin, were in the headwaters of the Rappahannock River and other watercourses in southside Virginia. By the 1750s these waters had seen extensive dam construction for grain mills. Colonists began to complain of the decline of spawning runs on the Rapidan River. Similarly, Maryland residents complained of mill dams that ruined fishing and pressured the assembly to give them relief from the rapacious grain millers. While Virginia colonists were aware of what was happening to spawning runs in Chesapeake waters, they did not understand the role that soil erosion and agricultural runoff had in ruining the fishery. As Hardin observed, there was "no evidence that Virginians realized what was happening to their waters and there was certainly no legislation designed to deal with the problem."[50] The only legislation focusing on a decreased fishery was a Virginia law in 1680 that established an off-season during which no fish could be taken by gigs and harpoons.

Not until after 1750 did market fishing become a significant industry in the Chesapeake. In Fauquier County, planter Landon Carter offered seines for sale, one of which was 75 fathoms long and 36 feet deep in the middle with five-eighths-inch mesh. Such nets heralded the arrival of broad scale commercial fishing technology to the waters of Chesapeake Bay.[51] By 1753 Maryland had begun to export herring commercially to the West Indies, and sturgeon—pickled and smoked—was slowly finding its way from the Chesapeake to the London market. George Washington became well-known on the Potomac as an enterprising herring and shad provisioner who supplied Alexandria merchants with five hundred barrels of seafood each season. The Byrd family of Virginia also operated several fish-harvesting businesses on the James River that were valued at more than two thousand pounds sterling annually.[52] But in the long term the British Navigation Acts protected the fishery by denying Chesapeake seafood merchants the right to import the large quantities of inexpensive salt from southern Europe

50. David S. Hardin, "Laws of Nature: Wildlife Management Legislation in Virginia," in Larry M. Dilsaver and Craig E. Colten, eds. *The American Environment: Interpretations of Past Geographies* (Lanham, Md.: Rowman and Littlefield Publishers, 1992), 137–62.

51. John C. Pearson, "The Fish and Fisheries of Colonial Virginia," *William and Mary Quarterly*, series 2, vol. 22 (1942): 358–59.

52. Middleton, *Tobacco Coast*, 222–25.

necessary for curing and pickling fish. Also, given the small population and the natural abundance of the Chesapeake, notes archeologist Henry M. Miller, "it is unlikely that the colonists had any impact upon the fish populations."[53]

Studies of fish usage in the Chesapeake indicate that at least until 1745 the fishing equipment used by colonists was "nothing more elaborate than hooks and lines."[54] The Chesapeake fishery during the colonial period remained plentiful largely because it served a limited regional market. Numerous accounts mention the large quantities of rockfish, drum, catfish, sheepshead, herring, and eels taken by local fishermen.

Consumption of fish and fish products in the Chesapeake followed strict class lines. Slaves, poor whites, and rich planters were major fish-eaters, but in Maryland and Virginia it was often remarked that the average colonist preferred salt-pork or beef to sturgeon and oysters. For the working classes of the Chesapeake the principal diet was hominy and pork washed down with large amounts of homemade cider and ale. Though cheap, fish was found more frequently on the dinner tables of the upper class than on those of the less affluent. The tobacco-rich Carter family of Nomini Hall in Virginia, for example, dined on fish and crabs every Wednesday and Saturday in summer, and Philip Fithian wrote of the great "Fishfeasts" frequently hosted by Robert Carter. The Virginia gentry consumed large amounts of Maryland oysters, and Robert Carter regularly sent his schooner *Hariot* to the Eastern Shore of Maryland in winter for cargoes of the tasty bivalve. For the Carters, oysters were a favorite breakfast staple.[55]

Given the overwhelming agrarian nature of Chesapeake Bay in the later colonial period, its inhabitants experienced no dearth of food. Most farms and plantations were self-sufficient. Corn, pigs, venison, and fruit were sufficiently plentiful. Although smokehouses were in use, little attention was given to smoking fish for future consumption. Cultural behavior, more than environment, determined the eating habits of colonists in the Chesapeake.

Archeological evidence indicates that during the colonial period the bay's

53. Miller, "Colonists and Ecological Change," 179.
54. Ibid., 175.
55. Philip Fithian, *Journal and Letters of Philip Vickers Fithian, 1773–1774: A Plantation Tutor,* edited by Hunter D. Farish (Williamsburg, Va.: Colonial Williamsburg, Inc., 1965), 29.

waters had a high salinity. Henry Miller observes that, until the forest cover of the Susquehanna and James River watersheds was removed in the eighteenth century, "it is likely that the rate of fresh water inflow was considerably less than today." Much of the time, the weather was dry. Oysters were plentiful in shallow waters and flourished in this saline environment.

In the eighteenth century soil erosion and deforestation in the piedmont came to be a serious problem, and as a result, greater freshwater runoffs into the Chesapeake began to alter salinity. Increases in siltation and nutrient content in Chesapeake streams and rivers transformed fish habitat. The development of long oyster tongs in the eighteenth century may be an indication that the pollution of streams was forcing Chesapeake fisherfolk to harvest in deeper, cleaner waters. Deforestation, soil erosion, and sedimentation would begin to have a noticeable impact on the waters of the Chesapeake by 1820, in what Henry M. Miller calls "a clear example of the impact that changing land use practices can have on estuaries."[56]

## Anglo-American Land Use Attitudes

The ten-million-acre Chesapeake coastal plain that was put to tobacco and timber production was a land known for swift and sluggish streams and rivers and for imperfectly drained soils. Despite its richness the land had a shallow topsoil easily injured by excessive agricultural use. Tobacco exhausted the soil after about seven years, and Chesapeake planters had to own large tracts of land in order to replace their depleted fields. The most serious loss to Chesapeake soils, though, came from water drainage. Seasonal storms carried off potassium, phosphorus, calcium, and other important minerals from the land. Nitrogen also washed easily out of the soil, leaving behind a poor, infertile countryside. As Avery Craven and others have shown, frontier communities like the Chesapeake at this time were "notorious exhausters" of the soil. In a region where land was abundant and capital and labor scarce, added Craven, "only the most fertile soils will be used and only those methods which give greatest immediate returns regardless of future consequences. The problem is one of rapid spending, not of conservation."[57]

56. Miller, "Colonists and Ecological Change," 186.
57. Craven, *Soil Exhaustion*, 19–21.

Tobacco is a heavy consumer of nitrogen, and the removal of the entire crop from the field encouraged soil rot and the proliferation of harmful micro-organisms. Often after as few as two planting seasons, planters abandoned tobacco land to sorrel and sedge. In fact, the term new land and tobacco land soon became synonymous in the Chesapeake. As early as the middle of the seventeenth century, visitors to tidewater Virginia noted that the region was beginning to have a worn out appearance that resulted, it was argued, from the sloth and negligence of its residents. In Maryland devotion to tobacco resulted in a disordered landscape of scrub trees and ravaged fields. At this time, writes historian Gloria Main, "Maryland appeared half-civilized to the European eye."[58] As early as 1649, less than a generation after Captain John Smith, Virginia lands on the south side of the York River had become barren from cultivation. By the 1690s Virginians began to refer to land that had passed out of cultivation as "Old Fields" that relapsed into thickets and second growth.

It was difficult to convince planters to develop more responsible attitudes toward the land when land itself seemed an unlimited and cheap commodity compared to the high price of labor. The Chesapeake had no sense of community or commonality of enterprise like that of Puritan New England. Furthermore, in Maryland delegates to the Assembly believed exhausting of the soil by tobacco planting took the wildness out of the soil and made it better for tillage.[59] It should be mentioned that nature limited planter options. The disappointingly low rate of livestock production in the region is explained by the corresponding unwillingness of planters to take a chance on committing land to timothy and alfalfa. "The risk of rain during the period of mowing and curing was very great," wrote Julius Rubin, and yields of livestock products "suffered from the direct effects of the climate."[60]

Most of the region's population during the colonial period was youthful, with large numbers of farm servants between the ages of fifteen and twenty-five. These servants as well as slaves who were forced to work on the plantations had little appreciation of the European concept of the stewardship of

58. Gloria L. Main, *Tobacco Colony: Life in Early Maryland, 1650–1720* (Princeton: Princeton University Press, 1982), 43.
59. *Archives of Maryland,* 19:540, 580.
60. Julius Rubin, "The Limits of Agricultural Progress in the Nineteenth Century South," *Agricultural History,* 49 (1975): 365.

land. John Clayton, a Yorkshire clergyman who visited Virginia in the 1680s, discovered how impervious Virginians could be to land management. When Clayton attempted to persuade a plantation overseer to use enlightened husbandry in draining marshland, the overseer replied scornfully that "he understood his business well enough, and did not desire to learn of me."[61] Most planters had little ecological consciousness of the value of wetlands and simply referred to them as "large rank morasses." Hugh Jones in his *Present State of Virginia* advocated systematic draining of marshes for livestock use. For Jones and his contemporaries, marshlands were "useless and incommodious."[62]

A similar attitude prevailed when it came to hunting. Deer were relentlessly hunted in the Chesapeake for leather, and by 1770 their numbers in Maryland, one observer noted, were exceedingly diminished. "These people, whose only motive was to procure the hide of the animal, were dextrous, during the winter season, in tracing their path through the snow; and from the animal's incapacity to exert speed under such circumstances, great multitudes of them were annually slaughtered and their carcasses left in the woods."[63]

## Property Rights and the Environment

The colonial Chesapeake represents an interesting historical transition in the conceptualization of property rights. What emerged in the region at this time was a conception of ownership that was in many respects different from what had prevailed in Europe over the centuries. As late as the seventeenth century many European farmers were engaged in landholding rather than landowning. The crucial difference was that in the former case a man had a right to land that he and his family could work with their own labor. Property was not yet completely an abstract or fungible thing that could be owned, speculated upon, and not worked. Many Englishmen who came to the New World brought this land practice with them. The unique-

---

61. "Letters of John Clayton to the Royal Society," in Peter Force, ed., *Tracts and Other Papers*, 4 vols. (1836–46, repr., Gloucester, Mass.: Peter Smith, 1963), 3:22.

62. Jones, *Present State of Virginia*, 143.

63. Aubrey C. Land, ed., *William Eddis, Letters from America* (Cambridge: Harvard University Press, 1969), 32.

ness of the frontier environment, however, lent itself to another property concept then being articulated in the mother country at this time by John Locke in his *Two Treatises of Government*. Writing with the excesses of Charles I and the Puritan Revolution in mind, Locke argued that property rights existed independently of kings, government, and the collective rights of the community. Thus, for Locke, if a man mixed his labor with nature, he was entitled to the fruits of that mixture and could enjoy it independently of any social context. Enjoyment of property was therefore a presocietal natural right. Later Thomas Jefferson would expand on this concept by referring to the "allodial rights" of Virginians. This hoary Saxon term, which referred to the English idea that property or an estate can be held in absolute dominion without obligation to a king or superior, appealed greatly to Jefferson and his tax-avoiding generation of 1776.

As Eugene C. Hargrove has shown, this new idea of property would greatly influence American attitudes toward the environment. Writes Hargrove: "Because it involved nothing more than the economic interest of the individual, it was devoid of moral obligation or moral responsibility." The ownership of land relieved planters of any individual or collective responsibility to the land itself. In effect, Chesapeake planters mythologized property rights by appealing to ancient traditions and to new political theories that appealed to their purses.

The Lockean or allodial concepts did not eliminate all other ideas about property. According to Hargrove, the idea of landholding independent of landowning was reflected in the Morrill Land Grant Act of 1862 and was "influential in American political and legal thought in the nineteenth century." Duke University Professor Laura Underkauffer has argued that, in the "Founding Era" of America, "property in the historical view did not represent the autonomous sphere of the individual to be asserted against the collective; rather it embodied and reflected the inherent tension between the individual and the collective." For Underkauffer and many current scholars of American property rights, property had meaning only insofar as it recognized the individual's need for freedom "in the context of relatedness to others."[64]

64. Eugene C. Hargrove, "Anglo-American Land Use Attitudes," *Environmental Ethics,* 2 (1980): 145. See also Laura S. Underkaffler, "On Property: An Essay," *Yale Law Journal,* 100, No. 73 (1990): 129.

The disposition of Calvert manor lands, for example, is instructive of the ways that landowning and property rights impacted harshly on the regional environment in the colonial period. Put simply, manor lands were nothing more than large tracts of land owned by the Calvert family which could not be bought or settled without the express permission of the proprietor. In the eighteenth century the Calverts owned some 190,000 acres of land in Maryland, and, as the biggest landholders in the region, sought to profit from land speculation. When available farm land became scarce in the Chesapeake after 1750, the proprietor invited colonists to settle on manor lands as tenants. The leaseholder was required to clear the land, build a house, and establish a fruit orchard. The tenant would have land to farm, and its owner would have rent and an improved piece of property to sell in the future at an inflated price. There were twenty-three manors in Maryland; the largest were on Maryland's western shore.

The landlord-tenant relationship on the manors worked better in theory than in practice. The proprietor was an absentee landlord and had difficulty extracting rent from his poor tenants. Tenants also abused the land. They cut down most of the trees on the manor in order to raise money and were slovenly farmers. As tenants had large families, they were forced to plant their fields in subsistence crops of vegetables, corn, and tobacco. Using hoes, tenants planted thousands of hillocks of corn that drew the nitrogen out of the soil, so that soil erosion took a particularly heavy toll on manor lands in Maryland. When much of the Chesapeake was shifting to new forms of agriculture, tenants stubbornly clung to tobacco. According to historian Gregory Stiverson, they grew tobacco as a cash crop "because they understood the culture of tobacco and the marketing system was well developed."[65]

Thus did corn and tobacco continue their destruction of the Maryland landscape in an age when agriculturalists advocated a four-field rotation system and the planting of potatoes, peas, and beans to restore the health of the soil. As Stiverson notes, it was basically a problem of poor farms continuously farmed by poor people. Tobacco and corn were the only crops that impoverished small farmers could plant to pay their rents and maintain their families. Necessity kept the tenants locked in a cycle of destructive agriculture.

65. Gregory A. Stiverson, *Poverty in a Land of Plenty, Tenancy in Eighteenth-Century Maryland* (Baltimore: The Johns Hopkins University Press, 1977), 92

Another problem with tenantry in the Chesapeake was the transformation in tenant leaseholds after 1750. Until that time tenants in Maryland usually had a life lease, which encouraged careful husbandry and a modicum of land stewardship. As proprietors and planters shifted to short-term leases that would provide greater immediate revenues, their tenants, hard pressed to make the rent, strove to produce ever greater crops of marketable tobacco, especially in the post-Revolutionary 1780s and 1790s. They also cleared more land for market crops like corn and wheat, but as Lorena Walsh has remarked, land that needed frequent rotation and long fallows could not sustain such intensive cultivation. These farmers extracted as much as they could from the land because they had no long-term interest in it. "It was the failure of both landlord and tenant to follow traditional agricultural practices rather than the practices themselves that were at fault."[66]

## Did Colonial Farmers Waste Our Land?

Recently the interpretation and understanding of environmental change in the colonial Chesapeake has become an important subject for historians, geographers, and ecologists. Since the 1950s a conservative school of scholars has followed the line of thought developed by economist Warren Scoville that colonial farmers did not waste our land. Planters in the Chesapeake acted economically and minimized waste in an age of scarce labor and capital.[67] By using up land quickly, farmers could get a higher rate of return on their investment. In that era, land was plentiful, and it would have been wasteful to squander capital instead of land. To do otherwise, argued Scoville, would have been to mismanage resources in ways that would have prevented subsequent generations from having a higher standard of living. The extra income gained from exploiting the land allowed for capital accumulation that supported economic development in America. This was an interpretation of history based on the concept of intergenerational economic advantage.

While few Chesapeake scholars have embraced this land wastage thesis

---

66. Lorena S. Walsh, "Land, Landlord, and Leaseholder: Estate Management and Tenant Fortunes in Southern Maryland, 1642–1820," *Agricultural History,* 59 (1985): 390, 394.

67. Warren Scoville, "Did Colonial Farmers Waste Our Land?" *Southern Economic Journal,* 20 (1953): 178–81.

in its entirety, they have been critical of the opposing viewpoint that has portrayed Chesapeake planters as "land butchers." Scholars like Carville Earle, Russell Menard, Lois Green Carr, Edward Papenfuse, and Lorena Walsh have produced a number of provocative and intriguing studies of seventeenth- and eighteenth-century Maryland, and their investigations constitute an important and fruitful Chesapeake *oeuvre*. (For convenience here we refer to these scholars as the Chesapeake School.[68]) They believe that judgments about agricultural practice in the colonial Chesapeake must take into consideration that a new husbandry was required, one that exploited land that was cheap without destroying it and conserved labor, which was expensive. The Chesapeake School further argues that planters were not the "land butchers" that they have been portrayed. While tobacco monoculture made for an untidy landscape, it did not severely deplete the soil.[69]

For the Chesapeake School, neither planters nor the tobacco staple led to the undoing of the Chesapeake environment. For over a century, these scholars argue, the hoe had been the chief agricultural tool, and the agricultural method of planting tobacco in hills created a land surface that resisted erosion. Fields cleared by slash and burn techniques left borders of vegetated tracts and forest to absorb water runoff. Soil erosion produced by humans, they argue, was minimal. It was Enlightenment-inspired agricultural reforms—plow agriculture, the introduction of fertilizers, and continuous systems of cultivation—that displaced an ecologically sounder, if primitive, land rotation system. Enlightened planters imposed order on an unkempt and unruly landscape and in effect destroyed it.[70]

To accept the thesis of the Chesapeake School, however, is to overlook

68. Among the best examples of the Chesapeake School of scholarship are: Carville Earle, "The Myth of the Southern Soil Miner: Macrohistory, Agricultural Innovation and Environmental Change," in Worster, ed., *The Ends of the Earth*, 191, 194–200; Edward C. Papenfuse, "Planter Behavior and Economic Opportunity in a Staple Economy," *Agricultural History*, 46 (1972): 310; and Lois Green Carr, Russell Menard, and Lorena S. Walsh, *Robert Cole's World: Agriculture and Society in Early Maryland* (Chapel Hill: University of North Carolina Press for the Institute of Early American Culture, 1991).

69. For a critical review of the Chesapeake School's position on colonial land use, see John R. Wennersten, "Soil Miners Redux: The Chesapeake Environment, 1680–1810," *Maryland Historical Magazine*, 91 (1996): 157–79.

70. Carville Earle, "The Myth of the Southern Soil Miner," 191, 194–200.

the fact that many of the destructive forces of environmental change in the Chesapeake were at work *before* agricultural innovation became widespread. Enormous flooding and sedimentation processes were at work in Chesapeake waters well before the Revolution and certainly before the wholesale introduction of grain agriculture into the region. During the eighteenth century the Chesapeake was in the throes of a population explosion that placed great pressure on the landscape. Fertility rates during this period were exceptionally high, and emigration to the region remained steady. In Maryland and Virginia black slaves composed in the eighteenth century 30 and 40 percent respectively of the total population, and between 1700 and 1740 Maryland's total population mushroomed from 34,000 to 300,000. Local figures in the tidewater are instructive. In 1705 All Hallows Parish contained eighteen people per square mile. By 1776 the parish had forty-two people per square mile. Prince George's County on the western shore was experiencing similar exponential growth at thirty-nine people per square mile.[71] Even if they had wanted to maintain the old ways, planters were essentially running out of space to continue the long fallow system. Population pressure helped to force a switch to cereals and higher yielding crops like potatoes, which heretofore had been used as fodder crops. As David Grigg has noted in his important work, *The Dynamics of Agricultural Change,* population growth causes agricultural change rather than being a function of it.[72]

Long fallows were seldom capable of reproducing the traditional forest. In the Chesapeake, pine invaded the old fields that had been cleared of oak and other hardwoods, and pine did little to reconstruct the forest floor humus. In the pine forests, cattle were allowed to range freely, eating green shoots of hardwoods attempting to reestablish themselves. Planters and poor whites alike thought pine forests to be good range for cattle, reducing the likelihood of the great oak forests springing up again.[73] Under the system of deforestation at work in the colonial Chesapeake, the vegetation was so degraded that it was impossible for the forest to reclaim its original self.

Tobacco culture and deforestation, especially, were at work in the region

71. See Miller, "Colonists and Ecological Change," 182.
72. David Grigg, *The Dynamics of Agricultural Change* (London: Hutchinson, 1982), 43.
73. See Gray, *History of Agriculture,* 40, 45, 139, 150.

long before other technological and agricultural innovations harmed the land and its waters. Like tobacco, the forest had become a money crop un-encumbered by feudal restrictions and historic restraints and was an excel-lent source of profit to foreign and local markets. In the end, tobacco, tim-ber, grain, and landscape were swept into the individualism and material-ism of the market. That irresistible tide led to the commodification of the Chesapeake environment and set the pattern for the exploitation of the region's natural resources in the future. James T. Lemon, a historical geog-rapher, summed up the matter well when he said that in the mid-Atlantic in the eighteenth century accumulation outweighed egalitarianism as the stronger value. "Only now," he writes, "when growth is checked and the cost of resources is eroding the real incomes of many, is it possible to recog-nize the nakedness of the accumulation impulse and to identify what it has done to the environment and ourselves."[74]

74. James T. Lemon, "Early Americans and Their Social Environment," *Journal of Historical Geography*, 6 (1980): 127.

## CHAPTER THREE

# Ecological Transformations
## Agriculture, Internal Improvements, and Town Development

"Every part of the landscape — woods, soil, and waterways, and the animals that used them — was altered by the demands of a society with many wants of its own, and foreign markets to serve, as well."
— Albert Cowdrey, *This Land, This South*

"Let us boldly face the fact, our country is nearly ruined."
— John Taylor, *Arator*

## Economic Growth and Development

Human progress in the Chesapeake during the colonial period resulted from man's increasing ability to interfere with ecological processes. Farmers, planters, and woodsmen tamed the Chesapeake wilderness and made it serve the purposes of commodity agriculture. In the seventeenth century the consequences were unimportant because the population was small, and colonials could only feebly disturb the environment. Those conditions did not last. In the eighteenth century, the revolution in commodity agriculture began to disturb the balance of the Chesapeake ecosystem. Nature does not take forever; it can be altered within a short period of time. By 1750, the Chesapeake had reached the point where its population had the capability to alter the region's natural cycles. Admittedly, colonial economic and social development by the mid-eighteenth century was hardly sophisticated. It resembled in tenor and scope and power that of Third World societies today. Nevertheless, anyone who is aware of the ecological transformations taking place in Third World societies can appreciate the power of the inhabitants of the eighteenth-century Chesapeake.[1]

Unlike New England which experienced bitter Indian warfare in its wilderness border zone, colonists found that Chesapeake waters and western

---

1. For additional comment on this subject, see Jack Larkin, *The Reshaping of Everyday Life, 1790–1840* (New York: Harper and Row, 1988), xv.

landscape were relatively peaceful. Indigenous tribes had long since been destroyed or expelled westward. By 1776 only the enfeebled Catawba Indians of the Carolinas and southern Virginia remained within the travel orbit of Chesapeake Bay. Further, by 1780 the population of Pennsylvania, Virginia, and Maryland had passed one million. An agricultural complex of grain and livestock kept the population reasonably well-fed, and Chesapeake society took on a life of its own.

Research on the colonial Chesapeake has shown that growth in the region was neither smooth nor uniform. While the population soared by 80 percent, there were recurring cycles of prosperity and depression.[2] After the Revolution farmers turned to mixed grain agriculture as improvements in transportation allowed shipment of bulky agricultural products to feed the new urban markets of Philadelphia, Baltimore, and Norfolk. Canals and steam power encouraged a shift away from older agricultural processes.

Pressure on the Chesapeake environment continued unabated. Farmers aggressively modified the environment by bringing in new species of plants that flourished in open country, and eliminated through bounties the population of wolves, bear, and other animals that preyed on livestock.[3] Chesapeake society with its high demographic vigor pressed against the limits of environment. Desirable lands in the tidewater could no longer be acquired except through purchase. Land enclosure by property-conscious elites propelled settlers westward.

Despite the explosive changes in politics wrought by the American Revolution, those who settled in the Chesapeake displayed little common purpose save money-getting. Capitalism and patriarchy existed side by side. Through much of the region's history people lived in nature without ever really formulating a social compact among themselves. West of the Blue Ridge evolved a rough-hewn pioneer society that did not bear the indelible stamp of tobacco monoculture and planter supremacy. Political authority was more local than national in scope, and small landholding and diversi-

2. Richard D. Brown, *Modernization: The Transformation of American Life, 1600– 1865* (New York: McGraw-Hill, 1976), 107. See especially Brown's remarks on localism giving way to cosmopolitanism and the novelty of invention and enterprise after 1776.

3. E. L. Jones, "Creative Disruptions in American Agriculture,1620–1820," *Agricultural History,* 48 (1974): 519.

fied farming had less deleterious effects on the environment. The yeoman economy of the western Appalachian region did not plunge the farmer into a downward spiral of indebtedness, dependency, and environmental decline, and was thus ultimately easier on the land. If anything, the growth of communities beyond the reaches of the Chesapeake illustrate how forms of collective life that knitted people together over vast stretches of space could lead to new ways of living with the environment.[4]

The Chesapeake Bay in the early nineteenth century, on the other hand, was a land of dreams. Progressive agricultural reformers dreamed of a restored landscape that would offer pastoral democracy to Chesapeake farmers. Business promoters and engineers dreamed of a region dominated by a matrix of rivers and canals that would open up the Chesapeake country and beyond to economic development. Neither group got exactly what it wanted, and no one anticipated that soil erosion, floods, and water pollution would turn a proud estuary into an "Ultimate Sink."

The period from 1750 to about 1820 marked the Chesapeake Bay country's transition to modernity. Farmers employed new methods, and a generation-long revolution in canals and other internal improvements precipitated new forms of environmental consciousness. Agricultural innovation paved the way for the triumph of commercial over subsistence farming, and the rise of new towns and commercial centers changed notions of environmental use and propriety. With the advent of canals, steam power, and new forms of transportation on the bay, farmers and businessmen intersected with a growing national market economy. The transformative power of the market in turn altered the face of the countryside.

## The Basic Problem of Agriculture

The basic problem of Chesapeake agriculture in the late eighteenth and early nineteenth century was that farmers paid no attention to their land or

---

4. See Malcolm J. Rohrbough, *The Trans-Appalachian Frontier: People, Societies and Institutions, 1775–1850* (New York: Oxford University Press, 1978); Warren R. Hofstra, "The Virginia Backcountry in the Eighteenth Century: The Question of Origins and Outcomes," *Virginia Magazine of History and Biography,* 101 (1993): 494–500.

to their craft.[5] Farming was simply the means to making a fast dollar. During the French Revolution and the wars of Napoleon, when Europeans cried for wheat at two dollars a bushel, Chesapeake farmers could sell even their poor quality grain full of weeds and dirt and the ravages of the parasitic Hessian fly. The European wheat boom lasted until 1825, by which time nearly five generations of Chesapeake farmers had misused the landscape.[6] William Strickland, an agricultural reformer, visited Virginia and Maryland in 1800 and thought it impossible to make a living farming in the Chesapeake. Virginia farms, he wrote, had reached "the lowest state of degradation," and Maryland was little better.[7]

Had anyone taken the time to look at it, the research, experience, and informed opinion necessary to save the region from desolation was readily at hand. The writings of Chesapeake agricultural reformers between the Revolution and the Civil War permit us to see what exactly was required to restore the Chesapeake landscape. The English passion for agricultural improvement and experimentation transferred easily to the new Republic, where leaders' thoughts focused on turning swords into plowshares. George Washington maintained an active correspondence with the English agronomist Arthur Young, who attempted to popularize manuring and the use of

---

5. Carville Earle, the historical geographer, objects that much "American environmental history is reduced to a morality play of good versus evil, of capitalist rapacity versus natural innocence." Why, asks Earle, would farmers destroy the very lands that sustained them in the pursuit of profit? Earle, in his examination of what he calls "human agency," does not see Chesapeake farmers ruining the landscape. He dismisses eyewitness testimony to environmental damage as biased and anecdotal. "Southern agrarian practices were more complex than environmental historiography usually allows." Yet throughout the period, visitors to the region who were skilled agriculturalists provided eyewitness accounts of a dilapidated and barren landscape that are difficult to reject. Thus in his work Earle displays the same hostility to the environmentalists that the environmentalists display toward capitalism. Much of his critique is ahistorical, projecting current social science models on past economic practice. For the clearest statement of this thesis see Carville Earle, "Into the Abyss . . . Again: Technical Change and Destructive Occupance in the American Cotton Belt, 1870–1930," in Larry M. Dilsaver and Craig E. Colten eds., *The American Environment: Interpretations of Past Geographies* (Lanham, Maryland: Rowman and Littlefield, 1992), 53–88.

6. E. L. Jones, "Creative Disruptions in American Agriculture, 1620–1820," 528.

7. Quoted in Craven, *Soil Exhaustion*, 84.

root crops like turnips that would provide good food and restore the soil. Progressive farmers like Thomas Jefferson and Landon Carter read Young's influential book, *Rural Economy,* and imported improved breeds of livestock from England, which they hoped would lead to some diversification of the Chesapeake agricultural economy.

When the spring freshets of 1771 caused Virginia rivers to run red, the aristocratic planter Landon Carter noted in his diary that bad farming was killing the region. Carter owned several hundred thousand acres of farmlands and worried that the laziness and indifference of his overseers and tenants would eventually ruin him. At that time the plow was coming into wide use, and hoe culture was considered old-fashioned. But Carter was a great believer in hoe agriculture because it created less soil erosion than the plow. Carter disliked plows because "they just scratched the surface," and oxen ate too much of the corn crop. "I cannot but observe," he complained in his diary, "that no single yoke of oxen could do the work fit for any growth."[8]

John Beale Bordley, a respected "scientific" agriculturalist and planter in Queen Anne's County on Maryland's Eastern Shore, grumbled that farmers were more interested in pursuing "folly" than husbandry. "They mount their horses and hurry to the tavern, the race, nine pins, billiards, excess upon excess of toddy, and their most nonsensical and idle chat [is] accompanied with exclamations and roarings, brutal and foreign to common sense as the mind of wisdom can conceive of a depraved man."[9] Bordley claimed that excessive corn production in the Chesapeake ruined the land as much as tobacco. Corn production was closely tied to the maintenance of "supernumerary negroes" and did little to create wealth in the region. He urged farmers to put exhausted tobacco and corn fields in beans, timothy, and hay and to make extensive use of manure.

John Beale Bordley's views as a progressive farmer and agricultural reformer merit serious study because he was one of the first advocates for a new way of looking at the land and the way of life that it engendered in the Chesapeake. As an apostle of agricultural education, he had ideas on everything from the making of pottery and beer to the seasoning of wood and the virtues of peas. He even had ideas about changing the behavior of convicts in Philadelphia jails through enhanced diet. Bordley believed that the

8. Jack P. Greene, ed. *The Diary of Colonel Landon Carter of Sabine Hall, 1752–1778,* 2 vols. (Richmond: Virginia Historical Society, 1987), 2:433, 575, 671.

Chesapeake landscape could be transformed if farmers in the region would relinquish their worst habits. There was nothing complex, he wrote, about being a good, dedicated farmer. All that it took was "well-digested systematic applications of labour." Bordley's ideal for the Chesapeake yeoman was a fifty-six acre farm with a small timber plot.

In 1785–86 Bordley kept a detailed diary of his agricultural experiments, most of which showed that it was not the specific crop that injured the land but the way in which it was cultivated. For example, noted Bordley, tobacco was not the culprit on Maryland's Eastern Shore. "I have known ground cultivated constantly in tobacco, many years; being frequently manured."[10] Excessive monoculture without restoring the soil, wrote Bordley, ruined the land. But farmers were indifferent to improvement, he complained, and were captive to "gloomy and barbarous practices." They never looked beyond their old habits to see the consequences of their actions.

Bordley was a champion of well-manured fields and crop rotation, and he devised a system of tables by which farmers could conduct their efforts "in regular rotation forever." The latter was probably too sophisticated for most Maryland farmers. He also wanted them to grow new crops like hemp that could be dried to make linen, and he was annoyed that Chesapeake farmers continued to practice the long fallow. "Rest," he wrote "is a friend of weeds and a hardness of ground." Far better, he believed to rotate fields in clover, beans, and peas. Bordley remained optimistic that a new Chesapeake farmer might be created, and his essays give us a glimpse of this new agricultural man. The fifty-six-acre model farm would contain several acres of spruce, larch, and fir trees planted 425 to the acre. These would mature in eight years and supply the farmer with lumber. A small stand of sugar maples on two-thirds of an acre could produce thirty dollars worth of maple sugar to buy a horse, two oxen, and two dairy cows. Significantly, Bordley's ideas on farming have been widely accepted in twenty-first-century progressive circles. The kind of small-scale agriculture that Bordley envisioned is alive and well in many areas of the country.[11]

Despite the dismal character of the environment in the early nineteenth

9. John Beale Bordley, *Essays and Notes on Husbandry and Rural Affairs* (Philadelphia: Budd and Bartram, 1801), 155–56.

10. Ibid., 226.

11. Wendell Berry is an especially noteworthy example of this tradition of agri-

century, the Chesapeake saw some notable agricultural successes. Of particular importance was the contribution of John Taylor of Caroline, a Virginia lawyer and country squire, who popularized agricultural study. After making a fortune in a tidewater law practice, he became a gentleman farmer and had the time, energy, and money to teach sound farming practice to his fellow planters. He personally showed them how to plant their fields and improve their estates. Land stewardship, he believed, was synonymous with the public good. The key to a sound plantation, argued Taylor, was a well-manured field enclosed with wandering livestock. The cattle would manure the field, which could easily be plowed up. Taylor researched and experimented with other innovative agricultural methods. He developed new and better seeds, sermonized on the use of fertilizer, advocated crop rotation, and utilized cedar hedges to stem wind erosion of the fields and to supply fire wood. In addition to showing the value of manure, he introduced the "enclosing system"—non-grazing of fields so that all vegetable growth was left to die and rot. Fields so used became self-manuring.

"Let us boldly face the fact, " Taylor wrote in his seminal 1813 work, *Arator,* "our country is nearly ruined." He blamed it on the incompetence of common farmers and the negligence of overseers, neither of whom were interested in restoring the soil. Taylor also condemned deep ploughing as "pernicious" and hoped that Chesapeake farmers would turn more to orchards, the planting of peas, and the fertilization of corn fields with animal dung gained from raising small herds of cattle.[12] Like Bordley and others, John Taylor of Caroline feared that the Chesapeake's agrarian society was threatened by farmers who were killing the land rather than improving it. Bordley might have mentioned something that all agricultural reformers came to recognize—restoring and building a farm was especially tedious business. It monopolized a planter's time and all but extinguished his social life.

In the years after 1800, tobacco prices plummeted because of foreign competition, and wheat rust destroyed crops all over Virginia and Maryland. Yellow fever spread in the coastal areas, and Gabriel's slave rebellion

---

cultural reform. See Wendell Berry, *The Gift of Good Land* (San Francisco: North Point Press, 1981), 257–58, 270–72.

12. John Taylor, *Arator, Being a Series of Agricultural Essays, Practical and Political* (repr., Indianapolis: Liberty Classics Books, 1977), 127–28, 160, 217, 231, 280.

spread panic out of Richmond. For Taylor this was evidence of both God's wrath and the moral and agricultural contagion of the Chesapeake landscape.

To Taylor, Bordley, and those who shared their pastoralist viewpoint, the purpose of sound farming was to rescue rural life from decay and to restore the natural order and abundance of the landscape. In our time they would be hailed by environmentalists as conscientious, well-informed ecologists. They saw that the Chesapeake social order was rooted in the land. If the land failed, so too would society. They strove to maintain a polity that sustained pastoral values and republicanism. Land stewardship, they believed, was synonymous with the public good. Yet, in their time they were voices crying in the wilderness. A slave-holding planter with a rich estate in Caroline County, Virginia, and a member of the Eastern Shore Maryland gentry carried only so much weight with the fiercely independent yeomanry.[13]

Land stewardship in the Chesapeake during the period 1819–1834 found its broadest and most influential expression in John Stuart Skinner, an able and highly energetic agriculturalist who edited *The American Farmer* in Baltimore. During his long editorship Skinner championed land restoration and agricultural education. He campaigned to get young farmers to study their craft seriously. Through pamphlets, speeches, and newspaper articles, Skinner made one of the most determined campaigns of all the agricultural reformers to bring the land back from the brink of destruction. In his articles and letters he also crusaded for internal improvements like canals and railroads that would ease the transportation problems of Chesapeake farmers and connect the agricultural base of the region with burgeoning towns and cities. Unfortunately, the small farmers ignored him, and after briefly enjoying the patronage of the planter class, *The American Farmer* limped along as an obscure publication.[14]

13. For an overview of Taylor's life and agricultural philosophy see, Robert E. Shalhope, *John Taylor of Caroline, Pastoral Republican* (Columbia: University of South Carolina Press, 1980).

14. See Harold T. Pinkett, "*The American Farmer:* A Pioneer Agricultural Journal. 1819–1834," *Agricultural History,* 24 (1950): 146–50. See also Margaret W. Rossiter, "The Organization of Agricultural Improvement in the United States, 1785–1865," in Alexandra Olsen, ed., *The Pursuit of Knowledge in the Early Republic* (Baltimore: Johns Hopkins University Press, 1976), 279–98.

The *American Farmer* lamented that the Chesapeake was known principally for its "benumbing poverty" and "broken spirits." The great estates were naught but memories in the 1820s, as farmers scratched for a living in truck patches of potatoes and cabbages. A devastating scourge of westward migration had lain waste to both tidewater and piedmont.[15] Rivers and harbors had silted up, and crop yields had declined generally across the region. Farmers had one-dimensional views of their craft and could not look beyond immediate return to the long-range consequences of agricultural misuse. Visitors to the region until well into the 1840s continued to deplore unkempt fields littered with stumps, ragged old fields, and slovenly methods of cultivation. Northern reformers like Frederick Law Olmsted blamed the region's demise on the institution of slavery.

It is easy to impose the moral and agricultural standards of today on yesterday's Chesapeake yeomen. Unlike our own times, they did not enjoy access to agricultural experiment stations and extension agents who would dispense expertise in sound farming. In the antebellum period, these farmers lived on isolated homesteads that were poorly connected by dirt roads to villages and distant towns. Edmund Ruffin, whose name is unfortunately more associated with secession and civil war than agricultural reform, discovered just how ill-informed his Chesapeake countrymen were when he tried to introduce new methods of agriculture in the tidewater. It would take more than pamphlets, speeches or moral exhortation to get farmers to change, and Ruffin hit upon an ingenious method to win farmer support of the reforms he envisioned. He would educate by doing.

Ruffin was scornful of those who left Virginia and the Chesapeake to emigrate to new lands—one could not solve environmental problems through flight. Ruffin read with interest Sir Humphrey Davy's *Elements of Agricultural Chemistry* and discovered the value of marl to neutralize acid soil. Ruffin found that land which heretofore produced fifteen bushels of wheat per acre increased to forty bushels after using marl. Like his friend Fielding Lewis, another James River planter, Ruffin experimented with liming his fields with oyster shell. Although Ruffin had a comfortable plantation on the James, he risked his money and his reputation by purchasing a

15. Lewis C. Gray, *History of Agriculture in the Southern States to 1860*, 2vols. (1933, repr. Gloucester, Mass.: Peter Smith, 1968), 1:126.

dilapidated plantation in Hanover County. On an investment of five thousand dollars, Ruffin quickly restored the plantation to prosperity through conscientious marling, crop rotation, and land drainage. He knew that water and storms drained the thin soil of its alkalinity, leaving behind acid soils, so he took on the major work of liming the fields and using marl generously from local deposits. Although the use of "calcareous earth," as it was called in the antebellum period, was confined to a very small minority of planters, it was highly effective in transforming dead land into productive fields. By 1849 Ruffin's estate in Hanover County was worth $81,000 and served as a showcase for agricultural reform in the Chesapeake.

Ruffin's success as a farmer was forged on the difficult anvil of penury. As a young married man, Ruffin had taken over the decrepit family plantation at Coggins Point, Virginia. The soil was so depleted it was considered "dead," even by progressive agriculturalists. Experiments in planting clover and crop rotation failed to bring back the land. Shellbanks were another matter, however, and Ruffin dumped thousands of loads of marl on his depleted fields. With a large family and numerous slaves to feed, Ruffin demonstrated that shellbanks or "Calcareous manures" could revive the countryside and maintain its inhabitants within a relatively short period of time.

Ruffin sought an answer to the fundamental question of why an agricultural crisis threatened the Chesapeake when the means of the land's regeneration was available. Part of the answer lay in the fact that marling the land was a difficult, labor-intensive task. Only planters with large teams of sweating slaves could do it. But after 1820 Peruvian guano became a cheap and available fertilizer in the region, and educated men had access to the latest agricultural and scientific information through learned and popular journals. Why then, asked Ruffin, did less than 5 percent of tidewater Virginia planters pursue good agricultural practice? Ruffin identified six reasons that explained the environmental despoliation of the Chesapeake landscape in a nutshell:[16]

1. Farmers were illiterate and lacked the education to accept better agricultural practice.

2. Most farmers had little experience with diversified agriculture.

---

16. Quoted in Gray, *History of Agriculture in the Southern United States*, 2:804.

3. There were few role models of thrifty agriculture. Chesapeake farmers had to look to distant western Maryland and Pennsylvania German farmers to find them.

4. Marl and guano were expensive to transport over long distances.

5. It was difficult to have a land ethic in the Chesapeake when land values were either unstable or collapsing.

6. Too few European immigrants who could infuse the region with progressive agricultural techniques settled there.

The plow was the only part of agricultural reform that most farmers bought in the Chesapeake. They did not take to organic manures and soil building crops. The inevitable result was that by the 1830s soil fertility in the Chesapeake had seriously declined. Agricultural reformers have subsequently found that the kind of alternative husbandry that John Beale Bordley suggested could only flourish in areas where transportation fed new urban markets. The orchard and truck garden boom on Maryland's Eastern Shore in the late nineteenth century would demonstrate the soundness of many of Bordley's ideas.[17]

Aside from the plow, ditching was the one agricultural innovation that became popular in the Chesapeake at this time. Beginning in Virginia in the late eighteenth century and extending into Maryland, farmers sought to drain their fields of swamp water and excess rain through elaborate networks of ditches. The practice enabled farmers to reclaim fertile land without the expense of restoring its fertility.[18]

But until the Civil War era the agricultural order in the Chesapeake was so entrepreneurial and ecologically wasteful that its redemption required a scientific approach to farming beyond the reach of most everyday farmers. Also, two centuries of farm practice organized around wheat, tobacco, and corn had bred an economic and psychological dependency that was difficult to break. Add the further dependency of African slavery in the tidewater and one can see how Chesapeake agriculture was caught in the maw of history. Powerful Chesapeake planters who ostensibly knew better refused to reform their farming practices because they would have had to scale down

17. See Julius Rubin, "The Limits of Agricultural Progress in the Nineteenth Century South," *Agricultural History,* 49 (1975): 363.

18. Jack Temple Kirby, *Poquosin: A Study of Rural Landscape and Society* (Chapel Hill: University of North Carolina Press, 1995), 52–54.

their lifestyle. George Washington, in spite of his own best instincts, continued to plow exhausted lands and rely on grain and tobacco. By 1834 his estate was a financial disaster. Thomas Jefferson was an inconsistent farmer who could not turn three thousand acres to profit. Jefferson believed that it was the fluctuation of distant markets and transportation problems that led to his financial undoing. Others might argue that his love of the good life, frequent absences from his estates, and the employment of negligent overseers did him in.

Even farm architecture reflected the impermanence and mobility of the system. Everything had a temporary and worn out look to it that reflected the values of exploitation rather than careful husbandry. When Johann David Schoepf, a professionally trained German farmer and forester, visited the Chesapeake at the end of the eighteenth century he was amazed at how little farmers knew about hay, manures, and livestock. Although he complained about bad roads, slavery, and expensive inns, the excessive deterioration of the landscape worried him most.[19] The same situation prevailed nearly fifty years later. Late in 1833 John Craven visited Virginia and complained that "farm after farm had become worn out, and washed and gullied, so that scarcely an acre could be found for cultivation."[20] Illiterate and semiliterate farmers scoffed at agricultural reform ideas and did little to halt the advance of soil erosion and general decay. Montgomery County, Maryland, offers an interesting case in point. Despite widespread efforts to renew farmland in the 1830s, agricultural reformers referred to the local countryside as the "Sahara of Maryland." It would be another twenty years before Montgomery County's soils recovered sufficiently to offer a productive agricultural base close to Washington, D.C.'s growing market.[21] Instead of raising tobacco, planters overworked their marginal lands with grain. After 1800 most Maryland counties were better known for the exodus of their people westward in search of economic opportunity than for their agricultural products. Throughout the antebellum period, Chesapeake farm land did not rise above eight dollars an acre in value, while an acre of farm

19. Joseph Schoepf, *Travels in the Confederation, 1783–1784,* 2 vols. (Philadelphia: Campbell Company, 1911), 2:31–37, 89.

20. Quoted in Craven, *Soil Exhaustion,* 77.

21. George M. Anderson, "Growth, Civil War, and Change: The Montgomery County Agricultural Society, 1850–1876," *Maryland Historical Magazine,* 86 (1991):

land in Pennsylvania was worth twenty-five dollars. Farm land in Virginia's Fairfax County was so barren that local government officials advertised for northern emigrants to homestead abandoned tracts and rebuild the community.[22] Until the 1840s, anywhere from 600,000 to 700,000 acres of land were for sale in Virginia at any given time. Maryland's most important product was families leaving the land, though its population losses were in part hidden by the rapid growth of Baltimore. The Eastern Shore of Maryland was at a standstill from 1800 to 1840—Talbot and Queen Anne's Counties had fewer people in 1840 than in 1820. One way of restoring the landscape was through alternative husbandry such as orchards and truck agriculture, but this would not be possible until after the Civil War when improved steamboat and railroads could link rapidly perishable commodities with urban markets.[23] For much of the antebellum period the Chesapeake tidewater appeared an alien landscape that bothered visitors. The "splendid and delightsome land" once described by John Smith had simply vanished.

## River Systems and Canals

In the Chesapeake, rivers served as corridors of demographic and economic expansion. Much of the Chesapeake until the Revolution was narrowly riparian, and most habitations within Maryland and Virginia lived within the sight of water. By the 1750s residents of the bay country had fixed their hold and put the harbors, bays, and rivers to regular use. Regional rivers like the James, the Potomac, and the Susquehanna became part of the post-Revolutionary national vision of power and political destiny. First articulated by Thomas Jefferson and George Washington and later by a growing chorus of mid-Atlantic farmers and businessmen, the vision entailed the connection of the Potomac River with the Ohio Valley of the great West

---

396–406. One issue that must be considered is the impact that agricultural reform would have had on the waters of Chesapeake Bay. Certainly guano and other manures would have precipitated algae blooms and other nutrient problems much earlier in the Bay's history.

22. Frederick Law Olmsted, *A Journey in the Seaboard Slave States* (1856, repr., New York: New American Library, 1969), 170, 213.

23. See especially the comments of Julius Rubin, "The Limits of Agricultural Progress in the Nineteenth Century South," 364.

through a series of canals and highways. Farmers had lost patience with navigational obstructions on the James and Appomattox Rivers and demanded as early as 1749 that the government provide funds to clear the rivers. America had few roads at that time. By 1793 there were more than thirty canal companies incorporated in eight of the original thirteen states.[24] A new land-water transportation system created a web of commerce, writes John Seeyle, stretching from Mt. Vernon north to Lake Erie and south to New Orleans. National land policy, aimed at bringing land swiftly into settlement and production, complemented this vision.[25] This generation of leaders articulated a hydraulic vision of an America tamed and disciplined by canals and dams and locks. Rivers, notes Seeyle, had to yield to human needs as "mechanisms of transportation" or "sites of nascent towns." Thus did Chesapeake waters come to be defined as a means to assure the commercial order of the new nation.[26]

Of the region's watercourses, none played a more important role in the politics and economy of the early Republic than the Potomac River. The Potomac gave birth to dreams of wealth and inland empire that influenced the course of our political development and intrigued Americans from all walks of life. From Fairfax Stone in Grant County, West Virginia, the Potomac is 3,140 feet above sea level and plunges toward Washington, D.C. before calming its flow to enter the Chesapeake, a distance of 382 miles. At its mouth the Potomac is eleven miles wide. In its northern reaches it slices through the mountains, creating narrow valleys and high ridges. At Great Falls, some ten miles above Washington, the Potomac flows through a rocky palisade to complete its drop of more than one hundred feet from its mountain height to the awaiting coastal plain.

During much of the early colonial period few settlers inhabited the mountainous lands of the western Potomac. According to historian Frank Porter, the presence of large barrens, land without forest cover, discouraged set-

24. Harry Sinclair Drago, *Canal Days in America: History and Romance of Old Towpaths and Waterways* (New York: Clarkson N. Potter, 1972), 41.

25. See John Seeyle, *Beautiful Machine: Rivers and the Republican Plan 1775–1825* (New York: Oxford University Press, 1991).

26. Ibid., 21. This hydraulic plan became part of America's future vision of the trans-Mississippi west after the Civil War. See Donald Worster, *Rivers of Empire, Water, Aridity, and the Growth of the American West* (New York: Oxford University Press, 1985).

tlers from moving there. Many thought it a desolate, harsh, and unfertile region, not conducive to agriculture. "Despite the probability that the barrens were simply a large area burned over by the Indians in pursuit of game, the stigma of sterility remained."[27] In the late colonial period most of the land was owned by the powerful extended family of Lord Culpepper and his relation by marriage, Lord Fairfax. The size of their holdings was truly baronial; together they owned all the land between the Potomac and the Rappahannock—what is called the Northern Neck of Virginia. The Culpeppers, Fairfaxes, George Washington, and others became involved in an elaborate real-estate venture, known as the Ohio Company, which planned to build a road through the mountains to the forks of the Ohio at the present site of Pittsburgh. The French and their western possessions stood in the way of these English entrepreneurs, and the French and Indian War must be viewed as an English attempt to link the Ohio Valley with the Chesapeake country by force.

George Washington recognized the Potomac's great potential as a highway of commerce as early as 1754 when he was a young surveyor. He probed the region again in 1784 during a trip that lasted five weeks and seven hundred miles in the saddle to the headwaters of the Potomac and the Ohio. The trip left Washington convinced that the Potomac as well as the Shenandoah River could be made navigable. The famous general also owned land along the upper James and Kanawha River routes. For Washington, rivers were avenues of business and land speculation, and toward that end the general and his associates organized the Potowmack Company. During its charter (1785–1828), the company's purpose was to open the Potomac River to navigation and build by-pass locks and canals for boats with a minimum clearance of one foot of water. Washington and his partners lacked practical knowledge of navigation and canal engineering in the early stages of the project, and their boats were subject to the whims of the river. The Potomac was fully navigable only about forty-five days a year, during floods or freshets in winter and spring. When the river was in flood, boats called "sharpers" that were pointed at both ends and could navigate rapids or "sharp water" carried loads of whiskey, flour, tobacco, hemp, and meat from the

27. Frank W. Porter III, "From Backcountry to County: The Delayed Settlement of Western Maryland," *Maryland Historical Magazine*, 70 (1975): 337.

hinterland to the bay country. It was dangerous work, and boat owners risked more than their fortunes during the freshets.

Washington called canals and internal improvements in the Chesapeake "fundamental to nationhood." He believed that without developed and navigable waterways—canals were preferable to dirt roads and turnpikes that bogged down transport during the wet season—the nation would not advance to its full potential. Like many of his generation of tidewater squires, Washington was possessed of the "Chesapeake dream," which consisted first of a canal along the Potomac to the West. Investors and engineers would then connect the James River with the Kanawha River in western Virginia, which led to the Ohio.

The Potomac River was also the source of the first major political conflict between states in the years immediately following the Revolution. Virginia had long sought the right to fish in the Potomac, which was legally owned by the state of Maryland. Given the states' rights orientation of the Articles of Confederation, the Potomac controversy figured largely in the decision to call a national Constitutional Convention in 1787. Under the Articles, states could not be forced to surrender or limit their sovereignty. Thus it can be argued that Chesapeake waters helped give birth to the new centralized nation of the constitutional era. The Compact of 1785, which the new government ratified, gave Virginia more than just access to fishing grounds. It gave Virginia a whole new border in the Chesapeake with greatly enlarged territory that included more than twenty thousand acres of valuable oyster bars. Washington and a handful of tidewater aristocrats, meeting at Mt. Vernon to iron out the Compact, were much more interested in the smooth flow of commerce between Virginia and Maryland than in fishing rights and the delimitation of state borders in the Chesapeake. As one historian has put it, "the Potomac River Compact showed the utility of a more centralized, better coordinated system of government."[28] Many tidewater Maryland communities thought otherwise, and the border would be a source of friction between the two states for nearly a century afterward. The border controversy would affect everything from shoreline development to resource utilization and pollution problems.

The impetus for this dream of massively transforming the riparian environment of the Chesapeake came from across the Atlantic. In England,

28. Seelye, *Beautiful Machine, Rivers and the Republican Plan*, 75.

Francis Egerton, the Duke of Bridgewater, succeeded in building a canal from his coal mines at Worsley to the new industrial city of Manchester. This engineering triumph gave the Duke of Bridgewater "immortality and $130,000 a year," quipped Robert Fulton, the steamboat promoter and inveterate canal enthusiast, but the dream was much older than the duke. Ever since the days of Canal de Midici, which connected the Bay of Biscay in France with the rich walled city of Carcassone in 1681, men had dreamed of inland canal empires.[29] The Chesapeake, with its vast watery expanse, gave a dramatic intensity to that dream.

With the opening of the Erie Canal in New York in 1825, Potomac planters and businessmen feared that they soon would be shut out of the lucrative markets of the Ohio Valley and the West. Within a short time the Potowmack Company was reconfigured as the Chesapeake and Ohio Canal Company, whose investors and lobbyists persuaded Congress to appropriate $3.5 million in federal money to begin construction. The driving force behind the canal scheme to connect the Potomac River with the Ohio was a powerful Virginia congressman from Loudoun County named Charles Fenton Mercer. As chairman of the House Committee on Roads and Canals, Mercer's vision exceeded George Washington's wildest Potomac dreams. Mercer envisioned nothing less than a canal that would join the waters of the Chesapeake and the Gulf of Mexico. From an engineering and business standpoint, the Potomac route, now called the Chesapeake and Ohio Canal, should have originated in Baltimore rather than Washington, because by 1800 Baltimore had become an important flour milling and shipping center. Congressman Mercer and his backers, though, would have none of it and turned a deaf ear to Baltimore's entreaties. "As events were to show," writes one historian, it was the canal that needed Baltimore, not the other way around. "By failing to go to the Chesapeake, the canal lost its chance for a booming trade that might have given it the strength to reach the Ohio."[30]

Canal construction was always a major undertaking, but the C&O posed exceptional engineering challenges. A ditch had to be dug wide enough and deep enough so that boats could travel over 340 miles through and around

29. Russell Bourne, *Floating West: The Erie and Other American Canals* (New York: W. W. Norton, 1992), 15, 24, 27.

30. William M. Franklin, "The Tidewater End of the Chesapeake and Ohio Canal," *Maryland Historical Magazine*, 81 (1986): 302–3.

mountains, climb elevations of 190 feet, and pass through 398 locks. The canal's chief engineer, James Rumsey, struggled with an unruly labor force— a thousand Irish immigrants who fought among themselves and were often drunk. The canal's agenda was also to link the rich bituminous coal beds of the Cumberland Valley with the Chesapeake. Once the canal was open to Cumberland, Maryland, millions of tons of coal could be freighted down the Potomac Valley. Ultimately the Chesapeake and Ohio Canal cost $22 million and never got farther west than Cumberland. Shippers who wanted to get to the Monongehela Valley had to portage their goods over the mountains to the Cheat River. Nevertheless, in its time the canal was an engineering marvel and was testimony to the unfolding hydraulic vision of America. During its ninety-six-year lifetime the canal earned little money for its investors, but it did play an important role in opening up the Allegheny back country. In 1875, its peak year, the canal carried over a million tons of commerce. Nearly eight hundred boats annually left the warehouse locks of Georgetown for the long ride up the Potomac Valley. The riparian system of Chesapeake Bay was given a vast new commercial extension westward. Soon that extension would be complimented by steam railways like the Baltimore and Ohio, which reached the Ohio River and Wheeling in 1850.[31]

Unfortunately, in the flurry of canal building which followed the opening of the Erie Canal in 1825, promoters gave little attention to the environmental and social consequences of these vast engineering projects. The construction of the Chesapeake and Ohio Canal brought tons of silt into the Potomac from muddy streams in the hinterland. Given the storms and flood surges of the Chesapeake region, the canal basin near Rock Creek Park in Washington quickly silted up and could only handle a small amount of traffic. The Chesapeake and Ohio Canal substantially increased flooding in the region, becoming a muddy sluice in the wet season. As money and power gravitated uphill and westward toward the Ohio, angry floods surged toward the Chesapeake.

Planters along the James River in Virginia had similar canal dreams. From the standpoint of trade and culture, the James was Virginia's most important river in the early national period. It crossed Virginia from west to east and traversed the Alleghenies and Blue Ridge mountains and thence made

---

31. See Richard L. Stanton, *Potomac Journey: From Fairfax Stone to Tidewater* (Washington, D.C.: Smithsonian Institution Press, 1993), 51, 75, 95.

a journey of three hundred miles to tidewater and the sea. In most respects, the James River aristocracy was *the* aristocracy of Virginia. Most of Virginia's important families had plantations along the James, and the river connected the capital of Richmond with the transmontaine, upland, and tidewater regions of the state. If cities and towns of the mid-Atlantic suffered from canal enthusiasm, Richmond's canal dreams reached feverish intensity before the last shot of the American Revolution was fired. Virginia's leaders saw the James as an artery of cheap transportation for floating hogsheads of whiskey, tobacco, grain, and beef, but rapids and falls hindered navigation. Flatboats powered by poles and human muscle could get only as far west as Lynchburg. Beyond that lay rapids and a dangerous gorge where boats were lost and crewmen drowned. Richmond itself had shown the way by constructing a modest little canal along its left bank that helped maritime commerce avoid the local boiling and island-studded rapids.

With Richmond's prosperity linked to the James, the city enthusiastically backed canal projects that would open the west beyond Lynchburg. Canal projects began in earnest along the river by 1789, the most notable being the efforts of the James River Canal Company, which from 1796 to 1801 kept an army of rented black slaves toiling on the upper river between Lynchburg and Crow's Ferry. Citizens' groups denounced the canal's excessive cost and argued that the promoters of the James River Canal Company were more interested in enriching themselves than in improving the James. The company dawdled while Richmond fumed that its fellow citizens and customers in Lexington were being denied access to their capital because the western part of the James was not being improved. Finally, Richmond and the State of Virginia sued in court and took over the company while handsomely compensating its stockholders. Only a few parts of the canal were ever built in the west—a canal around Balcony Falls and a twenty-seven-mile extension westward from Richmond. The dream of opening up the James River country so beloved by Virginia squires would not become a reality until 1835, when a newly chartered business, the James River and Kanawha Company, capitalized $5 million and three thousand slave and free black laborers to complete the 146-mile stretch between Lynchburg and Richmond in 1840. Despite the fact that excessive cost overruns forced the company into default, thousands of grateful citizens and businessmen cheered the James River and Kanawha Company when the first boat from Richmond, the *William Henry Harrison*, reached Lynchburg. According to one canal historian, "cannon boomed, the militia fired its rifles, bands blared and all Lynchburg cheered. It had been waiting forty-four years for this momentous day."[32] Because of the southern climate, the canal remained open year round until the great "freshets" of 1842 closed it for a long period of reconstruction. During the Civil War the canal, an important Confederate supply route, became a Union Army objective, and General Philip Sheridan's Union cavalry destroyed the canal's locks, buildings, dams, and boats.

The other canal scheme of that era that would have an important influence on Chesapeake life and its environment was the great Dismal Swamp project. This 500,000-acre wilderness stretches from a few miles south of Norfolk to the vicinity of Elizabeth City, North Carolina, and is mostly what is called cypress-gum swamp. Lake Drummond, which lies at the center, is the focal point of the swamp. Although today it is close to rapidly developing areas in suburban Norfolk, the swamp is still wild, though covered mostly in second growth forest.

The Dismal Swamp lies partly in Virginia and partly in North Carolina, and from the early colonial period business promoters had campaigned for a canal to connect Albermarle Sound and the Carolina trade with the town of Norfolk and the tidewater plantations of the lower Chesapeake. Public interest in the swamp was small until 1728, when noted planter William Byrd headed a special commission to survey the "dividing line" between Virginia and North Carolina. For Byrd the swamp was a morass, fit only to be drained and turned into hemp farms. During his surveying expedition he called the place "Dismal" and the name stuck.

In the 1760s George Washington and several prominent Virginia land speculators organized the Dismal Swamp Land Company. To get the lumber out, Washington envisioned a canal from the Chesapeake through the swamp to the Pasquotank River, a distance of about twenty-two miles. The little port of Deep Creek, six miles west of Norfolk, was finally designated as the point at which the canal should reach the Chesapeake.

The promoters who formed the Great Dismal Swamp Land Company planned to drain the entire swamp, then the last remaining, large, undeveloped tract of land in the eastern tidewater, for agriculture and lumbering. Standing undeveloped, the Dismal Swamp was pretty but useless, save for its stands of bald cypress trees, or so the company thought. Washington

32. Drago, *Canal Days in America*, 80.

and his associates figured it could be turned into rice plantations, and one of their experimental farms on the periphery of the swamp actually produced 10,000 pounds of rice.[33] And were someone to dig a canal through the swamp, Maryland and Virginia could ship agricultural produce and manufactured goods to the Carolinas. Their canal project, like most contemporary hydraulic dreams, began on a shoestring in 1787 with a small group of planters that included Washington, George Mason, and James Madison paying $500 each to subscribe. Later the Dismal Swamp Canal Company opened its ranks to the public.

Digging a canal through a swamp was such a hellish proposition that the company quickly turned to slave labor. The slaves frequently rebelled against working conditions, swamp muck, and insects, and of course the great swamp itself offered an inviting refuge from those opting out of servitude altogether. Inside the swamp lived a black refugee community of shingle cutters, trappers, and lumberjacks, making it a threat to the hegemony of the tidewater planters. Thus did the vision of a hydraulic empire have its liberating side effects.

The first section of the Dismal Swamp Canal, completed in 1794, could only accommodate flatboats of six-foot beam and drawing no more than two feet of water. The need for locks on the Pasquotank River delayed further work on the canal until 1807, by which time the company had expended over $100,000 on the project. When the canal reached the Pasquotank River it was still forty miles from Albemarle Sound. The only sign of habitation was the lawless town of Reading, soon to be known as Elizabeth City. Reading was little more than a shabby gathering place for wild lumberjacks and shingle cutters who had swarmed into the Dismal Swamp with the opening of the canal and assaulted the forest of juniper and oak. Juniper was especially prized by the shingle cutters, for juniper shingles would not rot. Shingle cutters made up their laws as they went along while their broadaxes sent thousands of bales of shingles up the Dismal Swamp Canal to Deep Creek, Portsmouth, and Norfolk. According to one local historian, the reputed terrors of the swamp—from outlaws to poisonous snakes—did not deter the shingle cutters, who made themselves at home in the vast wet morass called Dismal. "To get what they wanted,

33. Peter C. Stewart and J. Ariza, "Dismal Swamp in Legend and History," *National Geographic,* 62 (July, 1932): 120–30.

they scarred the swamp with fire and axe, but they did not tame it."[34] Yet Norfolk merchants continued to support canal projects in Dismal Swamp to connect the tidewater with the Carolina and Virginia backcountry.

Although they had claim to neither the swampland nor its timber resources, the shingle cutters throve in Dismal Swamp. The canal company and other groups, like the Great Dismal Swamp Land Company, made no attempt to eject them, figuring that they were far more useful in clearing land and opening the swamp with their axes. The swamp soon functioned as a kind of unofficial, non-legal commons that would prefigure in many respects the subsequent way resources were used in the Chesapeake Bay in the nineteenth century. Shingle cutters did more than rape the timber; they set fire to vast areas of peat bog, some of which burned for years. They did, however, facilitate the drainage of thousands of acres of swampland, which would open the region later to the concentrated efforts of large lumber companies.

The canal opened the great swamp to economic development, and for many years the Dismal Swamp Canal was the most important means of transportation and communication between the northeastern counties of North Carolina and the ports and markets of tidewater Virginia. A parallel canal, the Albemarle and Chesapeake, was completed in 1828, a year after the Dismal Swamp Canal.[35] Three steamboats with barges plied the waters from Roanoke through the swamp to Norfolk, at last completing the dream of a commercial waterway connecting the Virginia tidewater with the backcountry.

The Susquehanna and Tidewater Canal Company added to the network of canals in the Chesapeake country. Begun in 1839, the canal linked Havre de Grace and Baltimore with the Pennsylvania canal system and Philadelphia. During the 1840s the upper Chesapeake was busy with maritime barges and canal boats, and the volume of traffic on this network of waterways kept the Susquehanna and Tidewater Canal prosperous for more than twenty years. Like its brother along the James River, the canal fell victim to the military campaigns of the Civil War.[36]

34. Drago, *Canal Days in America,* 43.

35. The Dismal Swamp Canal is now part of the Intercoastal waterway of the United States. For the Dismal Swamp culture see also Porte Crayon, "The Dismal Swamp," *Harper's New Monthly Magazine,* 13 (September, 1856): 441–55.

36. George B. Scriven, "The Susquehanna and Tide Water Canal," *Maryland His-*

The hydraulic vision of the bay country did not begin with General Washington and his patriotic investors. It dates all the way back to William Penn, who in 1690 proposed to connect the Delaware River with the Susquehanna to attract the commerce of central Delaware to Philadelphia. If anything the canal revolution in mid-Atlantic transportation and commerce demonstrated how Chesapeake waters were from the earliest period defined by private business and state governments as engineering problems standing in the path of business expansion. Cost was always uppermost in the builders' minds. In building a canal in the Chesapeake little attention was given to the primary rule of establishing the shortest possible distance between two points and following it. Instead, the companies cut a canal as cheaply as they could, figuring the added miles were of no consequence. When necessary, canals flowed through mountain tunnels and traversed rivers on colossal aqueducts, sometimes at tremendous cost. But at no time were costs reckoned, except in dollars. The Chesapeake and Delaware Canal connecting Baltimore with Delaware City on the Delaware River, for example, in 1829 was hailed for its "Deep Cut" through a granite barrier. In fact this "internal improvements" project showed how black powder, primitive tools, and Irish labor could build a canal capable of altering the salinity of the entire bay as well as its hydraulic patterns, though no one as yet noticed. Viewed collectively, these hydraulic projects were part of a national vision worthy of the pharaohs of ancient Egypt. The use of slave and coerced labor was not lost on abolitionists who saw the environmental engineering of the Chesapeake country leading to the further degradation of the Republic. Like most environmental transformations of our early history, no one could foresee the difficulties and skyrocketing costs that accompanied canal-building. Most canal engineers had no previous experience and knew little or nothing about hydraulics. Surely, if the public had known what most canals were going to cost before being completed, it is doubtful that they would have been constructed. Suffice it to note that the engineering approach that stresses hydraulic manipulation through construction of canals, levees, dams, and channel dredging transcends the history of our republic and is still part of today's environmental calculus.

---

*torical Magazine,* 71 (1976): 522–26. This canal was also used to transport small rafts of logs to nearby lumber mills.

## The Susquehanna Forest Empire

No river caused engineers, investors, farmers, and businessmen quite so many headaches as did the Susquehanna. Through a fluke in geology, the Susquehanna was a shallow waterway, yet it flowed from Lake Otsego in upstate New York near Cooperstown all the way to the bay. Surely, argued businessmen and canal developers, a way could be found to make the river navigable. The problem was that the Susquehanna had either too much water or not enough. Canals branching out from the river into Pennsylvania sustained flood damage as the river coursed its own way during storm surges. Steamboat companies suffered disasters during flood surges and droughts. The Conowingo Falls a short distance from Havre de Grace, Maryland, were not harnessed and made pliable until the twentieth century.

A moody, powerful river, the Susquehanna over the millennia has knifed through rocky valleys, hills, and five mountain ridges to reach the Chesapeake, a distance of 448 miles. As the bay's major source of fresh water, conservationists assert that "the Susquehanna is Chesapeake Bay." Its 27,500-square-mile drainage basin provides an affluent habitat for its citizens today as it did for its explorers and pioneers in the colonial era. At times the river winds lazily back and forth through the wooded hills of New York and Pennsylvania. In its lush valleys, like the Wyoming of Pennsylvania, Indian and colonial settler alike found abundance and security.

The history of the Susquehanna River is more a story of timber and coal than it is the story of the canal builders. Upriver, midway between Cooperstown and the bay, the Susquehanna branches. The northern branch cuts through the rich coal veins of Wilkes-Barre. Since 1700 approximately seven billion tons of anthracite coal have been taken out of those hills, and the river flows with the murky brown sediment of coal mines and slag dumps. The western branch cuts through the Appalachian Mountains to Clearfield, Pennsylvania, and beyond. The region is rich in timber and haven for turkey, deer, and bear, and the water for the most part now flows clear and free through the forests.

In Captain John Smith's time, approximately four thousand Indians, who were called Susquahannocks, lived along the river.[37] The river valley system

---

37. Susan Q. Stranahan, *Susquehanna: River of Dreams* (Baltimore: Johns Hopkins University Press, 1981), 41.

was rich in fish and beaver, and the Indians traded downriver with English merchants as early as 1631, when William Claiborne established a trading post at Palmer Island at the river's mouth. The Indians did not surrender easily to European settlers penetrating the Susquehanna, and the area became notorious for its fierce Indian wars and racial bitterness. The Susquehanna was also part of the border warfare that raged for nearly a century between Maryland and Pennsylvania. The line surveyed by Charles Mason and Jeremiah Dixon took four years of work in the late eighteenth century and fixed the 332-mile border between the two sparring colonies. The new border denied Maryland's claim to the vast Susquehanna watershed, and today the Chesapeake must endure the consequences of decisions made along the river that are beyond Maryland's and Virginia's ability to control.

During the colonial period, the forests of the Susquehanna river system were estimated to have contained 700 billion feet of lumber, enough to build, estimates historian Susan Stranahan, "sixty-three million single family homes or about two-thirds of the current housing units in the United States."[38] Within the river system of the colonial Susquehanna stood the great forest of Pennsylvania. Vast expanses of pine, hemlock, and oak grew along creeks and river banks.

By the end of the eighteenth century the Susquehanna Valley had been transformed from a pristine wilderness of Indians and fur traders into a bustling landscape that was fueled by an insatiable demand for land, timber, and mineral wealth. The one great environmental casualty of the period was the native population of Susquehannocks and Iroquois. Prior to the Revolution, Indians and settlers had worked together peacefully in the region to develop healthy networks in trade, hunting, and agriculture. The Revolution soured ethnic relations after large numbers of Indians took the British side and led marauding expeditions in the valley. According to Peter Mancall, after the Revolution few settlers wanted Indians for neighbors. "They associated the Indians with war and would never trust them again. The Indians could not reestablish stable communities in the region because their economy was in disarray." In a new age of freedom, the Indians of the Susquehanna found themselves dispossessed. Many moved to northwest-

---

38. Ibid., 77–78.

ern New York and Canada.[39] Meanwhile settlers from Vermont and other areas of New England poured into the valley in search of cheap land and new homes. Most of the land came from confiscated landholdings of large Tory real-estate magnates.[40] By 1795 boats loaded with grain and other staples began arriving at the Maryland port of Havre deGrace at the mouth of the river. In that year nearly 180,000 bushels of grain were transported down the Susquehanna. A riparian economy now replaced the woodland fur trading culture. A rough trading nexus extended from Cooperstown, New York, south to Chesapeake Bay. Population soared dramatically in the region from five thousand settlers in the upper Susquehanna in 1770 to nearly seventy-five thousand by 1800.[41]

Until the War of 1812 the Susquehanna region retained its wildness, but after the war loggers swarmed into the forest to harvest its timber resources. The loggers made a virtue of seasonal necessity and cut down the forest in the early spring when the river was at flood and lumber rafts could be floated easily. For about ten weeks a year the "stripping season," as it was called, gave Pennsylvania a thriving lumber business. Log rafts from the Susque-hanna's west branch floated down to towns like Lock Haven and Williamsport where they were turned into processed lumber. Then either the river or the Chesapeake canal system carried forest products onward to the homes and factories of Baltimore, Wilmington, and Philadelphia. In 1820, when crude figures became available, 1,638 rafts containing 25 million board feet of lumber were brought down the Susquehanna to Baltimore alone.[42] Logging took off in earnest in the 1830s when the best logs had been taken out of New York and New England, and overseas demand for lumber made the hazardous business financially practicable. Deep snow falls in the Appalachians gave forth to heavy and

39. Peter C. Mancall, *Valley of Opportunity, Economic Culture Along the Upper Susquehanna, 1700–1800* (Ithaca: Cornell University Press, 1991), 25–26, 148–149; Paul A. Wallace, *Indians in Pennsylvania* (Harrisburg: Pennsylvania State Government, 1961).

40. James A. Frost, *Life on the Upper Susquehanna, 1783–1860* (New York: King's Crown Press, 1951), 10.

41. Mancall, *Valley of Opportunity,* 176, 180.

42. David F. Magee, "Rafting on the Susquehanna," *Papers of the Lancaster County, Pa. Historical Society,* 24 (1920): 193–202.

dangerous spring floods, and swollen streams carried thousands of log rafts southward to the sawmills. So heavily was Sinnemahoning Creek on the western branch logged that by 1890 not even deer could survive in the raw, cut-over landscape. White pine floated well in vast rafts, many of which went as far south as Havre de Grace.

The period from 1840 to 1860 saw the heyday of lumber rafts on the Susquehanna. As many as ten thousand men traveled downstream on the dangerous, bobbing contrivances. The trees came from a seventy-mile-wide swath of forest that ran north and south along the Appalachian plateau. It was during these years that a hard-bitten businessman named John DuBois moved to the region and quickly acquired a 32,000-acre tract of white pine in Lycoming County, Pennsylvania. DuBois, a native of Oswego, New York, had been raised in lumber and mercantile businesses and was eager to exceed the accomplishments of his successful father. With the Civil War and the transcontinental railroads intensifying the national and international demand for lumber, DuBois acquired a private fortune of twenty million dollars. A city that was once a Pennsylvania lumber yard bore his name, and DuBois flourished as a Pennsylvania robber baron. Along the west branch, notes forest historian Paul Wallace, "the trees came down like grass before a giant scythe."[43] Before the Civil War observers could see each season during high water some thirteen thousand logs bobbing in the river's raging, boiling current, a giant log boom destined for the lumber mills at Williamsport. More than a hundred men and eight teams of horses worked like hellish fiends along the shore line and on the boom to keep the logs floating downriver. John DuBois's crew was a regiment of lumberjacks on the move, with chuck wagons, ambulances, and a bank on wheels with a paymaster so that his men did not run short of cash during the logging season. It took two months to get the log boom to Williamsport. History records that the "lumber run" of 1867–68 contained over 44,430,000 feet of timber cut from 321 acres.[44] The work was backbreaking and dangerous. Sometimes the boom broke and the logs rushed pell-mell downstream, costing the crew a season's work. In 1860 DuBois lost 4.5 million feet of timber when the boom broke open.

43. Quoted in Stranahan, *Susquehanna, River of Dreams,* 97.
44. Ibid., 98.

Logging practices in this era were notoriously wasteful. The mills utilized only 20 or 30 percent of the trees; the rest was cast off as waste. Warnings from citizens and community leaders about the consequences of indiscriminate logging along the Susquehanna fell upon deaf ears. Forester Gifford Pinchot noted that in Pennsylvania and the nation generally, "forest devastation was going like a runaway locomotive." The success of the timber industry in the Susquehanna Valley exacted its own toll early in the region's history, writes Peter Mancall. "Once lumberers had thinned the woods, the many species of birds and animals that depended on forest resources lost much of their habitat and either died or, more likely, migrated to areas where forests remained."[45]

Deforestation not only accelerated erosion, it caused runoffs in abnormally rapid concentrations. Each wet season the floods were wilder and more devastating to human life and property.[46] After the Civil War it was not unusual for the Susquehanna to rise thirty feet over its normal course when at flood tide. In 1865 an angry flood wiped out the Susquehanna canal system. The scarred landscape of the Appalachian Plateau would make the Susquehanna one of the more dangerous flood rivers in the mid-Atlantic in the late nineteenth and early twentieth centuries. Even in 1972, long after flood control came to the river in the twentieth century, the people of Wilkes-Barre and the Wyoming Valley had reason to live in fear of the raging waters of the Susquehanna.

## Chesapeake Climate

On the eve of the great logging rush of the mid-Atlantic tidewater and the Susquehanna River system, the Chesapeake had not been visited by any violent climatic shifts for at least three thousand years. Population expansion and economic growth, however, provided the conditions necessary for what was to become a wholesale assault on a relatively stable riparian environment. While the link between changes in the economy and shifts in climate is not always strong, it is worth mentioning that the period 1674–1820 was an era of abrupt weather patterns characterized by periods of ex-

45. Mancall, *Valley of Opportunity,* 25–26.
46. Henry Eakin, "The Influence of Deforestation Upon Stream and Valley Resources," *Journal of Forestry,* 34 (1936): 983–87.

treme cold. The years 1805 to 1820, especially, constituted one of the coldest eras in North American history.[47] Thomas Jefferson kept a weather memorandum book until 1816, noting how bad winters gave way to cool summers. Jefferson recorded mean summer temperatures of seventy-two degrees at Monticello, hardly the hot weather associated with the old South. He also noted that the first ice appeared on Virginia ponds around November 7 and the last ice remained until March 20. His weather memoranda book also contained data on snowfalls when as much as twenty-nine inches fell in a single storm. Such severe winter weather played havoc with the Chesapeake Bay, forcing mariners to combat severe blizzards on the open water and fight ice packs that could tear open a ship's hold. Often, as was the case in the winter of 1783, ice jams halted all commerce on the bay.[48]

Events taking place far away from the bay also profoundly influenced the Chesapeake. In the spring of 1815, Mount Tambora in the Dutch East Indies made one of the most explosive volcanic eruptions in human history, the sound of which was heard in Sumatra, 970 miles away. Mount Tambora ejected some twenty-five cubic miles of dirt, ash, and debris 4,200 feet skyward. Millions of pounds of dust were drawn into the higher stratosphere. According to historians of this event, "large islands of floating pumice were seen at sea and were encountered by ships up to four years later. Mount Tambora's dust cloud, which encircled the earth for several years, has been cited as the cause of the cold year that followed." Falling summer temperatures were recorded in both New England and the Chesapeake. That summer, corn crops became the main weather casualty in the mid-Atlantic. At Monticello, Jefferson was so affected by the poor corn harvest that he was reduced to applying to his agent, Patrick Gibson, for a bank loan of a thousand dollars.[49] In the Chesapeake, fish, crabs, and oysters replaced corn and meat on the dinner table.

47. Helmut E. Landsburg, "Past Climates From Unexploited Written Sources," in Robert I. Rotberg and Theodore Rabb, eds., *Climate and History: Studies in Interdisciplinary History* (Princeton: Princeton University Press, 1981), 61; Paul Sears, "The Archeology of Environment," *American Anthropologist*, 34 (1932): 620.

48. John Thomas Scharf, *The Chronicles of Baltimore* (Baltimore: Turnbull Brothers, 1874), 235.

49. Henry Stommel and Elizabeth Stommel, *Volcano Weather: The Story of 1816, the Year Without a Summer* (Newport, Rhode Island: Seven Seas Press, 1983), 11, 12, 85.

For the remainder of the nineteenth century, cold winters sorely afflicted the Chesapeake Bay. The winter of 1857 froze the bay solid, and frost spread its hoary conquest as far south as Havanna, Cuba. In winter, bay and river traffic often stopped for weeks, while communities lived in fear they would freeze without fuel. Late winter ice jams occasionally broke free and drifted in the Potomac, crushing boats, wharves, and warehouses in their great sweeping mass. Railroad bridges snapped before the ice flow. In 1881 the ice broke up in Washington, the *U.S. Monthly Weather Review* noted, "carrying away a large section of Long Bridge, the lower portion of the city completely inundated by ice, water highest ever known. Hotels, depots, houses, and stores flooded."[50] Since that time, winter climate in the Chesapeake has shown a steady tendency to become milder with fewer ice jams in the modern era. Yet those who know winter on Chesapeake Bay fear ice and floods and worry that high waters and destruction could be commonplace again.

## Town Development

By the end of the colonial period most tidewater counties in the Chesapeake were fully settled. Migrants populated the valleys of the James, York, and Rappahannock Rivers, bringing more than three million acres of land under cultivation.[51] Out of what were once struggling villages and wharf depots grew towns that served largely as shipping centers for wheat destined for Portugal, Spain, the West Indies, and the northern United States. Norfolk grew rapidly from 1760 onward and after the Revolution had a large and powerful merchant community. Urban historians like James O'Mara have remarked that the decline of the tobacco industry facilitated urban growth in the Chesapeake by shifting excess laboring population to milling centers and warehouses in Richmond, Petersburg, Baltimore, and Norfolk. The new powers in the Chesapeake would be commercial centers that would not be dominated in the way that Annapolis and Williamsburg

---

50. "Ice Blockade," *Alexandria Gazette*, January 18, 1875; *U.S. Monthly Weather Review*, February 12, 1881.

51. James O'Mara, *An Historical Geography of Urban System Development: Tidewater Virginia in the Eighteenth Century* (Ontario: Atkinson College, York University, 1983), 103.

had been by tidewater planter elites. With the supremacy of wheat as the reigning commodity in the Chesapeake, economic and social links between town and piedmont became stronger. The improved fortunes of Richmond and Petersburg made the James River a leading area for urban development.

Baltimore by 1800 was a boom town of 26,000 on its way to becoming America's third-largest city and an important milling and manufacturing center. Baltimore benefited from its location at the convergence of wheat farming economies, national road projects, and the needs of frontier development in western Pennsylvania and Ohio. Demand for grain in European markets assured Baltimore's future, and the town spread out over 850 acres around the mouth of the Patapsco River. Deep water at Fells Point on Baltimore harbor accommodated vessels of five hundred tons; Jones Falls on the Patapsco provided water power for more than thirty flour mills. The river and the port basin were important factors in determining the social and political interaction of its citizens.

European population growth, the Napoleonic Wars, and the industrialization of England spurred the grain trade in the Chesapeake. The grain boom revitalized a long dormant trade with the Caribbean and Latin America, and the flour trade became especially active between Jamaica, Peru, and Baltimore. The trade with Lima had salutary environmental effects as it led to the introduction of Peruvian guano into Maryland in the 1820s and 1830s. Gary Lawson Browne, a historian of early Baltimore, believes that Baltimore's "merchant-flour millers" may have contributed to a temporary respite from the increasing stress on the bay arising from the rapid advance of cleared land in the piedmont and the erosion brought on by tobacco.[52] By the 1830s Baltimore was abuzz with flour mills. Its noisy ironworks forged metal products to be sold world-wide. It was a young, social and manufacturing center that seemed in constant motion. A town that in 1752 had only twenty-five houses and two hundred people was a thriving urban center of 250,000 by 1860.[53]

52. Gary Lawson Browne, *Baltimore in the Nation, 1789–1861* (Chapel Hill: University of North Carolina Press, 1980), 55.

53. See Richard M. Bernard, "A Portrait of Baltimore in 1800: Economic and Occupational Patterns in an Early American City," *Maryland Historical Magazine*, 69 (1974): 341–60.

Norfolk also grew during the Napoleonic Wars because of its thriving shipbuilding industry. After being sacked and burned by Lord Dunmore's army during the American Revolution, Norfolk had risen Phoenix-like from the ashes. According to one local historian, in the 1790s "one might walk from Norfolk to Portsmouth on the decks of the vessels at anchor in the harbor."[54] Norfolk benefited from a thriving trade on the Elizabeth River with backcountry farms, a flourishing pitch and turpentine economy from the pine woods, and the Dismal Swamp lumber trade. As a city Norfolk was a rough and raucous port that grew helter-skelter and was known more for its alcoholic disorders, riots, and Negro disturbances than for its municipal development. It might have prospered mightily were it not for the Jeffersonian Embargo that literally shut the port tight during the Napoleonic conflicts. Dependent on European trade, Norfolk lacked Baltimore's economic diversity, leadership, and defiant will. Throughout the embargo Norfolk's warehouses were locked, its wharves empty. After the War of 1812 the introduction of the steamboat made seacoast towns irrelevant as commercial centers. Steamboats brushed aside Norfolk's merchants, siphoned off canal traffic, and followed the rivers to hinterland markets. River towns like Richmond battled in the legislature to prevent Norfolk from having the kind of canal and rail links they enjoyed. Norfolk, writes historian Thomas Wertenbaker, though it was admirably suited for trade, never lived up to its geographic potential as a seaport. Though blessed by environment, it was sabotaged by world politics and local prejudice.

The new tidewater towns had their share of environmental problems, mostly in the form of floods, water pollution, and sewage disposal. Municipal government in the tidewater was a loose, voluntary affair, and officials devoted most of their attention to draining marshlands. Floods plagued Baltimore and often ruined flour mills and carried off farms. In the record deluge of August 8, 1807, floods swept away houses, mills, farms, and breweries and caused such destruction that Baltimore, according to a newspaper report in the *Maryland Gazette,* wore "the appearance of having been the scene of military operations; as if it had undergone the assault of the enemy."[55]

54. Thomas Jefferson Wertenbaker, *Norfolk: Historic Southern Port* (Durham: Duke University Press, 1931), 91.

55. Quoted in Ralph D. Nurnberger, "The Great Baltimore Deluge of 1817," *Maryland Historical Magazine,* 69 (1974): 407.

Chesapeake towns also came to be known as disease centers, a reputation they escaped with the greatest difficulty. Smallpox and other scourges came to the Chesapeake by sea, terrorizing local populations. During the colonial period, smallpox epidemics frequently disrupted the social and political life of Maryland and Virginia because it easily spread up the river systems. After smallpox peaked by 1770, yellow fever ravaged most coastal cities, hitting Norfolk and Baltimore especially hard. Yellow fever was transmitted by the mosquito *stegomyia fasciata,* and city residents had little in the way of knowledge or resources to combat it. The flushed face, scarlet lips, and yellow tinted skin of its victims produced local hysteria. Some cities like Philadelphia experienced mass flight that left only black slave burial details to inter the dead. Even those who survived suffered damage to liver and kidneys. In Baltimore and Norfolk they called the scourge "bilious fever." All they knew of the disease was that it was a summer plague, usually over by the end of October.

Norfolk continued to suffer from outbreaks of yellow fever well into the late antebellum period. In June 1855 the steamer *Ben Franklin* en route from the Caribbean docked in distress at Norfolk, its passengers overwhelmed by "bilious fever." The disease quickly spread throughout the town from the evacuated passengers until townspeople perished at the rate of one hundred a day. Yellow fever or "black vomit" as locals called it, raged until October. Long afterward, Norfolk residents would remember the hearses carrying away the dead while their city wrapped itself in gloom.

Yellow fever also struck Baltimore from time to time. The worst epidemic came in the summer of 1800 and lasted about sixty-five days. The Fells Point area became so thoroughly contaminated that the entire city fled to the countryside and points beyond. Until nearly the end of the nineteenth century, the local population believed that all disease in the city originated from the "foul cove" of Fells Point.[56]

Unexpectedly, a combination of human greed and environmental change prompted the disappearance of yellow fever from coastal cities. In Baltimore, as property values soared with urban growth, communities drained their marshlands—the home of *stegomyia fasciata*—to build homes and

---

56. Douglas F. Stickle, "Death and Class in Baltimore: The Yellow Fever Epidemic of 1800," *Maryland Historical Magazine,* 74 (1979): 293.

businesses. The large and highly problematic marsh at the junction of Harrison and Baltimore Streets was drained completely after 1800. The swamps and ponds on each side of the Patapsco River that had been particular hotbeds of malaria were also drained. The countryside, however, continued to suffer with malaria. September in the Chesapeake always marked the advent of the mosquito-induced malaria season.

Typhus, carried by lice and filth in crowded conditions, was more of a nuisance than a problem in the Chesapeake, though Annapolis was especially troubled by the disease in the colonial period. Living conditions in the Chesapeake were far less crowded than the warrens of the Old World. In the words of medical historian John Duffy, "isolation and lack of congested urban areas gave the American colonies a decided advantage in the matter of health, and this explains their rapid development."[57]

From an environmental standpoint, Chesapeake towns were often pestholes, with stagnant water, general untidiness, rubbish, and unpaved muddy streets. Norfolk did not have a single paved street until 1807, and local residents complained that the air was "impregnated with putrid effluvia arising from decayed substances of every sort" brought down the creeks and rivers. As late as 1856 one visitor described Norfolk as "a dirty, low, ill-arranged town, nearly divided by a morass." Chesapeake waterways served as garbage dumps and places for sewage disposal. In Richmond, Baltimore, or Norfolk in summer, visitors to the waterfront were usually repelled by the stench of filth thrown from the docks and ships. Norfolk's sister city of Portsmouth was notorious for its "powerful stench."[58]

Sewage runoff and other forms of human and animal debris that accompanied urban growth soon contaminated public wells and pumps. Baltimore's original water supply, the Gwynn's and Jones Falls, was contaminated by 1800. The Patapsco River was used as a public sewer. By 1817, most city water wells and springs had become contaminated. Water pollution as a public policy concept appeared in 1808 when Maryland's General Assembly voted to establish the Baltimore Water Company.[59] Nonetheless,

57. John Duffy, *Epidemics in Colonial America* (Baton Rouge: Louisiana State University Press, 1953), 247.

58. Olmsted, *Journey in the Seaboard Slave States,* 138.

59. John Crapper, Garrett Power, and Frank R. Shivers Jr., *Chesapeake Waters,*

as late as 1849 the aggregate of all sewers in the city of Baltimore did not exceed two miles in length, and health officials complained that the nuisances from overflowing privies were a constant source of annoyance and a danger to public health. The rapidly growing city used wooden water pipes that easily cracked and were polluted by urine and excreta leaching through the city soils. River water, especially the water consumed from Gwynns Falls, transmitted typhoid fever and other dreaded maladies.[60] Outbreaks of disease regularly resulted in renewed calls for a cleaner city. According to one urban historian, "Baltimore was notorious for its smells, especially during the hot and humid summer days, and increasing numbers of civic leaders warned of the health evils that the city was inviting with its poor system of waste disposal." Largely through poor budgetary supervision Baltimore frittered away millions on minor projects. Eminent domain litigation from real-estate speculators also stymied the city from developing a rational and effective waste disposal system. Not until after the great fire of 1904 did Baltimore build modern sewers.[61]

In practically every Chesapeake coastal city, the problem of human excrement became nightmarish, so much was in cesspools or on the ground in surface privies. By 1850 two-thirds of Baltimore's population was drinking water with high fecal matter content. The city's principal source of drinking water, Lake Roland, was contaminated by the 1860s and considered by many to be the source of regular typhoid outbreaks.[62] Night soil, regularly dumped into creeks and streams outside Chesapeake towns, steadily made its way into the bay, where it contaminated oyster bars and clam beds. Until the development of enforceable garbage laws in Baltimore in 1877, refuse of all kinds was thrown into city gutters. Norfolk, already well known for its stench, fed sewage from its cesspools and privies directly into streams and the bay. Baltimore's odor became so bad in 1811 that the city passed a law

---

*Pollution, Public Health, and Public Opinion, 1607–1972* (Centreville, Md.: Tidewater Publishers, 1983), 33.

60. William Travis Howard Jr., "The Natural History of Typhoid Fever in Baltimore, 1851–1919," *Johns Hopkins Hospital Bulletin,* 21 (1920): 8, 48.

61. Charles C. Euchner, "The Politics of Urban Expansion: Baltimore and the Sewerage Question, 1859–1905," *Maryland Historical Magazine,* 86 (1991): 274, 286.

62. John W. McGrain, "Historical Aspects of Lake Roland," *Maryland Historical Magazine,* 74 (1979): 257.

to prevent the erection of privies on the convenient walls overlooking the Jones Falls. City authorities attempting to persuade people to line their privies and cesspools with water-tight brick met with little success. Dead cows and horses floating in local waterways contributed to the public nausea. Finally, in 1886 the Maryland Board of Health was able to exert itself and again attempt to prevent stream pollution. It also forbade ships, scows, and steamboats dumping ballast, ashes, dead animals, and other filth in the bay above Sandy Point. It was nearly the end of the nineteenth century before Chesapeake towns and cities installed storm water and human waste sewers and enforced municipal codes for safe drinking water.[63]

All in all, there was little understanding of water pollution problems in the Chesapeake in the antebellum period. Virginia lost a landmark case in 1828 when it failed to prove that stagnant water in mill dam ponds was a public nuisance and health hazard, and for years it would be difficult to prove in court that the Chesapeake's polluted waters had an adverse effect on the citizenry.[64] Scientific knowledge of water pollution was minimal at best—the relationship between cholera and filthy water, for example, was not scientifically validated until 1884. As the brackish waters of the Chesapeake grew increasingly unsuitable for drinking or other uses, inhabitants suffered without knowing exactly why. Towns like Norfolk kept open sewage ditches; drainage systems carried the waste of tanneries, slaughterhouses, iron mills and other manufacturing establishments to the convenient sewer of Chesapeake Bay.

Similar patterns would be evident later in the municipal development of Washington, D.C. The growth of Washington during the Civil War and after placed great strain on water and sewage facilities. Local drains poured raw sewage into Rock Creek and the Potomac River. Sewage from the central part of the city found its way into the Potomac tidal marshes behind the White House. According to capital historian Constance McLaughlin Green, "as late as the 1890s the Potomac marshes were so polluted as to constitute a health hazard for tourists visiting the Washington Monument."[65]

63. William Travis Howard, *Public Health Administration and the Natural History of Disease in Baltimore, Maryland, 1797–1920* (Baltimore: Washington Carnegie Institute, 1924), 51–211.

64. Commonwealth *v.* Webb, *Virginia Reports*, 1828, 726.

65. Constance McLaughlin Green, *Washington: Capital City, 1879–1950*

Human and animal wastes mixed with ashes, street dirt, and garbage, all of which found its way into the Potomac.

Public attitudes toward water pollution in the Chesapeake during the antebellum period were often focused on short-term local expedients. After the colonial period, land use control had been the prerogative of local government, and the absence of effective control left most decisions about refuse disposal and shoreline development to what Chesapeake legal historian Garrett Power has called "the market mechanism." Public goals of sanitation and clean water have "not fared well in this market place."[66]

Most cities in the tidewater did not construct sewer systems until after 1880. The bay and its tributaries had no relief from the succession of lumber mills, tanneries, breweries, meat packing housess, and iron and steel mills that dumped their waste into local watercourses. The possible impact of these effluents on downstream water supplies was scarcely considered. While a variety of cases can be cited to illustrate this omission, one will suffice because of its overriding consequences. In 1882 the city of Baltimore sought to prevent the Warren Manufacturing Company, a cotton factory, from polluting the Gunpowder River. The sources of pollution were the company's hog pens and its factory waste. The Maryland court ruled that the company had to end the pollution from its hog pens because the pens were a "marginal" operation but could continue to pollute the river with factory waste because the factory created jobs and was an important and viable economic unit.[67] Jobs and the greater economic good would take precedence over clean Chesapeake waters. For Baltimore, Norfolk, Washington, and countless towns and villages in this mid-Atlantic watershed, Chesapeake Bay became in historian Joel Tarr's words, "the Ultimate Sink."[68]

Before the end of the eighteenth century, nature still dominated the Chesapeake country. Power was on the side of Nature, and it could be brutal. With the Industrial Revolution and its concomitant economic growth,

---

(Princeton: Princeton University Press, 1963), 44.

66. Garret Power, *Chesapeake Bay in Legal Perspective* (Washington: U.S. Department of Interior, 1970), 206.

67. Warren Manufacturing Company *v.* Baltimore, 59 *Maryland Reports,* 1882, 96.

68. Joel A. Tarr, *The Search for the Ultimate Sink, Urban Pollution in Historical Perspective* (Akron: University of Akron Press, 1996), 7–35.

the scale of power seemed to have been tipped in man's favor. Almost over-night, titanic energies had transformed the Chesapeake region into a grid of canals, cities, factories, railroads, and waterways that determined the region's future course in terms of business and technological agendas. Prop-erty, argued businessmen and their lawyers, was a tool of economic devel-opment and not an aesthetic consideration. Like most changes that have taken place recently in the Chesapeake, these developments did not occur gradually but went forward in great, sudden historic leaps provoked by tech-nological innovation, politics, and foreign and domestic wars. The period between the American Revolution and the Civil War was an era of rapid industrialization and urban growth that deprived the Chesapeake environ-ment of its independence as a natural force. For the first time, Chesapeake waters became as important as public sewers as they were arteries of trans-portation. The full impact of the pollution of Chesapeake rivers would not be felt until well into the twentieth century.

The industrialization of the Chesapeake accelerated dramatically in the post–Civil War period. The growth and development of towns and cities brought new, often deadly, problems of disease and water pollution to the region. It was the betrayal of a region surpassingly endowed. As a metaphor of human experience in the Chesapeake country, a "battered landscape" replaced the "garden."

Major changes in the look of the antebellum Chesapeake landscape re-flected a growing entrepreneurial culture taking place in the nation. Envi-ronmental change followed the cycle of the economy, and one simply can-not study the Chesapeake environment at this time apart from its economic context.[69] Both Virginia and Maryland were being drawn into the larger national culture of business and industrialization. New perceptions about individual wealth and public progress influenced notions about the Chesa-peake and its environment that were far from salutary.

The countryside endured the ravages of soil erosion, and localities bore the brunt of environmental changes. Most visitors to the region found that a blight seemed to have overtaken the Chesapeake landscape, making it a far less agreeable place to live and work than it had been a century earlier.

69. See D. W. Meinig, "Reading the Landscape," in D. W. Meinig, ed. *The Interpretation of Ordinary Landscapes: Geographical Essays* (New York: Oxford University Press, 1979), 228.

Anti-slavery writers like Henry David Thoreau and Frederick Law Olmsted tended to write off the Chesapeake as a horrible place. Thoreau called Maryland "a moral fungus. Her offense is rank; it smells to heaven."[70] More observant, but equally prejudiced, the famous New York correspondent Frederick Law Olmsted traveled by train from Washington to Richmond in 1856. From his window he speculated that only a quarter of the available farm land passing by was in cultivation, "the rest is grown over with briars and bushes, and a long coarse grass of no value." Altogether the Chesapeake countryside showed "less signs of an active and prospering people than any I ever traveled through before, for an equal distance."[71]

Actually, the Chesapeake's prognosis was better than Olmsted thought. The landscape began to show noticeable improvement after 1850, when rail and steamboat connections enabled farmers to develop reliable markets and pay greater attention to restoring their farms. On the eve of the Civil War, the use of marl and guano was everywhere in evidence, especially on Maryland's Eastern Shore north of the Choptank River. In Virginia marling was confined to the central tidewater counties. Lime kilns burning oyster shell for fertilizer also became important components of the agricultural economy. The lime trade and the explosion of truck and dairy farming to serve Richmond, Baltimore, and Philadelphia would help to restore and regenerate the Chesapeake landscape after the Civil War as tidewater cities grew exponentially. The term "worn out land" would soon apply to land trampled by marauding armies and not to bad agricultural practice.

Yet even in her most dilapidated state there was considerable beauty to the Chesapeake for those who wished to see it. There were pockets of progressive agriculture in the region that vindicated John Taylor's *Arator*. In the valley of the Monocacy River in Maryland and in the Virginia piedmont counties of Loudoun and Fauquier, farms delighted the eyes of foreign travelers and gave renewed hope for the future of the Chesapeake Bay country. An evening sail on the bay or a twilight cruise on the James or Potomac showed the beauty of the Chesapeake in all its splendor. The countryside still had sufficient allure to hypnotize writers like John Pendleton Kennedy; and after the Civil War newspaper men would rediscover the glo-

70. Howard R. Floan, *The South in Northern Eyes, 1831–1851* (Austin: University of Texas Press, 1958), 69.
71. Frederick Law Olmsted, *Journey in the Seaboard Slave States,* 17, 19.

ries of the Chesapeake Bay country and write popular essays about the Chesapeake's rich past and present potential.[72]

72. For example, see "The Chesapeake Peninsula," *Scribner's Monthly*, III (March, 1872): 513–23.

## CHAPTER FOUR

# The Age of the Oystermen and the Tragedy of the Commons

"The resources themselves were passive objects of technological and political manipulation, while the harvesters' freedom to use the fisheries as they saw fit was an article of faith."
— Arthur McEvoy, *The Fisherman's Problem*

"The state owns valuable fisheries which it cannot protect. Against the state stands every man who can use a pair of oyster tongs or a dredge. A fleet of water Arabs covers the bays and rivers."
— W. N. Armstrong, *Notes on the Oyster Industries of Virginia, 1879*

## The Tragedy of the Commons

Two great commons areas in the United States, the Great Plains and the Chesapeake Bay, came under stress and exploitation during the same period of our national economic development. Both had large areas held in common, and both experienced great human misery and resource depletion. Until the economic boom of the post–Civil War era, both the Chesapeake and the Great Plains functioned reasonably well as a commons because ecological stresses were manageable. But later, as Americans locked themselves into a system by which each man sought to gather as much wealth as was humanly possible, whether by shooting buffalo or gathering oysters, there came the inevitable tragedy. As ecologist Garrett Hardin has written so eloquently, "Ruin is the destination towards which all men rush, each pursuing his own best interest in a society that believes in the freedom of the commons. Freedom in a commons brings ruin to all."[1] A commons can

---

1. Garrett Hardin, "The Tragedy of the Commons," *Science*, 162 (1968): 1244. Hardin's thesis has been severely criticized by scholars like Barry Commoner, *The Closing Circle: Nature, Man and Technology* (New York: Alfred A. Knopf, 1971), 295–96 and Bonnie J. McCay and James M. Acheson, eds., *Question of the Commons: The Culture and Ecology of Communal Resources* (Tucson: University of Arizona Press, 1990). Like all explanations of social phenomena, the tragedy of the commons has

only function under conditions of low population density in a subsistence economy. The Chesapeake commons had neither luxury. And the tragedy of the commons for Chesapeake Bay was that men believed that the resources were available to all to exploit because the resources of the bay were inexhaustible. Thus did they ruin the Chesapeake oyster beds and bring certain species of fish and waterfowl to the brink of extinction.

## Follow the Water

To a great extent the social history of Chesapeake Bay is involved with the complex natural and economic history of the oyster. Until recently oysters were the defining natural resource of Chesapeake Bay and contributed greatly to the economic development of what heretofore had been subsistence societies in the tidewater. Since prehistoric times man has pursued the oyster, and it is not surprising that oysters would be part of the American experience. Even though oysters were cheap and plentiful in Europe, the abundance of the Chesapeake beds astonished early colonists. Sea captains reported oyster "reefs" large enough to sink boats and hinder navigation. During the "starving time of 1609," many families of early Virginia subsisted on oysters. A Swiss visitor, Francis Louis Michel, reported in 1701 that the passenger sloop taking him to Virginia struck an oyster bed in the Chesapeake, and the ship had to wait two hours for the tide to lift it off. Michel and his friends, meanwhile, dined on oysters so big that "I often cut them in two before I could put them in my mouth."[2] With the advent of the plantation in the Chesapeake, the oyster became a slave food, and mounds of oyster shells were an architectural feature of most slave quarters in the colonial Chesapeake. The presence of oyster bars enhanced the value of riverfront property in the colonial era. Oystering equipment was listed in probate inventories in Maryland as far back as 1796, writes historian Bayly Ellen Marks. In the 1830s Maryland law allowed private citizens the right to patent one acre of water for an oyster bed adjacent to their land.[3]

---

its limitations. His thesis, however, is still insightful and has application for understanding the human exploitation of the Bay's resources in the nineteenth century.

2. Quoted in a pamphlet by J. Wharton, *The Bounty of the Chesapeake, Fishing in Colonial Virginia* (Charlottesville: University Press of Virginia, 1957).

3. Bayly Ellen Marks, "Rakes, Nippers, and Tongs: Oystermen in Antebellum St.

Oysters grew in popularity in the early nineteenth century largely because of their association with men of wealth and gourmet dining. *Crassostrea Virginica* was but one of a number of species of oysters found in the waters of North America. It came relatively late to the American table because New York's Long Island Sound and Cape Cod contained a treasure trove of succulent bivalves that could be more cheaply marketed. By the time Chesapeake oysters came into demand in the nineteenth century, the American palate had long been conditioned by a shimmering variety of Narragansett, Cape Cod, Wellfleet, Fire Island, and Gardiner's Bay oysters.

Shellfish consumption was so prodigious in New York and New Jersey during the colonial period that their assemblies passed oyster conservation laws. Wellfleet oysters began to disappear in New England by 1775. At the beginning of the nineteenth century, Connecticut was the center of the oyster industry. Maryland's production was only about 500,000 bushels annually. But by the 1830s New England oyster schooners had taken up most of the Cape Cod oysters and had begun to loot the oyster beds of Long Island Sound. These oystermen used a dredge or "drudge" that consisted of an iron bar with teeth along one side. To the bar was attached a bag made of rope netting held open by an iron frame and a tow line. The dredge was then thrown over the side of the vessel and dragged along the bottom to pick up oysters which collected in the bag. When the bag filled, crewmen hauled the dredge aboard by a hand-winch. The dredge was efficient economically, but destructive to the beds.

Yankee dredgers did demonstrate that a demand for oysters existed far beyond New England and that this demand was for all intents and purposes insatiable.[4] In 1836 Caleb S. Maltby, a seafood packer in Fairhaven, Connecticut, became discouraged with the supply of oysters in New England waters and moved his entire business to Baltimore. In 1848 another Connecticut native, Abathiar Field, established an oyster canning plant in Baltimore, and soon many other New England oystermen were drawn southward by new employment opportunities on the bay. In 1850 six raw oyster

---

Mary's County," *Maryland Historical Magazine,* 90 (1995): 313–14, 320. Marks notes that "in all probability slaves made up a sizeable portion of the county's antebellum oystermen."

4. Joseph Conlin, "Consider the Oyster," *American Heritage* (February/March, 1980): 66–72.

packing plants operated in Baltimore and the total Maryland catch in that year amounted to 1,350,000 bushels. The newly completed Baltimore and Ohio Railroad provided a powerful marketing stimulus for the oyster industry, and by 1860 the railroad annually carried over three million pounds of oysters westward. The opening of the Chesapeake and Delaware Canal greatly expanded the Philadelphia market. What had originally been a tiny business on the Baltimore docks ballooned into a million-dollar business. More than sixty packing houses lined the city wharf on the eve of the Civil War.[5] The packing houses also had lime kilns and burned oyster shell for fertilizer. Oyster shell refuse from packing houses was used as ship ballast, landfill for swamps and marshes, and paving material for highways. In 1850 the mid-Atlantic and Chesapeake states alone recorded a catch of 145,000,000 pounds of oyster meat. As it turned out this was but the dress rehearsal of the oyster boom that followed the Civil War on Chesapeake Bay. Oystering, which in earlier years had been considered mainly an avocational adjunct to farming, after 1865 "offered lucrative opportunities on the water that could not be found on land," concludes Bayly Ellen Marks.[6]

With the near extinction of the New England beds, Yankee dredgers began to look at the Chesapeake Bay. Early on they operated chiefly in Virginia waters, where they promptly removed prodigious amounts of oysters for transport to Wellfleet and other northern ports. After 1810, when Virginia passed a law forbidding "foreign dredgeboats" in state waters, the "Yankee drudgers" moved up the bay to Maryland. Foreigners looting Chesapeake oyster beds produced a prompt outcry from local fishermen, and in 1820 Maryland's General Assembly passed an act prohibiting the dredging of oysters and forbidding the transportation of oysters by any boats except those owned by Maryland citizens. The law, however, did not outlaw Marylanders from building their own dredgeboats and scraping the Chesapeake bottom clean.[7]

On the eve of the great oyster boom, the Chesapeake Bay covered a fish-

5. "The Chesapeake Oyster Industry," *Harper's Weekly,* September 30, 1893; "The Oyster Industry," *Baltimore Sun,* November 16, 1947; John R. Wennersten, *The Oyster Wars of Chesapeake Bay* (Centreville, Md.: Tidewater Publishers, 1981), 14.

6. Marks, "Oystermen in Antebellum St. Mary's County," 328.

7. *A Manual of Oyster Culture in Maryland, Fourth Report* (Annapolis: Board of Shell Fish Commissioners, 1912), 279–348.

ery of 2,300 square miles. Of all the bay's marine inhabitants at this time, the oyster was undoubtedly the most valuable to the state of Maryland. Oyster beds or "rocks" could be found everywhere but in very deep water or in the mud of channel bottoms. In the bays, creeks, and river mouths where the water varied from two to thirty feet in depth, oysters thrived in large beds. The great bed of Anne Arundel County, for example, was estimated to cover more than twenty-eight square miles. Oyster beds covered much—about 193 square miles—of the Chesapeake Bay's bottom, and many pristine beds like that of Tangier Sound would provide an unparalleled source of seafood.

During the Civil War, Union gunboat activity seriously disrupted the Chesapeake oyster industry. Most oystermen served as guides and spies for the Confederate navy and were treated harshly by Union naval officers after a York River oysterman helped the rebels capture the *Alleghanian*, a 1,400-ton guano ship bound for London in October 1861. In Queen Anne's County near Centreville, a pro-Confederate planter employed oystermen to sail the sloop *Hard Times* to the South laden with men and contraband. Another oyster schooner, the *Nanjemoy*, owned by Captain A. S. Godwin, smuggled food and medical supplies through the blockade to distressed Confederates. After the war dredging was again permitted, and by the 1880s the industry in Virginia and Maryland attained its peak. Oysters were plentiful in the rivers as well, and watermen in the Potomac easily tonged fifty to seventy-five bushel of oysters in one day. At forty-five cents a bushel, oystering was a quick means to prosperity. Of the rivermen who tonged oysters, over 40 percent were ex-slaves.[8]

In 1881, Thomas Scharf, a Baltimore writer, estimated that during the height of the oyster season that year about 25,000 men worked out on the water. Not all of the thousands of boats sailed from Baltimore, but most of the crew members came from the poorer sections of the city. By 1890 the Maryland oyster industry would employ over 32,000 men and women with more than 11,000 of those being factory workers in the canning and packing houses. Nearly one-fourth of Maryland's total work force in 1890 worked

8. Eric Mills, *Chesapeake Bay in the Civil War* (Centreville, Md.: Tidewater Publishers, 1996), 183–86; Henry Wright Newman, *Maryland and the Confederacy* (Annapolis: n.p., 1976), 231; Edwin Beitzell, *Life on the Potomac River* (St. Mary's, Md.: n.p., 1967), 77.

in some sector of the five-million-dollar-a-year industry.[9] About 1,000 schooners and 3,500 smaller boats were employed in oystering during the fall and winter months. The harvesting, transport, and sale of oysters revolutionized traditional maritime industries. Oysters were the vanguard of a fifty-million-dollar seafood industry, and the activities of Baltimore oyster brokers were as closely watched by Chesapeake businessmen as the New York stock market. Oysters expanded Baltimore's economic role in the mid-Atlantic and fostered scientific interest in the Chesapeake Bay.

The oyster packing industry pumped life's blood through the towns and villages of tidewater Maryland and Virginia, and hundreds of boats bobbed at local wharves wrapped in sails and loaded to the gunwales with oysters. Blacks and immigrants arrived by trains to these seaside towns to work the oyster season as shuckers, stevedores, and cannery workers. The low-raftered oyster houses were smelly, sloppy places that nauseated patrons who relished Chesapeake oysters in the smart restaurants of New York and Philadelphia. During boom times packers at Oxford and Crisfield paid shuckers as much as $3.50 a day for twenty gallons of oysters, a wage heretofore unknown in the Chesapeake region. The economic impact of the boom was especially noticeable along Baltimore's Long Wharf, where hundreds of schooners annually disgorged four million bushels of oysters to the insatiable packing houses. In 1884, the peak year for the industry, watermen harvested a record fifteen million bushels of oysters from the Chesapeake. In his old age a waterman reflected on the excitement of the boom times: "If I had a chance to live my life over again, I guess it would be out on the water with the gulls when the sun come up on a boat, wheeling and whipping around for another pass across a bed where the oysters used to come up as big as a man's hand."[10]

American and foreign demand for oysters advanced faster than the supply. The avalanche of orders from the mining camps of Colorado and the restaurants of San Francisco overwhelmed Maryland packers. As James Richardson concluded in *Scribner's Magazine* in 1877, "if every acre of avail-

---

9. J. Thomas Scharf, *History of Baltimore City and County* (Baltimore: 1881); *Maryland, Its Resources, Industries and Institutions* (State of Maryland, 1893), 303, 312.

10. "Poached Oysters," *Harper's Monthly Magazine,* March 4, 1884; Ruley Covington, "I Remember Oystering in the 1890s," *Baltimore Sun,* March 7, 1971.

able coast water, from Cape Cod to the mouth of the Chesapeake were brought under cultivation, it is doubtful whether the supply of oysters could even outrun the demand." Added another Maryland observer, "Nobody tires of oysters. Raw, roasted, scalded, stewed, fried, broiled, escalloped, in patés, in fritters, in soup, oysters are found on every table, sometimes at every meal, and yet no entertainment is complete without them."[11] Both poor and rich alike were ravenous for oysters, if for different reasons. Oysters were cheap throughout the nineteenth century, and local consumption in the mid-Atlantic region averaged six pounds annually of the tasty bivalve compared to today's limited and expensive gourmet consumption. In Baltimore and Philadelphia workingmen flocked to oyster houses that advertised "all you can eat" for six cents. Gluttons were sometimes slipped a few spoiled oysters by the proprietors to discourage overconsumption. In New York City, Philadelphia, and Baltimore men enjoyed oysters and spirits at various hotel oyster bars. At many Chesapeake taverns, the front yard was not green with grass but white with oyster shells. And in private clubs, millionaires worshipped at the altar of the succulent oyster. In New York, "Diamond Jim" Brady, scorning pearls, slipped tiny diamonds into oysters to amuse his guests.

## Flush Times and Hell on the Hard Shell

The booming post–Civil War economy gave people additional money to purchase status-conferring comforts and delicacies. In the 1850s a hungry traveler lodging in Pittsburgh in winter considered himself to be among life's fortunate if he could have his oyster stew. During the postwar era, in regions as distant as the gold and silver fields of Colorado and California, miners hungrily consumed large helpings of tinned oysters as a regular staple.

Capitalizing on the oyster boom, Maryland Congressman John Crisfield and Eastern Shore investors in 1867 built a railroad to Somers Cove on Tangier Sound. The once sleepy fishing village of Somers Cove now had rail connection to Baltimore and New York and overnight became a seafood mecca. Renamed after its benefactor, the new town of Crisfield stood on a

---

11. James Richardson, "American Oyster Culture," *Scribner's Magazine*, December 1877; "On the Eastern Shore," *Lippincott's Magazine*, August 1876.

giant mound of oyster shells glistening in the sun. By 1872 Crisfield had the largest oyster trade in the state and provided employment for more than six hundred sailing vessels. Crisfield sent its oysters throughout the country and to distant ports in Europe and Australia. During the 1870s, every morning, Sundays excepted, from twenty to thirty railroad cars could be seen moving from the packing houses, heavily freighted with oysters.

Crisfield was a cluttered, muddy town, a Chesapeake honky-tonk of bars and brothels. Lured by the high price of oysters, hordes of men flocked to Crisfield to man the boats and fill the bars and brawl drunkenly in the streets. Despite its beautiful location on Tangier Sound, Crisfield reeked with the smell of "defunct oysters," a New York newsman reported in 1879. "Oysters, oysters, in barrels, in boxes, in cans, in buckets, in the shell and out. But little business is carried on here except oystering."[12] Huge oyster packing houses lined the shore for half a mile, all built upon shells. Canoes, sloops, and oyster schooners moved in every direction, all intent on one idea—oysters. A get-rich-quick spirit prevailed in Crisfield, and the attendant lawlessness of local life made this waterfront community resemble a rough, sprawling, mining town of the great western frontier. The burly watermen kept the saloons of Crisfield full. One saloon-keeper, Harvey Johnson, was appointed justice of the peace. Each morning he would rap on the table and announce: "Gentlemen, the court is now in session, but I call your attention to the fact that business is still going on at the bar."[13] Seafood packers in Crisfield were known for the brazen way in which they cheated customers. In the 1870s oyster packers put a scant five gallons of oysters in a ten-gallon keg, added a large hunk of ice, and filled the keg up with water. The bill called for ten gallons of oysters, and many ignorant "cityslickers" thought that oysters coming out of Chesapeake Bay brought a lot of water with them. What cost packers $2.25 netted them a profit of $7.75 on each barrel. Said one local reporter, "Oyster packers didn't know much about figuring costs and percentages then, but they were experts on water."[14] As in the mining towns of the West, those who made the most money were usually those who took the fewest risks. It was not the watermen risking their

12. "A Peninsular Canaan," *Harper's Monthly Magazine,* May 1879.

13. Quoted in Hulbert Footner, *Maryland Main and the Eastern Shore* (New York: Appleton Century Company, 1942), 209.

14. "The Oyster Gold Mine of the 1870s," *Crisfield Times,* January 7, 1944.

lives on the bay who made money from oystering. Seafood packers and hardware store owners reaped the lion's share of the profits during the oyster boom. Watermen were as captive to the storeowners for equipment, clothing, dry beans, salted codfish, coffee, and flour as were coal miners to the company store.

The same booster spirit and lusty optimism founded upon the oyster treasure of Chesapeake Bay prevailed elsewhere in the region. On the blue waters of the Choptank River, the thriving town of Cambridge sparkled in the sunlight. In 1871 Cambridge's population had grown to two thousand, and the town boasted new frame houses and four hotels. Cambridge's citizens and officials were quick to sing the oyster's praise. "It furnishes employment to thousands," declared Robert Wilson in *Lippincott's Magazine,* "and it contributes largely to popular education through oyster license taxes, promotes social intercourse, and keeps the lawyers and physicians in practice when other resources fail."[15]

With the advent of the autumn rains the fog banks stole up the Chesapeake and spilled onto the Eastern Shore in a dripping embrace. It was at this time that an oysterman's life began to lose its romance. The cold and damp of the bay prematurely aged men, and in water-locked hamlets like Crisfield, Cambridge, and Oxford, the most noticeable characteristics of watermen were iron-gray hair and a deeply lined brow. In countless waterfront saloons men complained of chest misery. Too many, local doctors knew, had cough-wracked bodies honeycombed with tuberculosis. Most dredgemen were dilapidated specimens of humanity. They usually wore ragged clothing, their hair went uncombed and their faces were purple red from exposure and frost. Many townswomen in oyster ports complained that dredgers were "indifferent to sanitary laws."[16] On shore the men of the oyster dredgeboats lost none of their fierce sea-worn look. Many of them suffered from a common malady, "oyster hand," an infection brought on by dealing with razor sharp oyster shells. Oystering was backbreaking, winter weather work, and each season watermen embarked on a voyage full of danger, subject to long odds against returning uninjured and possibly to be lost overboard. Many of the watermen were blacks supplementing their

15. Robert Wilson, "The Peninsula," *Lippincott's Magazine,* July 1876.
16. R. J. Robinson, "Life Aboard the Oyster Dredges In 1880," *Baltimore,* April 1952.

income as tenant farmers. On land the dredgemen were treated as rogues to be harassed out of sight by the police as quickly as possible. Even in pleasant weather the dredgers were not averse to slipping in to shore under cover of darkness to replenish their supplies from waterfront farms. Stolen pigs, chickens, and sheep never reached market but were cooked on the dredgeboats often over a blaze of logs taken from a luckless farmer's woodpile.

The sheer physical labor of oystering was almost unimaginable. Rivermen used long-shafted tongs that resembled two rakes bolted together with a scissor hinge. These tongs were twelve to eighteen feet in length and often weighed more than sixty pounds when full of oysters and bottom debris. Most rivermen acquired simian physiques, and long days on bobbing boats put a bounce in their gait. On the bay, where schooners used the dredge hauled in by a hand windlass, the process was often described as trying to haul in an anchor when the ship was under full sail. The windlass or "hand winder" was a cruel tyrant that could maim or break the health of the strongest oystermen. After a single voyage not even penniless ex-slaves would agree to serve on the dredgers. Most oyster captains had to resort to forced labor on their dredgeboats.

No man was safe around the Baltimore docks during oyster season. Ship captains shanghaied unsuspecting Irish and German immigrants from the Baltimore docks by giving them free drinks till drunk, knockout drops, and the blackjack. One captain boasted that he didn't care where he got his crew, "whether they are drunk or sober, clothed or naked, just so they can be made to work at turning a windlass."[17] Once on the water, they were made to turn the "handwinder," and men who refused to work received a cruel beating or a bullet. It was a classic case of evil conditions with irresponsible captains of irresponsible crews, the latter ill-fed, ill-clad and laboring long hours on icy, wind-swept waters. Those who did work were often thrown into the bay to drown when they were exhausted. The dredges carried no crew manifests, and who was to ask questions about those who perished? More than forty years later, Lorie Quinn, a Crisfield, Maryland, newsman, remembered how young men, drowned and frozen blue, were found in fish nets in Tangier Sound. Deaths on the Chesapeake were seldom investigated, and stories circulated throughout the region of captains who shot and killed

17. John R. Wennersten, "The Oyster Wars," *Country Magazine*, November 1981, 41.

men on the slightest provocation and afterwards claimed self-preservation in the face of mutiny. Reports of terrible suffering, cruel treatment, and horrible murders reached Baltimore. "The negroes of Baltimore, after the experience of a few seasons on these oyster vessels, refused to hire on any more, then there were some cases of shanghaiing negroes in the city for these vessels."[18]

Public protests by immigrant organizations like the German-American Society of Baltimore, and technological innovation rather than the intervention of the federal courts, put an end to involuntary servitude on Chesapeake Bay. About 1906 oyster dredgers began to get relief from the hand windlass as eight-horsepower gasoline engines for winding in the heavy dredges became available. With the power winders four men could now do the work of eight. The new gasoline winders also allowed the boats to obtain more oysters. By the end of 1908 many dredge boat captains had purchased gasoline-powered winders, and the tyranny of the hand windlass soon became only legend on the bay.

At first relations between tongers on the rivers and dredgers had been fairly amicable. By 1868, however, nearly a thousand dredgeboats had begun to invade the rivers, where dredging had been prohibited by state law. While the outraged tongers demanded that Annapolis enforce the law preventing dredging in the rivers, they also took the law into their own hands. When they went out on the water, tongers warned, they would have their rifles loaded. Soon the Chesapeake resounded to gunfire, and newspaper reporters noted that something new was floating in the Chester and Choptank Rivers—the bloated bodies of dead oystermen.[19]

Violence on Chesapeake Bay was not new in 1871. As early as the 1830s and 1840s Maryland watermen and out-of-state dredgers had clashed among themselves and with one another. In 1849 a flotilla of angry Eastern Shore watermen captured the Baltimore steamer *Osiris*, armed her, and used her to drive off a fleet of Philadelphia dredgers. In 1861 the sheriff of Dorchester County seized two steamboats, equipped them with small cannon, and used them to drive off illegal dredgers from Philadelphia, Baltimore, and New Jersey.[20]

---

18. Louis P. Henningham, *History of the German Society of Maryland* (Baltimore: The German Society of Baltimore, 1909), 125.

19. Wennersten, *Oyster Wars of Chesapeake Bay*, 36.

20. *Niles' Weekly Register*, November 23, 1833; Jacob Frey, *Reminiscences of Bal-*

In response to demands from the oyster packing industry for law and order on the bay, the Maryland legislature established the Board of Commissioners of the State Oyster Police Force in 1868 under the command of Captain Hunter S. Davidson. For Maryland politicians, Davidson was admirably suited for the position. He had commanded several ships for the Confederate navy during the Civil War, was a graduate of the United States Naval Academy and at the time of his appointment was journal clerk of the Maryland Senate. He was also a fearless sailor who took his mission seriously. Davidson quickly oversaw the outfitting and construction of three armed steamers and rebuilt the state-owned steamboat *Leila*, outfitting her with a twelve-pound Dahlgren cannon from a defunct Confederate gunboat.

Davidson tried to cooperate with Virginia authorities as well and traveled the Chesapeake to explain the oyster laws to watermen and distribute information about compliance with state dredging regulations. But for the oystermen of Chesapeake Bay, the laws were only paper. Nothing would deter them from getting the oysters. "Thems the Lord's Oysters," said dredgers defiantly, "and the Lord put them there so we could get them." Davidson wasted little time and soon filled local jails with "oyster pirates." His second-in-command, Captain Robert H. McCready, aboard the armed bay schooner, *Mary Compton*, used a howitzer to fire at dredgers and chase them out of the Annemessex River near Crisfield. In the upper bay, the presence of police boats diminished illegal dredging activity. Hunter Davidson's daring activities on Chesapeake Bay were quickly reported in the national press. Law and order had come at last to the "Mediterranean of America."

Oyster pirates subsequently plotted to murder Davidson, prompting him to remain armed at all times. Once, Davidson foiled an ambush. He stood in the bow of his yawl-boat and ordered his men to row towards the hiding place. When he got near enough, he said calmly, pistol in hand, "I will shoot the first man that moves." A few minutes afterward, he carried the ambushers all back as prisoners.[21] Soon packers were complaining that Davidson was

---

*timore* (Baltimore: 1893), 389; Elias Jones, *History of Dorchester County, Maryland* (Cambridge, Md.: 1926), 251.

21. Hunter Davidson, *Report Upon the Oyster Resources of Maryland* (Annapolis: George Colton, 1869), 16; "The Oyster War," *Harper's Weekly,* January 6, 1886. Davidson noted in his report that dredgers tended to be strong and rich men while the tongers in the rivers were weak and poor.

too successful because there was a noticeable falloff in the number of bushels arriving at their docks. Apparently the seafood brokers wanted law and order on the bay but not if it cut into their profits. Meanwhile, the rivermen sent petitions to the Maryland Assembly charging Davidson with not being aggressive enough in punishing the dredgers. Although the state cleared Davidson at an Oyster Commission Hearing, it was evident that the Oyster Navy was more a political vessel than a law enforcement tool. Davidson retired in disgust after a second tour of duty and emigrated to Paraguay, which was probably as far away from the Chesapeake as one could get at that time.[22]

Still there was no end to the violence on Chesapeake Bay. Dredgeboat captains seemed to be a law unto themselves and often had more ammunition and guns than the Oyster Police. For several years Maryland state authorities lost control over the dredgers, who worked both in-season and out, often within prohibited waters. In March 1881 the oyster police made another attempt to capture oyster pirates when police schooners came upon a fleet of oyster boats dredging in the mouth of the Chester River. The police and dredgeboats were so close to one another they could trade shotgun fire, but the dredgeboats had better sailors. Most escaped in a swift breeze, though not before the police confiscated the sloops Merrick and Kite. The owner of the vessels, Fred Bucheimer, lost no time but went to Chestertown and paid a $100 fine and costs for each boat, a mere financial slap on the wrist.[23] It was often difficult for commanders to arrest men they had grown up with, and local judges tended to be lenient. Yet, in the sea-borne battles over access to oyster beds on the Chesapeake, men were dying. In a United States government report, George B. Goode in 1887 described the oyster dredge men in ominous terms:

Dredging in Maryland is simply a general scramble, carried on in 700 boats manned by 5,600 daring and unscrupulous men, who regard neither the laws of God or man. Some of the captains and a few of the men may be honest and upright, but it is an unfortunate fact that

22. Norman H. Plummer, *Maryland's Oyster Navy: The First Fifty Years* (Chestertown, Md.: Literary House Press, 1993), 15–20.
23. "Dredging in the Chester River, Maryland Naval Engagement with Oyster Poachers," *Leslie's Illustrated Newspaper,* April 19, 1881.

they form a very small minority. Many of the boats are owned by un-principled men, and I am informed that a number of them are keepers of houses of ill repute.[24]

By the 1880s more than three thousand dredgeboats worked the Chesapeake Bay, and their depredations were beginning to seriously diminish the oyster beds. In Dorchester County, the Cannon family ruled over a flotilla of oyster pirates and openly defied the Oyster Navy. R. P. Cannon and his sons were known colorfully as the "El Mahdi," after the terrorists who had killed General Gordon in the Sudan. Like the Mahdi of the Sudan, the Cannon family obeyed no law and took no prisoners. To show their complete contempt for the Oyster Navy they fired salutes to the police boats before invading prohibited oyster grounds. When the police schooner *Julia Hamilton* attempted to stop them, they drove her off in a hail of gunfire.[25] Later the captain of the police boat, Jonathan Insley, complained that the pirates had been better armed than the police and that his men feared for their lives.

In February 1884, the legislature increased appropriations for manpower and rearmed the police steamers *Hamilton* and *Leila*. Each boat had a well-armed crew and the *Leila* had a twelve-pound cannon mounted in her bow. Taking the initiative, the *Leila* raided the Cannons in their home port on Fox Creek near Cambridge and confiscated several dredgeboats. Then the *Hamilton* went to the mouth of the Nanticoke River to aid a disabled police boat, and its crew showed great courage under fire from the dredgers. Yet when the pirates were arraigned before a local magistrate, they were promptly released from custody and their boats returned. Thus far the oyster wars had resulted in nothing but a string of setbacks for Chesapeake police authorities. According to the historian of the Oyster Police, "The 1884 confrontations ended without credit to the Oyster Navy. Few arrests were made and none of the oyster bandits appeared to be much in fear of the force."[26]

A similar kind of oyster anarchy in Virginia waters prompted the state

24. George Brown Goode, *The Fisheries and Fishery Industries of the United States* (Washington: 1887), 434–35.

25. Plummer, *Maryland's Oyster Navy*, 44.

26. Ibid., 47.

legislature to establish a Virginia fisheries police. Using both private boats and armed steamers like the *Chesapeake*, Virginia armed its men to the teeth and told them to arrest all Maryland watermen who came into Virginia waters to dredge illegally. With only three armed steamers the Virginia police drove off more than twenty Maryland dredgers who had invaded state waters. Virginia's police could and did fight.

By 1888 the Maryland Oyster Police fleet had two steamers and twelve sailing vessels. The dredging fleet found them about as annoying as green-headed marsh flies and not much more. Often for the sheer fun of it dredgers would chase police schooners like the *Eliza Heyward*, which they pursued into Oxford after pumping two hundred rounds of bullets into the boat. The captain and crew refused to take the *Heyward* out again. Another police sloop, the *J. B. Groome*, came upon dredgers near Slaughter Creek on the bay. The oystermen boarded her, threw the one-pound cannon overboard, and forced her to make sail and accompany them to the main anchorage where more than one hundred vessels were at anchor. The policemen feared for their lives but were later released in a tiny skiff and told to row home. The *Groome* was later found stripped and abandoned many miles away. The Oyster Police totally avoided some areas like Swan Point off Kent County on Maryland's Eastern Shore. Here dredgers and rivermen fought their own private civil war over access to the Swan Point oyster bar. The tongers obtained a cannon and attempted to blow the dredgeboats out of the water when they invaded the beds. Rock Point on the Potomac River was also known for its gunfights. As one watermen recalled, "Three killings a week created no civic resentment, while many weeks during the oyster season marked the departure from this life of as many as five or six men."[27]

In the late 1880s two developments occurred that would severely curb lawlessness on the Chesapeake. In 1888 Maryland elected a new governor, Elihu Jackson. A wealthy Eastern Shoreman with powerful connections throughout the state, Jackson vowed that he would no longer tolerate anarchy on the bay. "It is rebellion and nothing less," he said. "I shall adopt the most heroic measures for the enforcement of the law." The governor quickly dispatched Captain Thomas Howard, commander of the *McLane*, in De-

---

27. Sam Chamblis, "Battles of 1888," *Skipper Magazine*, November 1958; James W. England, "Survey of the Oyster Industry," *Eastern Shore Magazine*, November 1937.

cember 1888 to Queen Anne's County to do battle with the oyster pirates. The *McLane* encountered more than forty dredgeboats, who immediately opened fire. The *McLane* responded with a fury of bullets and cannon fire that had not been see before on the Chesapeake. Her howitzer accurately dismasted some among the dredgeboats, and Howard disabled several others by ramming them. The battle lasted four hours. Several dredgeboats fled. Two dredgers, the *J.C.Mahoney* and the *Jones* sank. Unknown to the oyster police, shanghaied crewmen had been locked in the forepeaks of both vessels. As the boats went under, the imprisoned crewmen pounded futilely on the battened hatches. The surviving boats were confiscated and their crews incarcerated in the Queenstown jail. This time, under Governor Jackson's watchful eye, the magistrate was not lenient.[28]

Public opinion both local and statewide turned against the oyster dredgers after a serious incident involving innocent citizens. That same winter oyster pirates attacked what they thought to be a police steamer in a fog bank. The pirates were excellent marksmen, and their bullets whined and crashed through the steamer's cabins. Unfortunately for the pirates, the craft was not a police boat but a passenger vessel, the *Corsica*, a steamboat owned by the Baltimore and Eastern Shore Line. On board the *Corsica* were many women and children who feared for their lives as the storm of bullets hit the vessel.

The *Corsica* incident sparked widespread indignation in the state, and Baltimore and Annapolis newspapers joined Governor Jackson in demanding an end to violence on the Chesapeake. But the oyster pirates did not surrender easily. In January 1889, Captain Thomas Howard took his armed police steamer *McLane* to Cambridge for a show of force. In the Little Choptank River the steamer traded fire with dredgeboats, and several pirates were wounded. Fighting was also brisk on the Patuxent River across the bay. In an urgent telegram to Howard, a police schooner captain declared: "The dredgers seem to be more determined to carry their point than ever before. The oysters are scarce in the bay and they seem determined to get the oysters from the rivers at any risk." Doubtless he had discovered that pirates sailing together in large well-armed fleets were more than a match

---

28. Wennersten, *Oyster Wars of Chesapeake Bay,* 80; Plummer, *Maryland's Oyster Navy,* 47, 50, 51.

for the police. Later the police schooner *Groome* attempted to drive the dredgeboats off the Choptank. The crew stood its ground firing rifles as the dredgers surrounded the vessel. Mate Charles Cator, commanding the *Groome,* blazed away with his Winchester repeating rifle. "But seeing how utterly powerless he was to cope with so many boats, each of which appeared better armed than his own vessel, the mate, Cator, reluctantly retreated, leaving the dredgers in possession of the ground." The battle lasted over two hours during which time a thousand rounds were fired.[29] Eventually, with public support and increased funding from the state, the oyster navy brought an end to "brigandage on the Bay." Dredgers were given swift punishment and prison sentences, and by 1891 the general mayhem on the bay had been reduced to sporadic fighting, mostly along the Virginia-Maryland boundary.

How effective were the Maryland Oyster Police in bringing peace to the troubled waters of the Chesapeake? Like most state commissions, the Oyster Navy was a blatantly partisan operation that offered sinecures to well-connected Democrats. Despite a mixed record, however, the Maryland Oyster Navy did police its own waters and protect them from invasion by dredgers from other states. It also enforced the state's oyster licensing laws. The oyster navy also learned, to its regret, that armed police sail boats were less effective in combatting lawlessness on the bay than armored steam boats with howitzers. Speed and power had become essential for the satisfactory work of Maryland's Oyster Navy.

Although Maryland and Virginia oystermen acted together to expel Yankee oystermen from their beds, they often turned against one another. Virginia did not enforce the Compact of 1785 and federal law requiring its watermen to remain in their own territorial waters, with the result that many Virginia oystermen poached oysters in the Maryland beds. Also the lack of a definitive agreement between Virginia and Maryland regarding a boundary line across the bay to the Potomac River was a constant source of friction. Before the Civil War and the emergence of the oyster industry, a modern trans-Chesapeake boundary line was considered unnecessary. After 1870 the boundary question became a burning issue.

29. "Dredgers Come Off Victors," *Baltimore Sun,* January 14, 1889, and "The State Should Enforce the Oyster Law Promptly and Vigorously," ibid., January 15, 1889.

An earlier attempt to solve the boundary issue had been made by representatives from both states, but local prejudice against change and the Civil War prevented serious negotiation between Virginia and Maryland. With millions of dollars of fishing rights at stake and a history of interstate territorial grudges that went all the way back to the early colonial period, it was not surprising that any discussion of state lines drew heated controversy. Maryland nursed a grudge that the Compact of 1785 had given Virginia 15,000 more acres of land and water than Maryland thought was her due. And Virginia complained that her fishermen were being denied access to their livelihood as oysters, crabs and fish did not follow state boundaries. To make the issue even more volatile, two island communities, Smith Island, Maryland, and Tangier Island, Virginia, were in the center of the disputed bay area, and their oystermen preferred to settle the issue with guns rather than surveyor's tools.

Specifically the issue involved who exactly had the right to harvest oysters in the Pocomoke River and in the Pocomoke Sound that was part of the Chesapeake. Maryland oystermen insisted that the entire Pocomoke Sound was a natural extension of the Pocomoke River. Since Maryland watermen could harvest oysters in the Pocomoke River under the Compact of 1785, the conditions of which applied to the Pocomoke Sound as well as to the Potomac River, they were guaranteed access to the oyster-rich Pocomoke Sound. Virginia disagreed, arguing vigorously that such an interpretation would deny her sovereignty over 40,000 acres of bay oyster beds. The 1785 pact, argued Virginia, referred only to the Pocomoke River; therefore Maryland was entitled to harvest oysters only in the river and not the sound. With lives and fortunes at stake, this was hardly an academic question. At issue was the economic well-being of the port of Crisfield as well as that of Maryland watermen.

In 1872 and 1873 numerous meetings between Virginia and Maryland commissioners resulted in a decision to submit the issue to binding federal arbitration. After three years of complicated negotiations, a boundary line was finally determined. Under the Jenkins-Black Award of 1877 the boundary was demarcated as beginning at a point on the Potomac where the line between Virginia and West Virginia strikes the river at low watermark, thence to Smith's Point and across the bay to Watkins Point on the Pocomoke. In terms of oyster beds, Virginia got the larger share of the Tangier and

Pocomoke sounds, and Marylanders who ran over the "line of '77" to take oysters risked having their boats confiscated. The Jenkins-Black Award did nothing to clarify other sovereignty issues between the two states arising out of the Compact of 1785. That compact would bedevil maritime rights between the two states until it was finally repealed unilaterally by Maryland in 1957 during a dispute over the Potomac River.[30]

Although Maryland retained sovereignty over the famous "Great Rocks" oyster beds of Tangier Sound, the Award of 1877 embittered large numbers of Maryland watermen. They had lost access to many of the oyster beds in the Pocomoke Sound upon which their prosperity rested. Maryland's Smith Islanders, especially, refused to accept the Jenkins decision, because their best beds were now in Virginia waters. The result was a small-scale shooting war that lasted until 1910, when many of the disputed oyster beds were finally played out. At least fifty men are known to have been killed in the boundary conflict. In 1894 the two states took their differences before the United States Supreme Court. In *Wharton v. Wise* the court ruled that the Pocomoke Sound and Pocomoke River were "separate and distinct bodies of water," and that Maryland oystermen were prohibited from harvesting shellfish in the Sound on Virginia's side of the "77 line."[31] As late as the 1980s occasional gunfights flared on the "line of '77" involving Maryland and Virginia watermen. In 1982 two Saxis, Virginia, watermen seriously wounded Maryland oysterman Ronald Burke with a full shotgun blast because, they said, Burke had been fishing over the boundary line. After all these years the boundary peace is still tenuous when it comes to oyster rights.[32] Locals quip that enough lead has been wasted in boundary fighting since colonial times to supply sinkers for all the fishing lines along the Atlantic coast.

---

30. Louis N. Whealton, "The Maryland and Virginia Boundary Controversy, 1668–1894" (Ph.D. dissertation, Johns Hopkins University, 1897). The award was ratified by Congress on March 3, 1879 (U.S. Federal Code, 20, Statute 481); Garret Power, *The Chesapeake Bay in Legal Perspective,* 76. See also, Wennersten, *Oyster Wars of Chesapeake Bay,* 47–48.

31. Wharton *v.* Wise, United States Supreme Court, April 23, 1894, *Opinions of the U.S. Supreme Court* (Washington D.C.:, 1894), 176.

32. John Kobler, "They've Been Fighting 173 Years," *Saturday Evening Post,* November 1, 1958. See also Chris Sullivan, "Oyster Wars Flare," *Salisbury Daily Times,* October 20, 1982.

To a great extent the conflict between Virginians and Marylanders grew out of a steadily diminishing supply of oysters that resulted from dredgeboats overfishing the bars. As early as 1869 oyster police commander Hunter S. Davidson in his *Report Upon the Oyster Resources of Maryland* had warned that the oyster beds of the lower bay were being recklessly depleted. Until this report, Maryland's interest in shellfish conservation had been minimal. A few counties like Dorchester, Somerset, and St. Mary's passed laws prohibiting the use of oysters for agricultural fertilizer or burning them for lime. Somerset County in 1854 passed the first law in the country authorizing oyster licenses to professional watermen. But overall, in the pell-mell rush to take the oysters out of Chesapeake Bay few envisioned conservation as a compelling public policy. Oyster licenses were generally unpopular with Maryland watermen, and refusal to follow license laws contributed in part to the founding of the Maryland Oyster Police. Watermen were rebellious and suspicious of attempts to manage oyster resources. Judges were lenient toward those who violated the oyster laws. The popular attitude on Chesapeake Bay, was summarized in the folk saying, "Get it today! Hell with tamar. Leave it till tamar, somebody else'll get it."[33] Championing the oystermen was a good way for politicians to win votes.

Significantly in this tumultuous period, the French government more than Maryland or Virginia was interested in the health of the Chesapeake oyster. France sent the famous zoologist Paul DeBroca to Maryland in 1860 to investigate Chesapeake oyster beds and possibly discover ways of rejuvenating depleted beds on the French coast. The Civil War disrupted his research.[34]

Others took up similar efforts. Oyster harvests continued to increase to a peak of fourteen million bushels in 1874 but then went into a five year fall, reaching only 10.5 million bushels in 1879. Such an abrupt decline raised eyebrows in Maryland's seafood and political communities and resulted in the commissioning of a survey of oyster grounds in the Tangier and Pocomoke Sounds, which had the richest "oyster rocks" and were sub-

33. M. Grave, *A Manual of Oyster Culture in Maryland, Fourth Report* (Annapolis: Board of Shellfish Commissioners, 1912), 279–348. Davidson, *Report Upon the Oyster Resources of Maryland (1869)*, 16; Davidson, *Report Upon the Oyster Resources of Maryland* (Annapolis: 1870).

34. Wennersten, *The Oyster Wars of Chesapeake Bay,* 52.

ject to heavy fishing pressure. On October 20, 1878, Lieutenant Francis Winslow, an engineer for the U.S. Navy, shipped out of Annapolis on board an Oyster Police boat to begin the first comprehensive survey of the Chesapeake Bay bottom. The young naval officer had cordial relations with the Oyster Police and in the days that followed he turned the boat into a floating biological and cartographic laboratory. On deck lay eighteen fathoms of chain used to take soundings and collect samples from the bottom of the bay, several pairs of oyster tongs, and a small dredge. Far from the "pirates" he had expected to encounter, Winslow found the dredge men good-natured and helpful. Often in reference to a particular bar a waterman would call out to Winslow, "What does she look like Captain?" Winslow had only bad news for the watermen. In his detailed and mathematically precise analysis of Tangier Sound, Winslow found only one oyster to three square yards of bed. Such low yields confirmed Winslow's hunch that the beds were being exhausted. In his report Winslow decried their destruction and urged returning more shell to the bay so that oyster larvae would have hard "rocks" on which to set and multiply. He also urged the creation of an independent regulatory commission to regulate dredging, protect young oysters, close beds when necessary, and rehabilitate oyster grounds.[35]

More pioneering work on Chesapeake Bay resources followed in the 1880s with the publication of Dr. William K. Brooks's widely acclaimed *The Oyster: A Popular Summary of a Scientific Study.* The director of the Chesapeake Bay Zoological Laboratory and a professor of biology at the Johns Hopkins University, Brooks knew more about the Chesapeake Bay oyster fishery than any man in the country. His research of the health of the beds throughout the bay supported Winslow's work on Tangier Sound, and his conclusion was resounding in its judgment: The Chesapeake's oyster resources were in rapid decline. By 1883 Brooks and his assistants were finding only one oyster for every four square yards of oyster bed, a major deterioration in only five years since Winslow's survey. Brooks called for prompt and decisive action and was soon joined by others.[36] In March 1889 *Harper's*

35. Francis Winslow, *An Engineering Study of the Chesapeake Bay Area Oyster Industry* (Annapolis: 1880); and Winslow, "Deterioration of the American Oyster Beds," *Popular Science Monthly,* 20 (1881): 29–43, 145–56.

36. William K. Brooks, *The Oyster: A Popular Survey of a Scientific Study* (Baltimore: Johns Hopkins University Press, 1891).

*Weekly Magazine* ran a long essay that chronicled the bay's problems and complimented Brooks for his pioneering research. "Thirty years ago," reported *Harper's*, "these beds were considered inexhaustible, but so merciless have been the depredations that the greatest oyster territory in the world is in serious danger of permanent depletion." Profit-hungry watermen with no respect for the law blatantly disregarded attempts by the State of Maryland to stake out certain portions of the bay for shellfish recuperation. The times now demanded conservation. "There are in the Chesapeake 640,000 acres of good oyster lands which can be utilized when the industry shall have been removed from the lawless grab game which it now is, and placed upon a basis of law and common sense." All that stood in the way were "demagogues" who solicited the watermen's vote and hindered "the prompt reform of existing evils."[37]

Ironically, the 1880s were the most prosperous decade in the history of the oyster industry. Although the physical volume of the business had declined, its total value reached an all time high. In Baltimore alone, more than 3,000 black shuckers were opening Chesapeake oysters, and the oyster canneries on Atlantic Wharf in the city's Canton District eagerly employed any man or woman willing to work. Warnings of imminent disaster went largely unheeded as daily oyster trains of thirty to forty railway cars passed out of the city to the West. The same kind of business practices that gave Rockefeller's Standard Oil Company infamy tarnished Baltimore's oyster packing industry. In the 1870s twenty-five oyster packers led by seafood merchant Sandy B. Platt and his sons formed the combine, the Union Oyster Company. The corporation, capitalized at $300,000, soon ran into trouble with other firms, who accused Union Oyster of monopolistic practices. State and city authorities found the quality of oyster meat Union was canning to be inferior to that of the independently owned firms and gave the company bad publicity. By 1883 Union had ceased to operate. Apparently the slippery industry could not be easily monopolized.[38]

In the winter of 1892–93, Chesapeake watermen began to reap the bitter harvest that Brooks had predicted. Oysters were scarce, and nine hundred dredgers scrambled on the bay to catch the few that were left. At the end of

37. "The Maryland Oyster Business," *Harper's Weekly*, March 2, 1889.
38. A. J. Nichol, *The Oyster Packing Industry of Baltimore: Its History and Current Problems* (Baltimore: 1937), 20.

that oyster season, the State of Maryland took its first faltering steps toward regulation of the industry. In the spring of 1893 the legislature passed a culling law that prohibited watermen from taking oysters less than two and one-half inches from hinge to mouth. As the oyster harvest continued to deteriorate, the bivalve found a champion in Baltimore lawyer B. Howard Haman, who defended the concept of oyster culture or "oyster farming." Maryland watermen opposed the idea, saying that they would not tend bay bottom to restore oysters. Oysters were to be taken out—the Lord would put them back. Eventually oyster planting on the bay took hold in Virginia waters, but even with the passage of legislation that allowed small oyster leaseholds under the Haman Act of 1906, Maryland watermen preferred the life of the "water Arab" to that of "oyster farmer."[39]

By 1909, three years after the passage of the Haman Oyster Leasing Bill, watermen recorded only 491 leases covering a total area of 2,230 acres. The state's effort to get 350,000 acres of barren bars back into cultivation failed to win watermen's support. As late as 1913 Maryland state officials reported that "oystermen are violently opposed to oyster culture in any form."[40]

Virginia discovered an interest in oyster conservation when their part of the industry took a serious downturn after 1900 owing to the rise of pests, disease, and municipal pollution in the Norfolk-Hampton Roads area. By 1912 the discharge of sewage from Washington, D.C. was seriously harming the Potomac oyster fishery. Inspectors from the federal government condemned all raw oysters in the Potomac above Blackston Island, a matter that alarmed Governor Philip Goldsborough of Maryland and Governor William Hodges Mann of Virginia.[41]

Interest in Chesapeake Bay oyster resources did have one long-range beneficial result. The State of Maryland financed a six-year, two-hundred-thousand-dollar study of the Chesapeake Bay bottom by Charles C. Yates, an engineer with the United States Coast and Geodetic Survey. After 159,530 soundings, Yates and his crew of thirty produced in 1913 forty-two large

---

39. James W. England Jr., "A Survey of the Oyster Industry," *Eastern Shore Magazine,* December 1931.

40. *Maryland Shell Fish Commission Report* (Annapolis, 1909). See also *Maryland Shell Fish Commission Report* (Annapolis, 1913).

41. *Report of the Potomac River Oyster Pollution Commission* (Washington D.C., 1912).

scale oyster charts, the *Yates Survey of the Oyster Bars of Maryland,* which is still in use today. The survey provided Maryland conservationists with one of the most scientifically precise studies ever made of the oyster reserves of the Chesapeake estuary.[42] This was the first major research effort under the direction of the newly created Maryland Shellfish Commission. Although it was the political arm of Maryland seafood packers, the Maryland Shellfish Commission argued that knowledge of the actual condition of the bay was the first step toward assuring a stable and prosperous industry. The legislature, unfortunately, appropriated money only to study conditions in the bay, not change them. Not until the 1930s would serious conservation leadership come out of either the political or scientific communities of Maryland.

At the same time that Chesapeake watermen took record amounts of oysters from the bay, they also over-harvested the great fishing grounds containing shad, herring, and menhaden. The first two were usually taken in the spring during the spawning runs along Chesapeake tributaries and gave employment to several thousand men. In autumn, the watermen cast their nets for menhaden, mackerel, pike, and any other fish in demand in the markets of metropolitan Baltimore and Philadelphia. Fish were cheaper than oysters; two large shad could be bought for twenty cents, and herring brought a dollar a hundred. The bulk of the profits went to the seafood packers while most fishermen lived in poverty.

A fisherman's life was as hard as an oysterman's. During the shad runs, when April nights were damp and chilly, they worked in their boats with wet nets and drenched clothing, often standing waist-deep in the water handling wet haul seines and struggling fish. Where the water was too deep for seine-hauling, watermen used floating gill nets to snare the fish. Shad and menhaden were spectacularly abundant and were turned into everything from fish meal to fish oil to fertilizer. In 1880, the first year that statistics on the Chesapeake Bay fishery became available, Maryland watermen took ninety-two million pounds of menhaden and almost seven million pounds of shad from the bay. A decade later those figures had soared to 135 million and 14 million pounds of menhaden and shad.[43] Purse nets, gear used mostly

42. Charles C. Yates, *Summary of Survey of Oyster Bars of Maryland (1906–1912)* (Washington: Government Printing Office, 1913).

43. *Proceedings of the Governor's Conference on Chesapeake Bay*, September 12–13, 1968 (Annapolis, 1968).

to trap menhaden, were ruthlessly efficient and killed large numbers of more valuable fish.[44] Resources seemed endless and little thought was given to what might happen if the oyster beds or fishing banks gave out. Even if they did give out, the thinking went, the bay and marshes were still rich with tasty Chesapeake blue crabs, clams, and Maryland terrapin. Fish harvests began to diminish in tandem with oysters after 1890. Seafood dealers grew seriously alarmed and lobbied the state legislature to have James C. Tawes, a Crisfield seafood dealer, appointed fish commissioner for the Eastern Shore of Maryland. An ebullient merchant who handled a hundred tons of fish a season, Tawes campaigned for the "artificial propagation" of fish in the bay. Only fish hatcheries, Tawes claimed, could help the bay regain its lost productivity.[45] In the 1890s fourteen million pounds of shad were taken annually out of the bay. By 1930 that harvest had diminished to 500,000 pounds. Overharvesting led to the wasteful and reckless destruction of young and spawning fish, and an alarmed Maryland legislature appropriated funds to encourage pisciculture and conservation of existing fish stocks.[46]

The Chesapeake in the nineteenth century also became the hunting ground of rich sportsmen and market gunners who loved to hunt canvasback ducks and other waterfowl for fun and profit. The bay was so rich in fish, crabs, and oysters that the enormity of its waterfowl stocks is occasionally overlooked by historians. No visitor departed without commenting on the giant flocks of ducks and geese that made their home in the Chesapeake. In their 1680 journal of a trip to Maryland, Jasper Danckaerts and Peter Sluyter, two Dutch immigrants wrote of ducks and geese: "The water was so black with them that it seemed when you looked from the land below upon the water as it were a mass of filth or turf, and when they flew up there was a rushing and vibration of the air like a great storm coming through the trees, even like the rumblings of distant thunder." Danckaerts and Sluyter reported that it was easy to get six ducks with one shot by firing into the mass.[47] Similarly journalists who visited the Chesapeake in the 1870s

44. Purse nets captured about everything that swam in the Bay and were not outlawed by the Maryland legislature until 1931.

45. "Pompanos in Chesapeake Bay," *New York Times*, July 31, 1896.

46. "On the Eastern Shore," *Lippincott's Magazine*, August 20, 1876. Maryland Conservation Department, *Annual Report,* Fiscal Year 1930 (Annapolis: 1931)

47. Quoted in John Thomas Scharf, *History of Maryland from the Earliest Times*

and 1880s were impressed by "clouds" of waterfowl that seemed at times to hide the sun.

After 1870, Chesapeake market hunters used "punt guns"—small cannon loaded with buckshot—to slaughter thousands of canvasback , redhead, and blackhead ducks for meat and feathers. The waterfowl were usually slaughtered at night when hunters used a bright kerosene reflector light to stupefy the birds in the dazzling glare and shoot them down as they took flight. Canvasback ducks were rich juicy birds, exquisite in flavor and rolling in fat, and brought a ready price of three or four dollars a pair on the Baltimore market. Meanwhile at the other end of the Chesapeake hunting spectrum, rich sportsmen with decoys and gun dogs used duck blinds and "sink boats" (boats that sank partially in the water and were covered with decoys to fool the birds) to shoot as many ducks as they wanted. They survived luxuriously in hunting lodges along the Susquehanna and Chester Rivers and other waterfowl flyways and their duck blinds were amply stocked with robes and blankets. The Chesapeake region attracted celebrity hunters like Theodore Roosevelt and President Benjamin Harrison and was well-known on the sportsmen's circuit. The Susquehanna Flats, a vast area of Chesapeake shallows created by river deposits, was the breeding and roosting area for millions of ducks and geese and a favorite celebrity hunting ground. Also the popularity of waterfowl hunting on the Susquehanna Flats indirectly contributed to the prosperity of Abercrombie and Fitch, an outfitting firm that provided sturdy clothes to protect hunters from the Chesapeake elements.[48]

Most people in the nineteenth-century Chesapeake believed that natural resources were a gift of God and existed for man's pleasure and design. In an age of Darwinian competition the bay was an exceptionally volatile economic region, ecologically vulnerable to any number of external influences, from pollution to changes in weather patterns. For packers, fishermen, and oystermen, the bay was an economic resource that responded to the demands of American consumption. Its use did not conform to established laws of property. Legal jurisdictional rights, as we have seen, were also problematic.

---

to the Present Day, 3 vols. (repr., Hatboro, Pa.: Tradition Press, 1967), 2:2–8.
48. John R. Wennersten, *Maryland's Eastern Shore: A Journey in Time and Place*

Given the size of the oyster and fish business in the Chesapeake, it is fairly easy to separate the ecological history of the bay in the nineteenth century into two harvest periods: a low-use and a high-use period. The Civil War divided the two. Although pollution and sedimentation were already noticeable by 1860, damage to marine resources was minuscule compared to the damage brought about by overharvesting after 1870. Despite scientific information that the fishery of the bay was being seriously depleted, little was done to restrain unfettered economic competition. State Commissions in both Virginia and Maryland found it difficult to accept the fact that declining yields on the bay might be permanent. Most officials thought that if fishing grounds grew barren, it was a relatively simple matter to move on to new grounds and give old ones time to replenish themselves. In this regard an early report of the state Oyster Commission is instructive. In 1884 the Maryland legislature established a special commission to investigate the health of the Chesapeake relative to the oyster beds. Within the year the commission concluded that "the oyster property of the State is in imminent danger of complete destruction." Oysters, the commission argued, had to be replenished through artificial cultivation. This meant the development by private oyster farming of five-acre leased beds, after the manner adopted by Connecticut and New Jersey. It noted that seed oysters taken from the Chesapeake to Connecticut waters had thrived and in turn were being used for plantings on the Pacific Coast. Now it was time for the Chesapeake itself to save its oyster beds in the same way that Connecticut and New Jersey were revitalizing theirs. Further, it argued that certain depleted oyster grounds had to be closed to dredging and that police boats would have to patrol the bay and river mouths to enforce this sanction.[49] Unfortunately, but not surprisingly, the Oyster Commission's report was launched on the troubled waters of greed and sank without a trace. No one thought that an entire ecosystem like the Chesapeake might be at risk. Oystermen and fishermen worked on the assumption that resource depletion was a necessary complement to economic progress and approached the problems of the bay with the same fatalism that Americans approached the destruction of forests or the passing of buffalo herds. Chesapeake watermen, it should also be mentioned,

---

(Centreville, Md.: Tidewater Publishers, 1992), 50–51.

49. *Report of the Oyster Commission of the State of Maryland* (Baltimore, 1884), 6–12.

tended to blame everyone but themselves for the problems they encountered on the bay. If only watermen were let alone by oyster police, conservation commissions, scientists, and "do-gooders," they could get their work done and the bay would ultimately replenish itself. Scientific research on bay problems held no meaning for them. In these years, the scientific and commercial fishing communities had relatively little to say to one another. Fish and oysters were like diamonds: commodities to be recovered from a state of nature and turned into cash. The "Lord" would do all the necessary work for Chesapeake Bay watermen. We can term this approach to resource utilization on the bay as the "Lord's Oysters" theory of nature. But divine providence seldom works out in ways understandable to man.

The Chesapeake's ecological problems were compounded by the fact that oyster and fish harvesting evolved during one of capitalism's most expansive phases, and there was little time to make adjustment to the rapid changes in industrialization, consumer markets, or economic ideology. A region defined by economies of subsistence was suddenly pulled pell-mell into an era of money, commodities, and resource exploitation. What had happened to farmers and planters in the great age of tobacco was now happening on the bay. Commodification of the seascape followed commodification of the landscape.

As the bay became an increasingly significant resource area, relationships among watermen evolved in which oystermen and fishermen were tied in networks of obligation with merchants, packers, and ship chandlers that prevented them from returning to simpler forms of livelihood once the bay went into decline. Even when oyster harvests were bad, watermen scrambled onto the bay. They had debts and bills to pay and were strung out in a remorseless web of dependency that cut across generations of fathers and sons and affected the life of entire communities. There could be no turning back the clock. Merchants in Crisfield joked that if a waterman found the last surviving oyster in Chesapeake Bay, he'd sell it.

Such character traits were hardly confined to the Chesapeake. Karl Mobius, a professor of zoology at the University of Kiel in the 1870s, remarked that oystermen along the coast of Schleswig-Holstein were astonished that the productivity of the beds diminished after millions upon millions of oysters had been taken from them. For Mobius, it was a classic case of the overwhelming power of human beings to destroy nature rather than work within its framework. In concluding his study on oyster beds, Mobius introduced the broader concept of extinction, mentioning the actual or threatened extinction of the dodo, turtles, beaver, and the Greenland whale. Looking at America, Mobius believed that the excessive exploitation of the oyster beds was directly related to the coming of the railroads. He noted also that the American railroad network raised the possibility, east and west, of the gradual extinction of the oyster and the buffalo.[50]

Eventually population growth in the oyster ports and fishing towns as well as the prosperity of local merchants who now had capital to diversify their businesses brought an end to frontier social conditions on Chesapeake Bay. Merchants invested in more economical vessels and turned to opportunities in truck agriculture and electricity generation. Oyster packers quickly mastered the art of electrical refrigeration to produce ice for seafood transport. Such refrigeration was soon expanded to include cold storage and refrigerated rail cars for vegetables and fruit. The packers sold electricity from their generators to their fellow townsmen and municipalities. Seafood packers soon had economic strength far greater than the watermen of the bay could hope to achieve as entrepreneurs. Packers grew richer from an industry that left Chesapeake watermen poorer.

The seafood industry of Chesapeake Bay expanded rapidly from the 1860s until the end of the century. After that the fishery went into decline, and market shifts and economic upheavals led to the deterioration of older fishing towns. By 1920 the great seafood ports of Crisfield, Oxford, Cambridge, and others were shadows of their former selves. All were both products and victims of the revolutionary economic transformation of Chesapeake Bay.

The nineteenth-century Chesapeake oyster wars were as much about property rights and privilege as they were about access to shellfish. The same process of commodifying natural resources that had taken place during the Tobacco Revolution now created commodities out of natural places and things. Increasingly by the end of the nineteenth century the tragedy of the commons permitted growing state intervention in the bay as a public trustee for public use rights. As anthropologist Bonnie J. McCay has pointed

---

50. Quoted in Clarence J. Glacken, "Culture and Environment in Western Civilization During the Nineteenth Century," in Kendall E. Bailes, ed., *Environmental History, Critical Issues in Comparative Perspective* (Lanham, Md.: University Press of America, 1985), 49, 53.

out, there is a danger in "romancing the commons." Fishermen were just as capable of ruining an environment as anyone else, even when such tactics went against the survival of their profession. Also, the commons as a legal concept ultimately could be used by businesses and industries to pollute the Chesapeake at will. Furthermore the "tragedy of the commons," writes McCay, was that it was all too often the "tragedy of the commoners."[51] Like many simple explanations of complex phenomena, the "tragedy of the commons" has its mythic component. It paints a one-dimensional picture of human nature. The individuals who ruin the commons do not talk to one another and have no social life. There is no attempt at community and sharing of resources, Rather, "as individuals, they are alienated, rational, utility-maximizing automatons and little else," noted historian Arthur McEvoy.[52] Exploitation of the Chesapeake commons occurred. But increased pressure on a common resource like the oyster did not result, as commons theorists might argue, in complete government management or privatization. What occurred on Chesapeake Bay was "some" management and "some" privatization.[53] Other factors must also enter the picture to get a complete explanation of the Chesapeake as a natural resource tragedy.[54]

Many of the policies put into place to "repair" the commons in fact tended to make it difficult for small-scale fisherfolk to pursue a livelihood. All too often in the Chesapeake and elsewhere the courts interpreted the doctrine of public trust to mean state ownership of natural resource properties, and

51. Bonnie J. McCay, *Oyster Wars and the Public Trust, Property, Law, and Ecology in New Jersey History* (Tucson: University of Arizona Press, 1998), xv–xxvi, 188–203.

52. Arthur F. McEvoy, "Toward an Interactive Theory of Nature and Culture: Ecology, Production, and Cognition in the California Fishing Industry," in Donald Worster, ed., *The Ends of the Earth: Perspectives on Modern Environmental History* (Cambridge: Cambridge University Press, 1988), 226.

53. "The response of the Maryland and Virginia legislatures to the problem of regulating and managing these resources has been erratic and piecemeal." Garrett Power, *Chesapeake Bay in Legal Perspective*, 217.

54. In his work on bison ecology and the Great Plains, historian Dan Flores suggests that even Indians had great difficulty working out a "dynamic, ecological equilibrium with the bison herds." As with the case of the Chesapeake oystermen, too many of the forces that shaped their world were beyond the power of the tribes to influence. See Dan Flores, "Bison Ecology and Bison Diplomacy: The Southern Plains from 1800 to 1850," *The Journal of American History*, 77 (1991): 484.

the state subsequently sold the commons to private enterprise. In the twentieth century, state governments often took the side of municipal and corporate polluters in disputes over water quality and preservation of fishing grounds. Giving substance to the notion of the Chesapeake as common property permitted legal and economic doctrines to evolve that strengthened the rights of individuals to use and despoil the environment. In the name of conservation management, Maryland and Virginia sold or licensed shoreline and oyster bars to private interests. Courthouse lawyers and cannery owners knew how to work the commons to their own advantage. We should not let the tragedy of the commons divert our gaze from the tragedy also imposed on the bay by corporate businessmen and public trust advocates. In order to preserve the oysterman's way of life, cautions Bonnie McCay, it may be necessary to "curtail absolute freedom" on the bay and impose "informal property rights and self-regulation" on those whose right to follow the water has been historically established.[55]

55. Bonnie J. McCay, "The Culture of the Commoner: Historical Observations on Old and New World Fisheries," in McCay and Acheson, eds., *The Question of the Commons*, 1–34.

## CHAPTER FIVE

# Engineering, Pollution, and Conservation
## Early Problems of Chesapeake Bay Management

"While city-wide sewer systems alleviated sanitation problems of the inner city, they often redirected waste to nearby rivers, lakes and bays, thus creating a new set of health and pollution hazards."
— Martin Melossi, *Environmental History Review,* Spring, 1990.

"I worked intensely researching Bay problems for nearly forty years, often without pay or support, though the Conservation Commission did thankfully provide boat travel."
— Reginald V. Truitt, 1982

## The Problem of Chesapeake Bay Management

In the first half of the twentieth century the problem of managing this huge natural resource focused on three main issues. The first was how the bay and its tributaries could be more efficiently utilized for navigation and commerce, an area in which the U.S. Army Corps of Engineers assumed leadership. The second issue centered on how the Chesapeake Bay could be made more productive as a seafood resource. There, state governments encouraged scientists to develop approaches to enhancing fish production, paying special attention to the matter of reviving a stagnant oyster industry. Lastly, in some ways connected with both the engineering and the maritime problems of the bay, was the matter of conservation itself. How was the Chesapeake to be conserved and the purity of its waters maintained for the benefit of all the citizens of the region?

Approaches to these questions in the first half of the twentieth century were tentative, as business communities cast a wary eye on attempts to regulate Chesapeake maritime life. Neither scientists nor legislators in Richmond and Annapolis were prepared to undertake the enormous and controversial effort, or create the bureaucracies necessary, to supervise the work of Chesapeake Bay management. The history of bay conservation in the first part of the twentieth century is a tale of frustration, legislative suspicion of scientific endeavor, and small successes.

## The Army Corps of Engineers

From the mid-nineteenth century onward, the U.S. Army Corps of Engineers was an important part of the environmental history of the bay and was significantly involved in river navigation, basin planning, flood control, and military construction. Organized during the American Revolution, the corps was concerned in the following years with the construction of fortifications in the Chesapeake at a time in the nation's history when the United States was weak and subject to invasion. After the War of 1812, the Corps of Engineers repaired the Cumberland Road and surveyed the Chesapeake and Delaware and the Chesapeake and Ohio canals, and helped lay out the land route of the Baltimore and Ohio Railroad.[1] The corps held a narrow view of water use and water development, viewing rivers primarily in terms of transportation, and did not interest itself in other possible uses of waterways.

After the Civil War, Congress placed the Corps of Engineers in charge of river and harbor projects throughout the country, and thereafter the corps' future would be closely intertwined with the Chesapeake Bay and the port of Baltimore. The Baltimore District of the Army Corps of Engineers' main thrust was in river and harbor operations. It became especially active in removing dangerous shoals at the mouth of the Susquehanna that restricted the passage of coal and lumber boats. The port of Havre de Grace became an important center for dredging operations on the upper bay and the Susquehanna. The corps also worked closely with the United States Commission of Fish and Fisheries, which needed channels cut for the movement of its boats in that area. The federal government further worried that ice storms on the Chesapeake would damage government facilities near the Susquehanna. Such concerns became fact when a violent snowstorm in December 1887 accompanied by the rapid formation of ice threatened to close navigation on the bay. The corps' tugboats worked around the clock bringing barges of soil to fill cribs and barriers to ward off the ice floes and to keep the channels open. Often the tugs had to crash through ice fields

1. Henry L. Abbott, "The Corps of Engineers," in Theodore F. Rodenbough and William Haskins, eds., *The Army of the United States, 1789–1896* (New York: Argonaut Press, 1966), 111–25; Franklin E. Mullay, "The Battle of Baltimore," *Maryland Historical Magazine,* 54 (1959): 61–65.

two feet thick. Without the corps' energy and resources, which put together a task force of ships and men who labored unrelentingly over a three-day period, the port of Havre de Grace and its channel to the bay would have been severely damaged.[2]

In similar fashion the Corps of Engineers worked closely with the city of Richmond to improve navigation on the James River in Virginia. The James had a unique problem: its navigational channel was littered with the hulks of Union and Confederate gunboats that had become dangerous obstructions to shipping. The corps needed several years to complete this task, and in the process it dredged a channel in the James 250 feet wide and eighteen feet deep. The dredging and excavating of rock around the Richmond area gave the Corps of Engineers invaluable lessons in ship channel construction that could later be applied to the Chesapeake itself.

Between 1870 and 1880 Congress approved several dynamiting and dredging projects and wing dams on the James, Potomac, and Rappahannock Rivers. In that same decade Congress appropriated more than $200,000 to deepen the channel of the Appomattox River from three feet to nine feet. Increasingly the corps' fleet of dredgers became a familiar sight in the Chesapeake, as it applied its engineering expertise in areas that ranged from dredging to lock and dam construction. The army, with public approbation and congressional funding, would soon be "managing" the bay and its tributaries.

The driving force behind these projects was Major William P. Craighill, a Civil War veteran and corps district commander who had constructed a floating dam to change water flows near Havre de Grace and the Susquehanna. To Craighill, the Chesapeake was one large engineering problem—two hundred-odd miles of waterway with a surface of 3,232 square miles to be mastered with levees, dredging, and ample amounts of money. Under Craighill's leadership, after 1870 hardly any creek or river that emptied into the bay escaped the corps' ministrations. By 1872 army engineers were at work on all but the most minor streams in the Chesapeake region. Most of these ventures were designed to improve navigation for the benefit

2. For background on this and other activities of the Corps of Engineers see W. Stull Holt, *Office of the Chief Engineers of the Army: Its Non-Military History, Activities and Organization* (Baltimore: Johns Hopkins University Press, 1923); Harold Kanarek, *The Mid-Atlantic Engineers: A History of the Baltimore District, U.S. Army Corps of Engineers, 1774–1974* (Washington: 1978), 65.

of the commercial fishing industry and involved routine contract dredging. In turn, maritime communities came to depend on the corps for navigation assistance and protested vigorously to Congress when appropriations for dredging and internal improvements in the bay were curtailed late in 1876.

The Corps of Engineers came to Maryland's Eastern Shore in the 1870s as well and embarked on an ambitious project to dredge Queenstown Creek to an average depth of six feet so that Queenstown could have a navigational outlet to the Chester River and the bay beyond. The engineers straightened and dredged the creek, providing Queenstown with a channel access to its harbor a hundred feet wide and eight feet deep. Similar harbor improvements took place at Cambridge on the Choptank River so that steamboats carrying heavy cargoes of peaches, grain, and ship timber could enter the port. Throughout the final decades of the nineteenth century the engineers worked on the Choptank to produce a channel 150 feet wide and twelve feet deep to a railroad wharf one mile distant from Cambridge. Cambridge officials hailed the corps as the protector of the town's economic life. By 1887 Cambridge had regular steamboat service that stimulated commerce with Baltimore. In Washington Major Craighill may have been a faceless military bureaucrat, but in Cambridge, Queenstown, and other Eastern Shore towns that benefited from having their rivers dredged, Craighill was an economic savior.

Resourceful and relentless, Craighill tackled any problem. The Wicomico River on Maryland's Eastern Shore, for example, posed special engineering problems because it was exceedingly narrow, crooked, and shoaled, with only a few inches of water in some places at low tide. Only small vessels could come up the river and even they had to anchor two miles below the town of Salisbury and offload their goods to ox-drawn wagons. Even at flood tide, the Wicomico offered a draft of only two feet.

Craighill began full-scale dredging of the Wicomico in 1875. This time the corps had to use special restraining dikes to prevent the river from refilling with mud. If mud were simply deposited on both sides of the river banks it would only be a matter of time before the action of passing steamboats washed the spoil back into the channel. To remedy this condition the engineers decided to tow scows filled with mud to Ellis Bay some twenty-four miles down the Wicomico. This plan, however, soon brought the Engineers into conflict with local watermen, who claimed that dumping mud in the river near them would destroy their oyster beds. The watermen sued successfully in court and forced dredge scows to offload much farther downstream. Apparently, everyone wanted navigable rivers. What to do with the dredge waste, however, would be an issue that would spill over into the environmental politics of the Chesapeake in the modern era. In the 1940s, for instance, Virginia watermen in the Norfolk area were at odds with the corps over the dumping of dredge spoil along the James River. This time the army was too strong for the watermen, for the state wanted the dredging to continue. Virginia therefore cancelled the watermen's oyster leases in the James and released the federal government from damage claims to the local oyster beds.[3]

In the 1890s it became apparent that not every riverine community in the Chesapeake could be helped by the dredging of ship channels. The Manokin River, an Eastern Shore tributary that flowed to the town of Princess Anne, was a barely navigable, heavily silted stream. Dredging did little to remedy its problems. Congress, however, appropriated over $30,000 to dredge a ship channel to Princess Anne six feet deep and a hundred feet wide. Dredging had its own powerful economic momentum. Corps dredgers labored on the Manokin from 1892 until 1899 with little effect. Every year the mud they had dredged slipped from its banks back into the ship channel. The corps concluded that only constant dredging would prevent the mudflats from refilling the channel, and there was not enough boat traffic on the river to warrant such an expenditure. Mud shoals also made trouble for the Engineers on the Pocomoke River along the Virginia-Maryland Eastern Shore border.

Despite these problems, river and channel dredging became an accepted fact of environmental life in the Chesapeake in the late nineteenth century. Dredging came in three periods of intense activity—1879–80, 1887–88 and 1896–97—during which time army engineers straightened rivers, dug ship channels, and eliminated numerous obstacles to navigation, from sunken ships to tree stumps. They refurbished harbors, and struggling Maryland ports like Rock Hall, Cambridge, and Salisbury received a new economic lease on life.

3. Steven G. Davison, Jay G. Merwin Jr., John Capper, Garrett Power, and Frank R. Shivers Jr., *Chesapeake Waters: Four Centuries of Controversy, Concern, and Legislation* (Centreville, Md.: Tidewater Publishers, 1997), 116.

Although the corps learned invaluable lessons while dredging the James River near Richmond, its greatest impact was on the Eastern Shore of Maryland. Dredging the waterways, writes historian Harold Kanarek, "opened new markets for Eastern Shore produce and allowed cheaper and more efficient transportation than nineteenth-century railroads could furnish." The Army Corps of Engineers, Kanearek concluded, offered the farmers of Maryland's Eastern Shore "a broadening of their commercial horizons."[4]

Making decisions about technology and environment, then and now, often involves critical tradeoffs. Sometimes the problem is a relatively simple one, like the dumping of channel dredge spoils on flourishing oyster beds. Usually, though, the problems are more complex and often require some kind of broader technological "fix." As it happened, these kinds of solutions did not become widely considered in the Chesapeake until after World War II. All too often the problems of the Chesapeake Bay in the late nineteenth and early twentieth centuries were characterized and shaped by local focus. The only agency that seemed to have even the most rudimentary regional environmental focus was the Corps of Engineers, and what the corps learned in the late nineteenth century Chesapeake it applies today. Its philosophy has inclined more toward transforming an environment for economic purposes than enhancing the health and amenities of the bay country.

## Garbage

In cities as diverse as Baltimore, Washington, and Richmond, clean water and efficient waste disposal became popular urban issues by 1880. The most popular urban technology was the capital-intensive water carriage system—the use of running water for the transportation of wastes. Given this technology, the rise in the number of water closets in Chesapeake cities and towns affected the bay's fate as most waste water found its way into streams and waterways that flowed directly into the bay. Little consideration was given to the problems effluent might create for downstream communities. How much pollution occurred in the bay toward the end of the nineteenth century is difficult to ascertain, for period records of emissions flowing into rivers and streams are nonexistent. The problem of sewage and garbage in the mid-Atlantic worsened by becoming more dispersed

4. Kanarek, *Mid-Atlantic Engineers*, 75.

after 1920, as transit lines and automobiles gave people greater access to outlying areas.

American ideas about the dangers of garbage, disease, and pollution had not crystalized by century's end. What today we regard as social and public health menaces were considered either a nuisance or a cost of everyday life that had to be tolerated. According to one concerned writer in 1893, "The average citizen, accustomed to endure nuisances as a humpback carries his deformity, saunters along sublimely indifferent to foul smells, obstructed sidewalks, etc."[5]

By the turn of the century, one-half of all Marylanders lived in Baltimore, a fact that lent some urgency to the problem of municipal waste. City wastes from Baltimore were routinely trucked out to Maryland farms and deposited on the landscape. The use of night soil was popular in Maryland agriculture, because commercial fertilizers were expensive and the region had a long history of soil erosion and depleted farms that would benefit by *any* kind of fertilizer application.[6] Garden and truck farmers in Maryland and Virginia as well as growers of orchards and vineyards were especially disposed to using urban night soil as fertilizer. Baltimore, which until 1912 lacked a comprehensive sewer system and had more than seventy thousand cesspools and privy vaults, routinely exported night soil by barge eight or ten miles down the Chesapeake Bay where it was sold to farmers who raised cabbage, spinach, and tomatoes. The practice continued well into the twentieth century despite sanitarians' protests about the possible dangers to public health from polluted streams and ground water. In Baltimore and other Chesapeake municipalities, night soil contractors constituted a powerful interest group opposed to solid waste controls. Such practices like the water carriage system and the use of nightsoil in Chesapeake agriculture did demonstrate one important point, however. Water and land, as historian Joel Tarr observed, united the city and the country, making them one when it came to the environmental health of the region.[7]

5. John S. Billings, "Municipal Sanitation: Defects in American Cities," *Forum*, 15 (May, 1893): 305.

6. Rosser H. Taylor, "The Sale and Application of Commercial Fertilizers in the South Atlantic States to 1900," *Agricultural History*, 44 (1947): 46–52.

7. For a full explication see Joel A. Tarr, "From City to Farm: Urban Wastes and the American Farmer," *Agricultural History*, 49 (1975): 598–612.

In the late nineteenth century, Baltimore was well-known for its short-comings in water management. A Baltimore County newspaper in 1877 described Lake Roland as a "receptacle of filth" from nearby slaughterhouses, and large pig pens and privies emptied enough refuse into the Gunpowder River to discolor it. This fact was especially unsettling to urban masses who drew their drinking water from the Gunpowder when it flowed into the Loch Raven reservoir. Sewer lines in outlying communities around Baltimore were often nothing more than pipes that led to nearby streams.[8]

By 1916, when statistics on garbage became available, Baltimore's population produced 37,915 tons of collected garbage. Washington, D.C., produced slightly more with 46,293 tons. In both cases, garbage mindlessly thrown into watercourses like the Potomac or Patapsco that led down to the bay was not tabulated. City or private contracting agencies collected less than 30 percent of all garbage; most was dumped on land, used as fill or buried. Few precautions were taken to insure that such practices were sanitary.[9]

Securing dump sites for urban areas became a problem as early as the 1880s. Rapidly multiplying neighborhoods and subdivisions in Washington, D.C., for example, created skyrocketing land values. This in turn made it difficult to secure new and ample dumping sites. A health officer for Washington's Office of Public Health complained: "appropriate places for (garbage) are becoming scarcer year by year. The waste that is taken from yards and dwelling places must be provided for, and that provision should not be longer delayed." Similarly, Baltimore was already hearing protests from citizens in its poorer neighborhoods over the creation of garbage dumps near them. Apparently the urban rich had their servants and elegant lifestyle, and the poor had their garbage.[10] In the 1880s the refuse problem finally came to the attention of city dwellers in the Chesapeake, and sanitarians and public health experts gave compelling health reasons for concern about it. Yet little real progress was made in bringing the garbage problem under control save extensive inquiries and collection of data by sewage experts about the sanitary needs of Baltimore and Washington.

8. See Billings, "Municipal Sanitation: Defects in American Cities," 306.

9. Martin V. Melosi, *Garbage in the Cities, Refuse, Reform, and the Environment, 1880–1980* (College Station: Texas A&M University Press, 1981), 24, 31.

10. Washington D.C., Health Department, *Report of Health Officer,* 1889, 31; Baltimore, Department of Street Cleaning, *Annual Report,* 1887, 19–20.

Treatment of the urban garbage nuisance in the Chesapeake became better organized in the early twentieth century. Sanitary engineers identified specific sewage and solid waste problems and offered bureaucratic and technical solutions. The 1893 Columbian Exposition in Chicago gave birth to a "City Beautiful Movement" that gained increasing momentum in the mid-Atlantic in the years before World War I. Since aesthetics could not prevail without sanitation, municipal leaders paid greater attention to garbage and pollution problems. In 1914, Richmond passed a rigorous ordinance to curb dumping in the James River and open disposal sites within the city limits. Those responsible for the campaign had realized that the spread of garbage was so pervasive in Richmond that strong measures were required to control it.[11] Fortunately, if that is the correct term, the problem of waste was alleviated somewhat by armies of "dump picker" immigrants who regularly scoured the dumps for paper and scrap that could be sold in Baltimore and elsewhere. Some of the Chesapeake's garbage, at least, was being recycled.

While most cities and towns in the mid-Atlantic had organized programs of street cleaning by the 1920s, garbage received little systematic attention. Contractors carried tons of Baltimore garbage bayward in scows to be dumped either in the Chesapeake or at sea. Most technological tools like the development of managed sanitary landfills seemed beyond the will of local governments, who lacked the means to finance them. After World War II the sanitary landfill would become a preferable alternative to open dumping, as it produced reclaimed land that could be converted into industrial or warehouse sites.

The development of environmentalist thought in the Chesapeake took place slowly in the last century, and early on the problem of waste and waste reduction was intertwined with issues affecting public taxation and the business community. Change came reluctantly. Only when the waste problem became critical were Chesapeake citizens willing to deal with it. After 1920 industrial and sewage waste paled as an issue beside the far more bountiful waste cast off by an age of soaring American prosperity. The throwaway consumer culture of the modern era would present the Chesapeake

---

11. For a detailed discussion of these "City Beautiful" ordinances, see Martin V. Melosi, ed., *Pollution and Reform in American Cities, 1870–1930* (Austin: University of Texas Press, 1980).

with two critical problems: a staggering amount of refuse and citizens who cared about the environment only as their own interests were affected. The defilement of the physical world of Chesapeake Bay continued unabated right though mid-century. In 1955 the *Baltimore Sun* reported that more than sixty sizeable Maryland towns on bay tributaries had either inadequate plants for sewage disposal and treatment or no facilities at all. The disgusting effluent was still spilling directly into Chesapeake waters.[12]

The Chesapeake's pesticide problem is also rooted in the nineteenth century. After the Civil War the growth of cash crop monoculture led to the clearing of forests, which in turn created a favorable insect environment by destroying insect predators. Maryland farmers soon turned to arsenical insecticides and sprayed their fruit trees to kill the pests.[13] Because the trees were sprayed while in bloom, the arsenic killed off the bees. Called Paris Green, this compound of arsenic and copper used extensively on fruit trees on Maryland's Eastern Shore soon entered the food chain and water tables. So deadly was the compound that after its introduction into the United States in 1867 scientists regularly published alarms and in the early decades of the twentieth century launched a national attack against it. The unrestrained, *ad hoc* development of arsenic-based poisons like Paris Green showed how risky undisciplined technological progress could be both to humans and the natural world. Pesticides deadly to man and insect alike were released in the Chesapeake long before DDT and other chemicals came into widespread use, and it would be a serious error to believe that the waters of the Chesapeake would have to wait for DDT and the controversy over *Silent Spring* to be troubled by pesticides.[14]

## Acid Mine Water Pollution

Mining companies, too, spilled their noxious wastes into Chesapeake tributaries. Before the Baltimore and Ohio Railroad had laid a single rail, coal companies in western Maryland were obtaining charters to exploit the

12. Edgar L. Jones, "Maryland Pollution: Raw Sewage, Industrial Waste and Acid Mine Water Poured into Chesapeake Bay and Streams," *Baltimore Sun,* March 6, 1955.

13. *American Bee Journal,* 23 (1887): 803.

14. James Wharton, *Before Silent Spring: Pesticides and Public Health in Pre-DDT America* (Princeton: Princeton University Press, 1974), 255.

landscape from the state legislature in Annapolis. After 1860 the Consolidation Coal Company swallowed up most of the coal mining operations in western Maryland, and by the 1870s the corporation, based in New York, owned about five-sixths of all the big vein coal fields in the upper Potomac Valley. What happened in the western Maryland coal fields was a reprise of what took place on a national industrial scale: corporations mushroomed into giant trusts with interlocking directorates and corporations more colossal in scope than anyone could have imagined in the pre–Civil War years. By 1927 this coal giant had metamorphosed into the Pittsburgh Consolidation Coal company with its feet firmly planted in the Potomac Valley. Consolidation routinely pumped water from hundreds of pits and mine shafts heavily tainted with sulphur and other chemicals directly into the streams of the Chesapeake watershed. By 1897 public health concerns about mine pollution of the upper Potomac watershed prompted the U.S. Department of the Interior to undertake a survey, which found large amounts of iron hydroxide pollution in George's Creek, a major Potomac tributary. Thousands of outdoor privies also flowed directly into the river, and the offal from slaughterhouses made the water a conduit of stench. Around Westernport, the study concluded, streams and the river "assume the nature of a public sewer."[15] Mining's voracious need for railroad ties and tunnel beams also led to "massive deforestation of the region."[16] Western Maryland became an industrial landscape as dangerous to Chesapeake Bay as the overflowing and primitive sewage systems of Baltimore and Washington and the Eastern Shore's arsenic-laced orchards. Pollution of the upper Potomac did not capture national press attention because it was an age of environmental exploitation. The businessman was a heroic figure in the national culture. In a more concrete display of power, the coal companies deployed legions of lobbyists in Richmond, Harrisburg, Annapolis, and Washington, who saw to it that pollution was dismissed as a trifling inconvenience. By 1915 Maryland's Allegany County was widely known for its stark and dismal mining land-

15. U.S. Senate, Department of the Interior, *Drainage Basin of the Potomac, Senate Document 90* (Washington, D.C.: U.S. Government Printing Office, 1898), 14, 27.

16. Geoffrey L. Buckley and Betsy Burstein, "When Coal Was King: The Consolidation Coal Company's Maryland Division Photographs," *Maryland Historical Magazine,* 91 (1996): 301. See also H. I. Stegmaier, David M. Dean, G. E. Kershaw, and John B. Wiseman, *Allegany County, A History* (Parsons, West Virginia: McClain Printing Company, 1976), 244.

scape, a testimony to the power of "King Coal" over the upper Potomac Valley.

Similar developments took place in the Susquehanna Valley, as coal mining became a dominant economic force there. On both the Potomac and the Susquehanna, the water glistened with a sheen of chemicals. Waves of dead fish, killed either by silt and lack of oxygen or mine acids, floated downstream all too regularly. If the Potomac became the hydraulic conduit of the western Maryland coal fields, the Susquehanna became one of the great national sewers. From 1880 onward it carried the waste of Bethlehem Steel. The west branch of the Susquehanna and the Juniata River carried refuse from tanneries and slaughterhouses. Additionally, there was the great Northern Field, a huge Pennsylvania vein containing over seven billion tons of coal that extended the length of the Wyoming Valley, some fifty-odd miles. In 1917, 156,148 miners worked in these fields, descending into the earth's bowels to blast the coal away from the rich veins and bring it to the surface. According to one recent study, it was "possible at this time to walk the twelve miles from Pittston to Nanticoke and never leave the underground maze of tunnels and shafts." Although miners' efforts were noble and at times heroic, the by-products of the mines were the devil's own brew. Iron hydroxide in mine water gives it a bright orange color, and as the pace of mining increased in the Potomac and Susquehanna Valleys, more and more of the streams took on this tell-tale hue. The chemicals raised acid levels to a point where no living thing could survive. In 1923 the Pennsylvania legislature created the Sanitary Water Board, empowering it to monitor the pollution of state waterways and to issue sewage discharge permits. Unfortunately, the board's guiding philosophy was that industrial prosperity was more important to the public's welfare than clean water. State authorities believed that nearly a third of the state's waterways were so polluted they were not worth saving. Reformers quickly found themselves hamstrung in pro-industry courts. As late as 1935 Pennsylvania law and public policy were summarized in a trial decision involving smoldering coal wastes. Judge Michael A. Musmanno wrote: "We cannot give Mediterranean skies to the plaintiff, when by doing so, we may send the workers and bread-winners of the community involved to the Black Sea of destitution."[17]

17. Stranahan, *Susquehanna, River of Dreams* (Baltimore: Johns Hopkins University Press, 1980), 165.

In 1954 the U.S. Bureau of Mines stunned the Maryland conservation and sport-fishing community with a proposal to construct a "big pipe" that would transmit mine waste from the coal fields of northeastern Pennsylvania and dump it directly in the bay. The bureau argued that the bay with its vast expanse would neutralize the acid waters. Unconvinced, Maryland doggedly fought the proposal until it died from procedural and political delay.[18]

Nature and not reformers finally controlled the environment of Pennsylvania's anthracite fields. During the winter of 1958, a flood on the Susquehanna crashed thorough a weak wall in a coal mine that had been dug too close to the river bank, and a torrent of water flooded the mine and its labyrinth of coal shafts. The flood threw more than eleven thousand miners out of work, because the owners considered pumping out the mines to be too costly. In that year mining ended along the North Branch of the Susquehanna, but mine acid continued to pollute the river. Although the Susquehanna looked clear, its water was deadly acidic. Even today abandoned-mine drainage constitutes a major source of pollution in Pennsylvania. The advent of clean water legislation in the state in the 1960s has left the Susquehanna far cleaner than it was in the Robber Baron era of coal and steel.

## Bay Conservation

From 1900 until World War II the main thrust of Chesapeake Bay conservation centered on shellfish resources in both Virginia and Maryland waters. In 1916 Annapolis created the Maryland Conservation Commission, which consolidated the older Shellfish Commission and the Oyster Police with state game wardens. The commission was unpopular with the Chesapeake business community, and in 1922 tidewater politicians reduced it to one man. Commissioner Harrison Vickers, however, was a prominent Chestertown, Maryland, businessman who could not be kept silent. In speeches and annual reports he articulated the view that conservation was not an experiment; it was a policy whose time had come.

Maryland scientists began to experiment with the extensive placement

18. "U.S. Proposes to Dump Mine Water into Bay," *Baltimore Sun,* March 1, 1954.

of oyster shell on the bay bottom to serve as cultch on depleted oyster bars. Oyster packers vigorously protested these measures, because they were doing a flourishing business in the sale of oyster shell for limestone and road paving material. The new program, they argued, was an intrusion into their property rights. Not until 1927 did Maryland enact legislation that required oyster processors to make 10 percent of their shucked shell available for planting. The law was expanded in 1947 to 20 percent and again in 1953 to 50 percent of oyster shell.[19]

One scientist has written that as early as the turn of the century "the essential core of information for enlightened management was there."[20] A satisfactory information base on shellfish resources had been obtained from the Winslow (1881, 1882, 1884) and Brooks (1905) surveys, but the public demonstrated little initiative for conservation.[21] The bay continued to exist in a laissez-faire business environment. Watermen and seafood packers were a powerful and vocal political constituency in both Maryland and Virginia and did not brook outside interference by meddlesome conservationists.

Developments in St. Mary's County revealed the problems confronting even the mildest form of conservation activity. In 1914–19, Robert Spedden and his brother J. B. Spedden, endeavored to take up twenty acres of depleted oyster grounds under provisions of the Haman Oyster Leasing Law. In the early fall of 1912 Spedden and his brother seeded the acres with 1,100 bushels of oysters. The following autumn, oystermen began to take notice of Spedden's activities and threatened to raid his "bar" to make a test case of the oyster leasing law. The Speddens had expected one or two boats to test their lease and were surprised when thirty boats from Calvert County came upon the leased ground and took up a thousand bushels of oysters. Reported Robert Spedden: "The Sheriff reached us late the next evening and by that time the oystermen had seen the state boat *Folly* and they all had scattered except for six, for whom they happened to have warrants." The

19. Victor S. Kennedy and Linda L. Breisch, *Maryland's Oysters: Research and Management* (College Park: University of Maryland Sea Grant Publication, 1980), 114–15.

20. Ibid., 121.

21. W. K. Brooks, *The Oyster: A Popular Summary of a Scientific Study* (Baltimore: Johns Hopkins University Press, 1905); F. Winslow, "Deterioration of American Oyster Beds," *Popular Science Monthly*, 20 (1881).

Oyster Police were in no hurry to go after the rest. The six whom they arrested were promptly released on $100 bail. The Spedden brothers for their efforts to conserve and develop Chesapeake resources lost a young growth of oysters on their leased bar and several thousand dollars worth of "marketable oysters."[22]

The incident demonstrates what was to be a continual theme in the story of bay conservation. Those who had the information and expertise to see what was happening to Chesapeake Bay lacked the political clout to have their ideas and strategies implemented. Meanwhile the legislature controlled bay scientists with its annual appropriation, and Annapolis was not friendly toward policies that might regulate the shellfish industry and cause economic hardship among maritime workers. Finally, after much contention, legislators reluctantly agreed to an oyster tax of two cents a bushel on oysters taken in Maryland waters to fund the work of the commission.[23]

By 1923 the Maryland Conservation Commission was self-supporting; the oyster tax made it independent of state appropriations. In his report that year, Commissioner Vickers stated that he had twenty-one game wardens and twenty deputy commanders in his Oyster Police fleet to enforce laws on the statute books dealing with the taking of ducks, fish, and oysters. Vickers specifically called attention to the need to protect the bay's oyster bars from overfishing and agitated for a tax of fifteen cents a bushel on all seed oysters taken out of the bay for planting beyond Maryland and Virginia to help pay for replenishment of the bars. Watermen, warned Vickers, could not "live for the day only and take everything from the bottom as they have done in the past."[24]

Maryland oyster law at the time reflected many of the shortcomings of Chesapeake Bay conservation. Although the state tried to conserve the oyster industry, its oyster licensing laws were limited and varied by county. In the words of one scholar, oyster conservation represented a "disjointed compilation of local laws." In its piecemeal fashion, the state presented a variety of criminal penalties that confused both the government and the watermen it

22. "Statement of Robert H. Spedden, of Sand Gates, St. Mary's County, Maryland, December 5, 1913," *Report of the Shell Fish Commissioners of Maryland, 1914–1915* (Annapolis: 1915), 40–42.

23. State of Maryland, *Maryland Manual, 1922* (Annapolis: 1922), 38.

24. Ibid., 38; *First Annual Report, Conservation Department of Maryland, 1923* (Annapolis: 1923), 23.

tried to control. These controls have had numerous side effects. "They discriminate generally in favor of Maryland residents; more particularly in favor of certain county residents," writes Maryland legal historian Garrett Power. "They interfere with the development of mutually advantageous, cooperative arrangements between Maryland and Virginia."[25] The net result in the 1920s was a kind of constitutional catharsis in oyster regulation that spilled over into other areas of Chesapeake Bay conservation.

Bay researchers in those years looked beyond the oyster problem and called attention to the fact that the "absolute necessity" of having a statewide fish law was becoming more evident each year. The state's inability to control the commercial use of fish nets by watermen was one of the most serious problems facing the Maryland Conservation Commission. Extensive netting at river mouths prevented fish from reaching their spawning grounds. The only thing the commission could do to alleviate this problem was to release millions of fish fry—shad and striped bass—into bay waters.[26] By 1930 Vickers had persuaded Pennsylvania and Virginia to participate in joint hatchery operations to restore fish to Chesapeake tributaries. Under Vickers' direction the conservation department also enforced more strictly the laws pertaining to the use of commercial purse nets in the bay and enjoined Virginia to contribute funds for the purpose of resurveying and restoring oyster bars on the Potomac River. The conservation commission enlisted Virginia's and Maryland's cooperation in banning oyster dredgers on the Potomac as an additional conservation measure.[27]

About this time a marine engineer named Swepson Earle began to make his mark in the field of Chesapeake Bay conservation. In a brief but widely read report in 1923, Earle called attention to the fact that those who believed Chesapeake Bay waters were clean and risk free did so out of misplaced faith in a myth rather than confronting reality. In frequent cruises on the bay to gather data, Earle noted how ships in increasing number were recklessly pumping their bilges into the bay and declared that "the fisheries of Chesapeake Bay will soon suffer from this pollution." Many of the bay's popular bathing beaches had become "fouled with oil and useless," and

25. Garrett Power, "More About Oysters Than You Wanted to Know," *Maryland Law Review*, 30, No. 3 (Summer 1970): 202, 204, 206, 210.

26. Ibid.

27. *Maryland Manual* (Annapolis: 1930), 54.

"patches of oil are seen floating in different localities of Maryland waters." With each passing year Earle warned, more and more oil-burning steamers entered the Chesapeake. Insofar as neither Virginia nor Maryland could constitutionally regulate this interstate commerce, Earle advocated national legislation to regulate oil-burning ships in Chesapeake waters. For Earle and others, the oil pollution of navigable waters in the Chesapeake was an early distress signal that the popular perception of the bay's health was out of step with reality.[28] The Maryland Conservation Commission agreed that oil pollution was a clear enemy of bay organisms, and Maryland in concert with other seaboard states successfully campaigned to have the federal government pass the Federal Oil Pollution Act of 1924, which prohibited ships from dumping oil in state waters. Earle succeeded Harrison Vickers as head of the Maryland Conservation Commission, where he provided continuity and vigor to the cause of Chesapeake conservation.

Although the Chesapeake Bay's embryonic scientific community was beginning to articulate problems confronting the estuary, it had until now remained relatively isolated from the general population, a state of affairs that would soon change. As is the case with so much conservation history, the beginnings of change in public perception about Chesapeake Bay would be largely the work of one man, Dr. Reginald V. Truitt. In the 1920s and 1930s no one bridged the gulf between the community of estuarine science and the tempest-tossed world of Annapolis politics better than Dr. Truitt.[29]

Born in Snow Hill, Maryland, in 1890, Reginald Truitt grew up in a wealthy family of powerful seafood packers who shipped Chincoteague oysters all over the nation during the heyday of the "oyster boom." As a child Truitt developed a love of nature and a fierce and protective devotion to the bay country in which he was rooted. Unlike his family, he was more interested in the biological end of oystering and fishing than the business

28. Swepson Earle, "The Pollution Situation in Chesapeake Bay," in Conservation Department of Maryland, *First Annual Report* (Annapolis: 1923), 31–33.

29. During his lifetime, Reginald V. Truitt was a pioneer in the field of Chesapeake Bay conservation and public policy issues affecting the bay. As a scientist, historian, and educator, Truitt served as director of the Chesapeake Bay Laboratory, director of the Maryland Department of Conservation Research and Education, and was a member of the Maryland Board of Natural Resources. In October 1982, I spent several days interviewing Dr. Truitt by phone and in person regarding his role in Chesapeake Bay affairs in the 1920s and 1930s.

part. After graduating from the University of Maryland in 1914, he taught science on Kent Island, where he became principal of Sudlersville High School. World War I interrupted his educational work; he joined the Air Corps and became a pilot in the air war of 1918.

After the war, Truitt earned a master's degree at the University of Maryland and a Ph.D from American University, then joined the faculty of sciences at the University of Maryland. In 1926 he studied for a year at the University of Berlin, Germany, where the scientific approach to politics and history had profound impact on public policy studies, an approach Truitt would bring back with him to Maryland and apply to studies on Chesapeake Bay.

Truitt first became involved in Chesapeake science as an entomologist at College Park. The title was fancy, but he was little more than an assistant scientist for programs funded by the U.S. Bureau of Fisheries and was paid only $1,500 a year. Like so many scientific organizations of the time, the Bureau of Fisheries was chronically underfunded and saw itself primarily as a research agency. It was not at all oriented toward developing a coherent fishery conservation policy. The work nevertheless gave Truitt experience working on the Albatross, a U.S. Fisheries vessel moored at Baltimore. Out on the bay Truitt learned first-hand from experience with oyster larvae that the bay was being literally worked to death. "In those days," he remembered, "there was a slack domestic market for oysters. In 1919 most of the oysters harvested were going to the canneries and thence shipped overseas" to food-starved postwar Europe. The Albatross regularly sampled the water of the Patapsco River and found it dangerously polluted.[30]

Truitt wanted to continue to take surveys of the oyster bars and asked for support from the University of Maryland, for he had "no keep and no travel money." But the university was a new institution created out of an older land grant college in 1920, and its governing authorities were reluctant to under-

30. The Albatross's notable career as a research vessel began in 1881 and ended in 1921. It was the brainchild of Spencer Fullerton Baird, the noted zoologist and Smithsonian researcher who was appointed the first U.S. Commissioner of Fish and Fisheries in 1871. He established the first marine laboratory in the United States at Woods Hole, Massachusetts, and started a fisheries program to rehabilitate the nation's fisheries resources. Truitt was the beneficiary of Baird's early efforts. See Henry Clepper, Leaders of American Conservation (Washington: Natural Resources Council of America, 1971).

take any research programs that might incite public controversy. Remembered Truitt: "The planters, politicians and watermen of Maryland thought that God would take care of the Chesapeake, and not some college man."[31]

It took Truitt several years of politics and persuasion to get a modest research budget from his school. Starting in 1924 the young scientist campaigned for the creation of a marine laboratory to study bay problems and to serve as an information clearing house for those interested in Chesapeake issues. Truitt was well-credentialed, financially independent, and from years of living on the Eastern Shore of Maryland had come to know most of the power brokers on bay matters in the legislature. Here was a different kind of scientist—one who could talk the language of politics and at the same time press for conservation of bay resources. Professor Truitt was also a snazzy dresser, a kind of Chesapeake Gatsby in a fast car who was in demand at all the Annapolis parties, in short, the kind of fellow who was as comfortable in a speakeasy as he was in a laboratory. Soon Dr. Truitt would be much in the company of Mary Harrington of Cambridge, the daughter of Emerson C. Harrington, former governor of Maryland. They married in June 1930, and their marriage gave Truitt all the access he could have wanted to the corridors of power in Maryland. Truitt never forgot that the bay was first and foremost a political problem. Only after politics, intrigue, debate, and compromise could the work of a Chesapeake scientist really bear fruit.

So Truitt discovered when he tried from 1920 to 1922 to enlist the help of watermen to improve oyster cultch by building oyster reefs from concrete crates. Although Truitt had the support of the conservation commission, watermen refused to support the program. The Lord put the oysters in the bay, they reminded him, and they were not going to spend their time and money building oyster reefs. Compounding Truitt's problem was the fact that in the 1920s the Chesapeake Bay, with the exception of Baltimore Harbor, looked good. It was hard to convince wary watermen and politicians that a bay that looked so inviting was actually in bad health and in need of rejuvenation. Additionally, oyster shell was a popular commodity with food producers. Chicken farmers used ground oyster shell for chicken grit and did not want to see oyster shell returned to the bay.

Truitt's successes were few and hard earned. Mountains of oyster shell that should have gone back into the bay to stimulate oyster production were

31. Truitt Interviews, September 23, 1982.

instead being used for chicken grit, roads, and land fill. About the only break Truitt received was when the legislature agreed to support him and stop the use of oyster shell in limestone production and as road paving material. Fortunately, though, some issues of conservation and progress converged, and Truitt was able to capitalize on them. As automobiles came into greater use in the Chesapeake Bay country, drivers began to complain that oyster shell dust stuck to their cars. It also pasted itself on shop windows and houses, giving all an ugly hue. Truitt and his allies dug back in their files for an early report on this problem, first published in 1899, and used it to good advantage to get shell returned to the bay.[32] They were also helped by a general awakening of the state to the greater need. In 1922 Maryland began to realize it had to replenish its rapidly depleting oyster bars, and in that year the Maryland Conservation Commission planted 100,000 bushels of oyster shell in the bay. The days of oyster shell roads were over.[33]

Developments far away from Chesapeake Bay also strengthened the conservation movement. In 1925 a typhoid epidemic in Chicago paralyzed the oyster industry of the Atlantic Coast and forced Maryland authorities to take a critical look at water quality in the bay. They found several areas "unsuitable for growing oysters" and invited Dr. Herman Bundesen, Chicago's health commissioner, to Maryland to monitor the investigation of bay waters. It was the first time the state had worked in cooperation with the U.S. Public Health Service to assure that oysters taken from the bay were safe. Largely through Truitt's efforts, the state discouraged packers from processing and shipping raw oysters in September, when Maryland's weather was still warm and chances of spoilage or infection high.[34]

32. William Bullock Clark, *Report on the Highways of Maryland* (Baltimore: Johns Hopkins University Press, 1899), 204, 207.

33. "Maryland Conservation Commission Report," *Maryland Manual,* 1922. By 1929 the Maryland Conservation Department, which succeeded the Maryland Conservation Commission founded in 1916, reported that "conservation is no longer an experiment." In that year the state became actively involved in eliminating purse nets from bay waters and in 1931 supported construction of the marine laboratory in Solomons. See "Report of the Conservation Department," *Maryland Manual* (Annapolis: 1929), 51–57.

34. Conservation Department of Maryland, *Third Annual Report* (Annapolis: 1925), 10. See also Conservation Department of Maryland, *Fourth Annual Report* (Annapolis: 1926), 9.

At the Chesapeake Bay Laboratory at Solomons in the 1930s, the principal mission was to study ways to rejuvenate the Chesapeake's sagging shellfish industry, which had declined 51 percent between 1910 and 1931.[35] The bottom of Chesapeake Bay was so depleted of oyster shell that in 1924 the Maryland Department of Conservation estimated that fifteen million bushels of oysters were needed to restore depleted areas. Further, the conservation department declared that "if the entire shell output of Maryland were available for planting it would require five years or more before the added increment would be felt in a large measure."[36] Using the Honga River as an experimental site, Truitt supervised the planting of 42,000 bushels of oysters over fifty-two-acres. Three years later, Truitt's research associates reported that 50,000 bushels of seed oysters had set. This strongly supported Truitt's theory of restoring the bay by rebuilding the oyster bars. The oyster is such a sophisticated animal that it filters tremendous quantities of water every day, and Truitt knew that more oysters would lead to a cleaner and clearer body of water.[37] Unfortunately, Truitt's experiment did not survive the opening of the Honga oyster bar to commercial shellfishing in 1935.[38] Throughout this period, conservation commissioner and outspoken advocate of conservation science Swepson Earle supported Truitt's work at Solomons.[39]

At the same time, A. J. Nichol, Truitt's friend and colleague at Solomons Island, published an important work on the Baltimore oyster packing industry which chronicled the oyster industry from colonial days to the boom times of the 1870s to oyster scarcity in the 1930s. Experience, Nichol wrote,

35. *Chesapeake Biological Laboratory: Its Facilities History and Program* (Solomons Island, Md.: University of Maryland, Natural Resources Institute, undated).

36. R. V. Truitt, "Conservation Through Shell Planting," in Conservation Department of Maryland, *Second Annual Report* (Annapolis: 1924), 42–43.

37. See especially R. V. Truitt, "A Policy for the Rehabilitation of the Oyster Industry in Maryland," in Maryland Conservation Commission, *Annual Report* (Annapolis: 1920).

38. B. H. Wharton, "The Maryland Oyster Industry" (Master's thesis, Rutgers State University, 1963), 1–64.

39. Romeo Mansueti, "A Brief History of the Chesapeake Biological Laboratory at Solomons Maryland," Maryland Department of Research and Education, Chesapeake Biological Laboratory, Solomons, Maryland, May 17, 1952.

demonstrated that the only solution to a depressed market was replenishing the supply. Watermen and packers of Chesapeake Bay, Nichol argued, "had to realize that their excessive independence has worked against their best interest, economically and socially, while at the same time, it has been dissipating a treasure which belongs not alone to them but to all the people of the State."[40] Although Truitt and his colleagues had demonstrated successfully how oyster grounds could be restored, the state was lukewarm in its effort to require the use of all oyster shell to rebuild the beds. As late as the 1960s, despite laws on the statute books, state resource managers were still pleading for oyster shell to be returned to the Chesapeake for oyster culch.

In 1928 Truitt seized the opportunity to publicize bay conservation when the Baltimore Chamber of Commerce, disappointed over the failure of the canned oyster industry, asked him to establish a special task force to study the problem. Overfishing and the export of seed oysters out of state had led to the collapse of Baltimore's $750,000 canning industry with the loss of two hundred jobs.[41] The chamber of commerce appointment also gave him the opportunity to meet and befriend Merle Towner, vice-president of the Western Maryland Railroad and a powerful voice in Baltimore business affairs. Towner's main interest, though, was timber conservation and not oysters. He was concerned about the depleted forests of western Maryland, generally, and specifically the decline of white oak, once the major source of railroad ties. But over the course of several dinner meetings in Baltimore, Truitt succeeded in convincing Towner of the need for a comprehensive state-wide conservation policy that would benefit both Chesapeake forests and waters. Towner was enthusiastic and secured co-operation from the chamber. Shortly thereafter, Towner and Truitt made a presentation to Governor Albert Ritchie about the need for conservation. The governor appointed a special task force, but woodlands proved to be a subject less controversial than the bay itself. In its presentation the task force urged the state to pass legislation allowing barren areas of the Chesapeake Bay bottom

40. A. J. Nichol, *The Oyster-Packing Industry of Baltimore: Its History and Current Problems,* (Solomons Island, Md.: Chesapeake Biological Laboratory Bulletin 1937), 32.

41. State Planning Commission, "Conservation Problems in Maryland," unpublished report by the Maryland Emergency Relief Administration (Annapolis: 1935), 54–64.

to be leased for oyster farming. This raised the ire of Preston Webster, a wealthy Maryland oyster dredger and political leader who did not want any change in the laissez-fare approach to oystering on the bay. Seafood interests who saw in conservation a threat to the livelihood of Chesapeake watermen, denounced Truitt, the son of an oyster packer, as a "snake in the grass." Faced with hostile watermen in the 1927–28 legislative session, Ritchie disassociated himself from the task force. "When Ritchie dropped it, the legislature dropped it," Truitt recalled. "Everybody feared the political clout of the watermen. We thought we were on the right strategy, but politics got in the way." Those were "tumultuous times" for conservation, he added.[42] Truitt learned one valuable lesson from the early fray: the need to organize civic groups outside of politics to bring about conservation.

The friendship of Merle Towner would be indispensable to Truitt and the growing idea of Chesapeake conservation. Towner gave leadership to the "conservation idea" in Maryland business circles and helped the fledgling Maryland conservation movement gain respectability among Maryland's social and economic elites. On several occasions Towner accompanied Professor Truitt to Washington to learn first-hand how natural resources could be successfully managed. At this time Truitt and Towner often joked that the Chesapeake conservation movement "had no money, no assistance and few to fight for conservation." Nevertheless, Truitt attempted to publicize any development that would help the cause, no matter how insignificant. Truitt also found himself under increased pressure from the University of Maryland, which had supported neither forestry nor bay research. Throughout the 1930s, when Maryland governors were not interested in conservation, Professor Truitt had to battle just to keep the idea of saving the bay alive.

Truitt approached the bay's problems with a broad perspective. He preached the efficacy of government studies and safeguards for the preservation of irreplaceable bay resources. Nature for Truitt was a "unity" and the problems of the Chesapeake could not be approached piecemeal. At times, Truitt was capable of surprising detachment from scientific viewpoints and could sympathize with the problems of packers and watermen as they struggled to wrest a living from the bay. Since the bay was a contest of politics and personalities, Truitt sometimes chose not to offend a present

42. Truitt Interviews, 1982.

foe who could be a future friend. Although many tidewater legislators in Maryland cared little for Truitt's views, they respected him as a fighter, a likeable fellow, and a good dinner companion.

The one break Towner and Truitt got came in 1938 when Governor Herbert O'Conor thought the conservation idea might give new vigor to his leadership of the state. To get around the packers, dredgers, and seafood interests, O'Conor proposed a new Department of Resource Management and put it to the voters of the state in a referendum in 1938. To everyone's surprise, the new department idea garnered over ten thousand votes, which scared the packers and sent their lobbyists into furious arm-pulling in Annapolis. O'Conor backed off somewhat but did succeed in using his executive power to force the legislature to create the Maryland Department of Research and Education and appointed Professor Truitt as its director. The measure passed the legislature by one vote.[43] Although the department lacked clout and legal power, it gave Truitt a public forum with the governor's support to advocate and publicize the necessity of conserving Chesapeake resources and protecting the bay for the future. What had started as an after dinner speech at the Baltimore Chamber of Commerce in 1928 had become an institutional presence. But even such a modest accomplishment had taken a decade of political opposition and gubernatorial indifference to overcome. The ten thousand voters who supported conservation and a Department of Resource Management had been much more enlightened than the state's political leadership.[44] In 1941 Maryland created a stronger administrative unit for bay conservation, the Board of Natural Resources under the leadership of Edwin Warfield, to address all of the state's natural resource problems.[45]

The first phase of Chesapeake conservation was based on wise use. Con-

43. Ibid.

44. Oyster harvests had been poor throughout the 1930s, and Governor O'Conor hoped that by placing resource conservation under a single powerful agency, he could help to rejuvenate the shellfish industry. Ten thousand voters supported the idea, but watermen in Annapolis saw the proposed agency as anathema and killed the proposal. The crony-ridden Tidewater Fisheries office continued as nothing more than a watermen's patronage machine. See Robert J. Brugger, *Maryland: A Middle Temperament, 1634–1980* (Baltimore: Johns Hopkins University Press, 1988), 561.

45. Acts of 1941, Chapter 508, Board of Natural Resources, *Maryland Manual*

servation ideas were deeply influenced by the sustained-yield theory, which rested on the assumption that the only influence on productivity was the number of breeding animals left after harvest. Chesapeake biologists were well aware of statistical research done by Danish scientist C. G. Peterson, who developed a model in 1903 that documented the perils of overfishing.[46] The theory, however, paid little attention to the nature and quality of the environment and lent itself easily to the nineteenth-century laissez-faire ideology of seafood harvesting. In fact, the most convincing argument conservationists could bring to bear for the defense of Chesapeake Bay waters was economic. The bay was just too productive to lose. For example, Maryland officials noted that it took at least four acres of pasture to support a dressed steer valued at $60. Four acres of relatively healthy Chesapeake Bay bottom could produce a harvest of oysters conservatively valued at $2,000.[47]

From World War I through the 1930s Chesapeake environmental policy was characterized by minimal protection and frequent outright abuse. It took the economic crisis of the Great Depression to force political leaders in the Chesapeake to adopt an environmental agenda that would include greater attention to equity and ethics. Small restoration projects dealing with shore erosion and replenishment of oyster beds became part of the National Recovery Administration relief effort in the state and showed how government intervention could be beneficial for the environment.[48] In Maryland forests the New Deal–funded Civilian Conservation Corps established thirteen work camps and enrolled 2,600 young men to work on projects that ranged from soil erosion to the conservation of fish and game. Many of the tidal dams and ponds that currently give such public delight have their roots in these early efforts to enhance marsh land and tidal areas. Of course, some issues divided the conservation community. One of them was the emphasis on the protection of forests at the expense of protecting the

---

(Annapolis: 1940–41), 94.

46. Larry A. Nielson, "The Evolution of Fisheries Management Philosophy," *Marine Fisheries Review,* 38 (1976): 15–23.

47. "Oyster Conditions and Future Oyster Production," Conservation Department of Maryland, *Fourth Annual Report* (Annapolis: 1926), 15.

48. For a more in-depth view, see Charles M. Kimberly, "The Depression in Maryland: The Failure of Voluntaryism," *Maryland Historical Magazine,* 70 (1975): 189–202.

waters of Chesapeake Bay. Conservation-minded citizens in the Chesapeake Bay country also had difficulty getting the attention of bureaucrats in Washington whose national policies focused almost exclusively on western land and water reclamation and the protection of Rocky Mountain forests. Dominating the conservation agenda were western political leaders like Governor George Pardee of California, Judge Ben Lindsey of Colorado, and Governor Joseph Dixon of Montana. Conservation battles in the American West did, however, produce one fruitful development: they diminished considerably the once nearly unanimous hostility of legislators against any regulation of forests and waters.[49]

There were two positive developments in this period. One was that Virginia and Maryland recognized the growing pollution problem in the Potomac River. Urged on by conservationists in Washington, the two states agreed in 1940 to a compact creating the Interstate Commission of the Potomac River Basin. The new commission could recommend standards for the cleanliness of streams but lacked legal power to punish polluters. Still, as a fact-finding and literature dissemination agency, the Potomac River Commission began to tabulate and summarize data on river conditions that future scientists and friends of the Chesapeake Bay would find useful.[50] The second development was the establishment of the Maryland Conservation Forum in 1944. Led by Edwin Warfield, Chairman of the Commission of Tidewater Fisheries, the forum moved conservation thinking in government circles beyond the economic values of Chesapeake commercial fisheries. In a keynote speech Commissioner Warfield noted that the state's failure to manage more effectively the bay's resources was "attributed to a lack of appreciation by the general public of the value of the bay to the people as a whole." If the bay was to survive as a resource area, a major public education program was necessary to show the average citizen in the region how important the bay was as a social and recreational amenity. The bay's future, said Warfield, was tied to the citizens' "wholesome diversion as well as the visitors who are attracted to its broad waters."[51] After World War

49. For an overview on the work of the American Forestry Association in the East see Samuel P. Hayes, *Conservation and the Gospel of Efficiency* (Cambridge: Harvard University Press, 1959), 179.

50. "Interstate Commission on the Potomac River Basin," *Maryland Manual, 1948–49* (Annapolis: 1949), 132–33.

II pollution control and recreation would become capstones of Maryland's Chesapeake conservation program.

## Chesapeake Forests

As the Chesapeake Bay increasingly became a question of resource management in the first half of the twentieth century, Maryland and Virginia also paid greater attention to their forest reserves. The basic question confronting politicians and businessmen was not "Are the forests worth preserving?" but rather "How should the forests be managed?" During this period, writes one forest historian, "there was a focus on planned, long-range management or some form of sustained-yield concept, which contrasted markedly with the 'grabbing and moving on' of the commercial lumbermen."[52]

Two developments occurred around the turn of the century that would have great impact on the forests of the Chesapeake watershed: the engrossment by the Baltimore and Ohio Railroad of upper Potomac basin timberlands and the migration of pulp and paper factories from Canada and the North to the Chesapeake tidewater. In 1886 John Garrett, president of the Baltimore and Ohio railroad, controlled more timberland in Maryland than any other businessman. His interests and world-view far outstripped that of his lumber-baron contemporary, John DuBois of Pennsylvania. Garrett envisioned the forests of the upper Potomac basin serving a two-fold purpose: first, as a reserve for railroad ties and wooden beams for coal mine shafts (the Baltimore and Ohio was a stockholder in Consolidation Coal) and second as a setting for mountain-top resorts in Western Maryland that would serve as a recreational outlet for the state's increasingly urbanizing population.[53] More businessman than conservationist, Garrett nonetheless knew that woodlands had esthetic value. Toward this end he constructed

51. Edwin Warfield Jr., "Conservation Problems and Progress in Chesapeake Bay," Board of Natural Resources, Maryland Conservation Forum, April 12, 1944, 61–62.

52. Michael Williams, *Americans and Their Forests, A Historical Geography* (Cambridge: Cambridge University Press, 1990), 411.

53. For an overview of John Garrett's business career and his multifaceted business dealings, see William B. Catton, "John W. Garrett of the Baltimore and Ohio: A

Deer Park Hotel in the county that bore his name and in 1886 hosted President Grover Cleveland and his new bride at the resort where guests were "strictly of the highest order" and earth, sky, and water joined "to render summer life a positive charm."[54] Thus in idyosyncratic fashion did a vision of the Swiss Alps come to the Chesapeake watershed. During Garrett's lifetime, his namesake county remained 70 percent forest and continued at that level as late as 1990. Whether by accident or design, the rape of timberlands, like those of the Susquehanna Valley, did not occur in western Maryland.

Garrett's conservation/business ethic may have protected Garrett County, but elsewhere Maryland forests continued to decline noticeably. In 1906 the Maryland legislature created a state Board of Forestry and recruited a professional forester, Fred Beasley, to address the problem. At the time of Beasley's appointment Maryland was down to about 35 percent total forest cover, which left about two million acres of woodlands. Using modern scientific management, Beasley hoped to improve forest yields.

One of the key problems was the diminished woodlands of the tidewater counties, especially on the Eastern Shore. Because much of the Eastern Shore was covered with scrub pine of no commercial value, Beasley proposed the introduction of loblolly pines, which were resistant to fire and in demand by the new and growing pulp and paper mill companies of the Virginia and Maryland tidewater.[55] Unlike deciduous trees, loblolly pines could be turned into uniform tree plantations that flourished under wise management and guaranteed corporate profits. With the advance of pulp companies like the Chesapeake Corporation and Union Camp of Franklin, Virginia, thousands of acres of tidewater land were transformed into loblolly plantations. Three areas were particularly affected: the decaying Virginia farm region of the

---

Study in Seaport and Railroad Competition, 1820–1974" (Ph.D. dissertation, Northwestern University, 1959).

54. Alison K. Hoagland, "Deer Park Hotel," *Maryland Historical Magazine*, 73 (1978): 346–347. Such ideas were not unique to Deer Park. In this same period steamboats took thousands of vacation-seeking Marylanders on excusions to Chesapeake resorts like Tolchester Beach and Betterton Beach in Kent County on the Eastern Shore. What was new was the growing acceptance of the natural world of the Chesapeake region as a recreational amenity.

55. For Besley's approach to forest management see Maryland State Board of Forestry, *Report for 1910 and 1911* (Baltimore: 1912), 5.

James-Albemarle hinterland, the Eastern Shore of Virginia, and Worcester and Somerset Counties on Maryland's Eastern Shore. By mid-century absentee pulp and paper corporations controlled almost half of the Virginia tidewater and riverine woodlands. A similar kind of pulp and paper barony prevailed in Maryland. Tidewater hinterlands in the two states soon became "plantation country beyond the imagination of the looniest champion of the antebellum Cotton Kingdom." The loblolly domain, once established, was followed by "human withdrawal or stagnation," wrote historian Jack Temple Kirby. "For where the loblollies spread in rows for miles and miles, human populations remain low, directly or indirectly, dependent upon corporate organizers and owners of the countryside."[56]

## Toward a Maryland Plan

World War II aided the work of the Chesapeake's emerging public conservation effort. With the manpower needs of the American military and manufacturing juggernaut at an all-time high, there was a corresponding decline in the number of watermen and fisherfolk harvesting Chesapeake Bay, a development that took some of the commercial pressure off the estuary.

The exception to that reduction in pressure was the menhaden fleet. Although menhaden have always been part of the bay, they did not become commercially viable as a source of fish oil until around 1910. Except for the oil, menhaden is not fit for human consumption. From 1910 until the 1960s a fleet of menhaden ships operated out of Reedville, Virginia, and took hundreds of tons of menhaden out of the bay for use as fertilizer, fish meal for livestock, and fish oil. In the 1920s millions of menhaden were taken in purse nets, and after World War II fish companies like the Baltimore-based Zapata-Haynie Corporation converted used military transports into commercial vessels capable of taking 750,000 to 2,000,000 fish. These giant factory ships employed pumps to suck the fish from the nets into refrigerated holds, and only twenty were needed to harvest the annual menhaden run. In the final boom year of 1965, factory ships harvested a record 359 million pounds of menhaden, nearly four times the amount of the first recorded menhaden harvest in 1880.[57] Thereafter the menhaden fishery declined sig-

56. Jack Temple Kirby, *Poquosin: A Study of Rural Landscape and Society* (Chapel Hill: University of North Carolina Press, 1995), 230–31.

nificantly, and six lean years doomed the industry. The Virginia Water Control Board began to monitor and discipline the fleet for dumping menhaden waste in Chesapeake waters. While menhaden is still processed for animal food at Reedville in the modern era, the day of the floating fish factories and giant schools of menhaden in Chesapeake Bay has passed away.[58] Unfortunately, the depletion of menhaden stocks has greatly reduced the food supply of other species like striped bass, perch, and bluefish.

In April 1944 Professor Truitt made a national presentation at the Maryland Conservation Forum, where he outlined the "Maryland Plan of Conservation" that had recently been approved by the General Assembly. Essentially the "Maryland Plan" sought to regulate the Chesapeake fishery through a program of controlled licensing of those who took marine life from the bay. It also sought to limit future licenses to bay watermen in order to control the amount of harvesting. As Truitt explained, "Fishermen now operating will not be put out, or have their gear reduced, but additional men will be kept from entering the already too-intensive industry."[59] Truitt insisted that what was happening to Chesapeake Bay was of national importance, for the results obtained there could be applied to the fishing banks of the Atlantic and Alaska's large fishery. While the symposium issued only a call for further study of American fisheries, it did show that Maryland was beginning to exert national leadership in matters of fishery conservation.

Prior to 1941, whenever fish became abundant or the price attractive, large numbers of Marylanders dropped their usual vocations, purchased a license for a nominal fee, and became commercial fishermen. After the fish were depleted, these fishermen returned to some other vocation. But after 1944 the state enacted a sterner law that regulated the entrance of "transitory fishermen" who formerly kept fish production at a low level. The results of the law were immediately apparent. In 1939 only 7 percent of the

57. Maryland Department of Tidewater Fisheries, "History of Bay Fishery Landings, Total Weight Landed," Annapolis, 1967.

58. John Frye, "The Menhaden Fleets of the Bay," *Baltimore Sun Magazine*, June 16, 1974.

59. *Remarks of R. V. Truitt, Director, Department of Research and Education, Symposium, Maryland Conservation Forum, April 12, 1944, Solomons Island, Md.*, Department of Research and Education, Educational Series, No. 4, June, 1944.

state's shad population reached headwaters to spawn. By 1945, 25 percent of the shad run escaped the nets and spawned successfully. The Maryland Fishery Management Law received widespread interest and was closely studied by fishery authorities in British Columbia, Canada, California, and New York.[60] From 1941 to 1947 Truitt and his staff at Solomons actively publicized their research findings documenting the precipitous decline in Chesapeake oyster production. The laboratory also became known for its statistics on crab production. From 1930 to 1940 the Maryland crab catch declined by two-thirds, from 36,938,783 pounds to 12,811,700 pounds, but the laboratory's loudest alarm in the 1940s sounded the impending collapse of the shad fishery due to over fishing.[61]

The conservation movement would later grow economically stronger and become more broad-based. It would profit from the instruction of a pioneering scientist-educator who showed how politics, scientific education, and civic awareness could be marshaled to help protect the Chesapeake Bay. Although others, like Johns Hopkins scientist W. K. Brooks, had studied the bay decades earlier, Reginald V. Truitt was the first bay scientist to approach the Chesapeake using both science and politics. As bay writer Tom Horton has noted, "with his pioneer's status came a good deal of frustration for Dr. Truitt. He was promoting notions of conservation and bay policies based on scientific understanding decades before they were embraced."[62] For example, in the 1930s Truitt and his colleagues at the Chesapeake Bay Laboratory conducted pollution related studies on the bay to gauge the impact of industrial effluent from Baltimore's steel mills on Curtis Bay just downstream from the city. In his studies, Truitt emphasized that in the future industrial waste could upset the bay's delicate biological balance.[63]

The career of Professor Truitt thus marks an important transition in bay conservation thought. With Truitt, ethics joined economics in making the

60. Board of Natural Resources, *Conservation Progress in Maryland* (Annapolis: 1951), 21.

61. Board of Natural Resources, "Conservation Progress in Maryland, 1941–1947," Bulletin 2 (Annapolis: 1951), 10–25.

62. Tom Horton, " Reginald Van Trump Truitt, His Laboratory: Chesapeake Bay," *Baltimore Sun Anniversary Issue, Our Land, Our Water,* May 17, 1987, 115.

63. Maryland Conservation Department, *Annual Report,* 1940, 59.

case to conserve the Chesapeake. The bay and its preservation mattered as an end in itself. It was more than a livelihood, more than an urban sink. Its continued maintenance and beauty was part of the American pursuit of happiness.

By the time of his retirement in 1954, Truitt had built the Chesapeake Bay Laboratory at Solomons to a staff of twelve scientists and a small campus of brick buildings with sophisticated laboratories and instrumentation. Later it would join with sister institutions of the University of Maryland at Horn Point on the Choptank River and at Frostburg State University in western Maryland to form a network for the scientific investigation of the bay country from the mountains to marsh and sea. Those who followed in Truitt's wake would have a much easier time.

Cooperation between states on economic and environmental matters is always problematic, and relations between Virginia and Maryland between 1880 and 1960 on Chesapeake Bay issues were typical. During the oyster wars of the late nineteenth century relations between the two states were so strained that they had to resort to the federal courts to settle issues affecting their sovereignty over the bay. From boundary lines to oysters, crabs, and the general regulation of boat traffic on coastal waters, each state preferred to act as if the other did not exist.

This strained state of affairs began to abate during World War II, when Virginia officials worried about diminishing crab populations and fish stocks and the general prosperity of their maritime industries. In 1941 Virginia took keen interest in how Maryland had organized its new conservation agency, the Department of Tidewater Fisheries, and a conservation policy agency, the Department of Research and Education, and sought new ways to approach its own conservation problems. In 1944 the two states agreed to meet in Washington at the behest of the U.S. Fish and Wildlife Service to study what courses of action they could take in partnership with the federal government to deal with the bay's steadily declining seafood harvests. The meeting was held in the Washington office of Secretary of the Interior Harold L. Ickes. The outcome of these deliberations was that Maryland, Virginia, and the U.S. Fish and Wildlife Service agreed to fund major research programs to explain the wild fluctuation in crab harvests, ascertain the general quality of the bay, and suggest means of maintaining satisfactory production of the Chesapeake fishery. These studies contributed to an ever-growing body of regional and national knowledge on the American shellfish industry and constituted a major data source for Chesapeake Bay policy planning after the war. Scientists and conservationists would be better able to study general trends of abundance and scarcity in complex fisheries. Prior to 1944, no one— Virginia, Maryland, or the federal government—had adequate records on commercial fish and shellfish taken from the entire estuary.[64]

Virginia's approach to bay conservation had been sluggish. It took the massive die-off of oysters in the York River in 1930 to spur Virginia's interest in regulating its waters. At that time pulp mill waste pollution was becoming a dangerous threat to Virginia's maritime communities and required remedial action. To improve the state's tidewater fisheries resources, the legislature established the Virginia Fisheries Laboratory at Yorktown to study the impact of industrial wastes on state rivers and the Chesapeake. Armed with new research data, Virginia convinced industry to make some changes in its production and control of industrial effluent, but the overall condition of the Chesapeake did not improve significantly. According to one recent bay study, "a clear opinion evolved that the situation was growing worse. Growth in population and industrial activity had simply outstripped the watchdog abilities of the two states."[65]

After World War II the Virginia Water Control Board and the Hampton Roads Sanitary District focused on pollution as the major problem affecting the Virginia Chesapeake. Massive oyster die-offs in 1949 and 1955 in the Rappahannock River prodded the state to action. Virginia watermen gathered data that showed how upstream pollution was killing their oyster beds and pressed the legislature for sterner pollution-control measures. Yet it was difficult to pinpoint legally which company was doing the polluting and whether the pollution of a specific firm had contributed to shell-fish die-offs.[66]

In the postwar period, both Virginia and Maryland suffered from problems of perception that hindered their ability to take action to protect the bay. Although each state was rapidly becoming an industrialized community with exponential metropolitan population growth, both tended to per-

64. Board of Natural Resources, *Conservation Progress in Maryland, 1941–1947*, 13–22.

65. Davison, et al., *Chesapeake Waters,* 118.

66. Ibid., 121–22.

ceive themselves as rural and small town political units rooted to an earlier and more sedate era of history. Furthermore, since resource areas tended to be defined by state lines, there was no general requirement to coordinate conservation management across the boundaries. As one ecologist has remarked, "it would be difficult to imagine a less ecologically sensitive way to operate a nature conservation program."[67] The political and economic climate of each state was so solidly pro-business that it was difficult for scientists and conservationists to persuade politicians that the bay was being irreparably harmed. Thus when major social and environmental changes came to the Chesapeake, they tended to take both Virginia and Maryland by surprise.

## Hurricanes and Chesapeake Storms

The period 1930–60 was an era of increasingly destructive hurricane activity in the Chesapeake region. Nearly sixty severe storms and hurricanes punished the Chesapeake shore. The Susquehanna River basin was notorious for its floods. From the time of the great flood of 1889, the Army Corps of Engineers had compiled data and studied the region with the idea of controlling nature with levees or embankments. Although the corps warned that the Susquehanna could be dangerous, populations in search of cheaper real-estate for housing in the Wilkes-Barre area and the Wyoming Valley spread out onto the river's flood plain. As the engineers had predicted, the concentration of population along the river ensured that flood losses would be substantial. In March 1936 the Susquehanna rose up again and caused $67 million in damages along its length. The Susquehanna prior to the flood had been relatively untouched by army engineers, because railroads to the Pennsylvania coal fields obviated the need for developing water transportation. But with flooding in this century the corps embarked on the business of transforming the Susquehanna River basin. It proposed large levees and dams on the Susquehanna, but until the flood of 1936 conservative congressmen like Senator Millard E. Tydings of Maryland were able to hold up the measures as burdening future generations with unnecessary debt.[68] The torrents of 1936 changed that kind of thinking. Flood control was an idea

67. Joseph L. Saxe, "Nature and Habitat Conservation and Protection in the United States," *Ecology Law Quarterly*, 20 (1993): 20.

whose time had truly come. In 1940 the Susquehanna flooded again, forcing thirty thousand Wyoming Valley residents to flee. These two tragedies finally spurred the federal government to undertake one of the largest flood control projects in the East. The Army Corps of Engineers built a $9 million levee system on the Wilkes-Barre and Kingston stretch of the Susquehanna designed to contain a flood crest of thirty-seven feet of water, four feet higher than the 1936 crest. But neither levees built by the army nor the pious wishes of local politicians could contain the river's fury. During Hurricane Agnes in 1972, the Susquehanna again rampaged in Pennsylvania and caused major disaster in a region that spread from Elmira, New York, to Havre de Grace, Maryland. Over and over again nature would show how mighty its presence could be and how easily it could trouble the waters of the bay country.[69]

On October 16, 1954, Hurricane Hazel struck the bay with murderous intensity after forming in the Atlantic a week earlier. Hurricane experts classified it as a Class 4 storm with an ocean storm surge of thirteen to eighteen feet and winds up to one hundred miles per hour. The hurricane claimed 295 lives and did an estimated $200 million dollars in damage from South Carolina to New York. The Delmarva Peninsula was extremely hard hit, and some Maryland tidewater counties lost extensive wetlands to the storm. Millions of gallons of fresh water roared down the Susquehanna and other Chesapeake tributaries, altering the salinity of the bay and flooding marshlands and farms as well as disrupting sewage systems. Somerset County, for example lost 25 percent of its total wetland to the storm, wetlands that were vital to the development of the Chesapeake maritime food chain. High water battered boats to pieces or carried them inland so far onto the marshes that salvage was later impossible.[70] Hazel's surge was made worse because it struck at the exact time of the highest lunar tide of the year—the full moon of October. As a result Hazel's storm tide may have been boosted several feet by the unfortunate timing of its approach. The hurricane ripped out and wrecked the shoreline like an armored division smashing through infantry. Muddy freshets from a thousand torrential streams covered the Chesapeake oyster beds with silt.

68. Kanarek, *Mid-Atlantic Engineers*, 121.

69. Stranahan, *Susquehanna, River of Dreams*, 126–29.

70. John Bozman, "Somerset Waterman Remembers Hurricane Hazel Experience," *Salisbury Times*, October 15, 1978.

The following year three more storms battered Chesapeake Bay with destructive effect. Unfortunately, efforts to stem Chesapeake shoreline erosion were feeble at best. Bay agricultural scientist John Cotton noted that there was very little scientific knowledge about the impact of soil erosion on the Chesapeake coastline and its prevention.[71] When Maryland in the 1930s had sought to develop a program of groins and jetties to protect homes and vacation cottages in Anne Arundel County, it ended up spending thirteen dollars per front foot, an excessively high cost that doomed future shoreline protection projects. Apparently the Maryland legislature preferred to let nature takes its course in refashioning the Chesapeake shore.

Hurricane Hazel became a benchmark in the lives of many in the Chesapeake tidewater as it demonstrated the destructive effect and tragic losses that the human community could suffer. Though storms of such magnitude were historically rare, hurricanes seemed all too frequent in the region after 1954 and would give impetus to a variety of public demands for flood control, shoreline erosion programs, civil defense evacuation, city planning and wetlands preservation.

In the first half of the twentieth century, Virginia and Maryland focused their evolving conservation efforts on the efficient utilization of Chesapeake Bay.[72] Though the fishery was depressed by low harvests and diminished prices, conservationists adapted their proposals with an eye to competitive markets. Fishery stocks were not managed in a rational way. As one conservation historian has noted, "In a competitive economy, no market mechanism ordinarily exists to reward individual forbearance in the use of shared resources."[73] Conservationists, therefore were only moderately successful in persuading both the voters and the legislators of states in the Chesapeake basin of the need for better management of the estuary.

Yet in the first half of this century, conservation ceased to be an experiment in the Chesapeake and became instead an acceptable way of utilizing and protecting the Chesapeake's environment and maritime resources. Both

71. Mauritz Hallgren, "Old Man Chesapeake, He Just Keeps Chomping Along," *Baltimore Sun Magazine*, September 22, 1946.

72. Theodore M. Miller, *Utilization Plan Maryland Marine Products* (Solomons Island: Maryland Department of Research and Education, May 1947), 3.

73. Arthur F. McEvoy, *The Fisherman's Problem, Ecology and Law in the California Fisheries, 1850–1980* (Cambridge: Cambridge University Press, 1986), 10.

Virginia and Maryland asserted some government responsibility in limiting the rights of private parties over natural resources and managing them for the long-term good of society. This kind of conservation was utilitarian in focus and did not calculate the costs of economic growth or the disruption of landscape and seascape by development and pollution. By the 1960s the challenges confronting the Chesapeake estuary would far outstrip any experienced by an earlier generation of bay conservationists. Defenders of the bay would have to re-think their approach to the Chesapeake and develop an understanding of the system as a whole. The Chesapeake was more than a body of water. It was a region that included people, history, politics, economics, lifestyle, and culture. Failure to recognize the Chesapeake in its entirety significantly reduced the effectiveness of both scientific and political leadership in the region as it entered its most critical period.

## CHAPTER SIX

# Is the Chesapeake Dying?

"Somewhere we should know what was Nature's way; we should know what the earth would have been had man not interfered."
— Rachel Carson

"We don't need a new sewer plant. We've already got the best in the world. The tide comes in, and the tide goes out."
— Accomack County, Va. official

## Save the Bay

In the 1960s and 1970s the Chesapeake figured significantly in the environmental affairs of the United States. Subject to more than four thousand reports, studies, and scientific investigations of subjects ranging from the fishery to water quality and urban growth, the bay became widely known as the most intensely studied estuary in the world.[1] In part, the new interest reflected changing conservation values nationally—a departure from ideas of conservation based on "efficient management" of natural resources. Scientific knowledge grew exponentially and with it the awareness that the Chesapeake's problems should be addressed not only by scientists but by social scientists, economists, historians and public policy analysts as well.[2]

Emerging, too, was a new, better-educated generation with money and interest in education, leisure travel, recreation, and environmental protection. Leisure-oriented, environmentally expressive organizations like the

---

1. See especially U.S. Army Corps of Engineers, *Chesapeake Bay Existing Conditions Report,* 7 vols. (Baltimore: 1973) and U.S. Army Corps of Engineers, *Chesapeake Bay: Future Conditions Report,* 12 vols. (Baltimore: 1977).

2. "How We Studied the Bay: Asking and Answering the Questions," *Chesapeake Bay Program Technical Studies: A Synthesis* (Washington: United States Environmental Protection Agency, 1982). David Hoffman, "The Suffering Chesapeake: It's Not Dead Yet. But the World's Most Productive Estuary Could Be Killed by Politics and Pollution," *Washington Post Magazine,* April 29, 1979, 27–37.

Sierra Club provided a focus of civic action.[3] Television highlighted bay problems and placed them in dramatic context before an increasingly discerning public. Awareness of the environment melded conveniently with ideas of personal health and the pursuit of the good life just coming into vogue. A close historical correlation exists between the rise of "health and lifestyle" books and magazines throughout the country and the movement to protect the environment. Ultimately these sentiments reflected values that would lead to greater tensions between an environmentally conscious public and those who exploited Chesapeake Bay. Environmental affairs in the 1960s reflected a new phase of consumer politics, as Americans began to equate consumption with the recreational use of natural resources. This was especially true in the Chesapeake, where boating and fishing increased in popularity.[4]

The most vigorous response to new environmental objectives came from the business community, especially from those sectors with high economic stakes in pollution control. Many businessmen looked upon environmentalists with incredulity, anger, and fright. At first the business community operated on the assumption that new environmental initiatives were only part of the short-lived excesses of 1960s college youth. Yet as time passed the give-and-take of environmental politics, notes historian Samuel Hays, "led to steady environmental gains to which industry, with varied mixtures of reluctance and acceptance, made major contributions."[5] One thing was certain. Polling agencies warned their clients that public interest in and support for protecting the environment was here to stay and should be accepted rather than resisted.

In 1968 the engineering department of the University of Maryland launched a new course of study, training the first specialists in air quality and air pollution inspection. Similarly, educators like Eugene Cronin at the Institute of Natural Resources at Solomons Island and Donald W. Pritchard

3. For more perspective on the role of leisure in the environmental movement see, Ronald G. Faich and Richard P. Gale, "The Environmental Movement: From Recreation to Politics," *Pacific Sociological Review*, 11 (July 1971): 381–93.

4. George Reiger, "The Chesapeake: A Troubled National Treasure," *Field and Stream*, 83 (February, 1979): 20.

5. Samuel P. Hays, *Beauty, Health, and Permanence, Environmental Politics in the United States, 1955–1985* (Cambridge: Cambridge University Press, 1987), 308.

at the Annapolis-based Chesapeake Bay Institute recruited and trained hundreds of scientists in researching the productivity problems of the bay. Their discipline acquired a new name—estuarine science.[6]

What did the new environmental thinking entail? For many it meant that the environment was more than a commodity resource; it was something to be experienced, savored, explored, and protected. Rachel Carson's 1955 book *The Edge of the Sea* had profoundly influenced many Americans. As a science writer capable of explaining the threat to American waters by American technological progress, Carson was without equal, but until *The Edge of the Sea* was published most Americans had very little idea of what estuaries were or of their ecological and social value. In telling prose Carson explained the critical role of wetlands "crowded with animals and plants," the beginning of the marine food chain.[7] She made an invaluable contribution to the new environmental thinking by championing unpopular causes like preserving wild seashores and protecting fish. *The Edge of the Sea* is a manifesto for the necessity of marshes and the intrinsic value of wild things. When she began her career as a science writer in the 1930s, public concern for the fate of estuaries like the Chesapeake was at low ebb. Her writing raised the public level of consciousness about the meaning of an estuarine preservation ideal. More popularizer than scientist, Carson preferred to explain the works of others to a lay audience. Yet, as Joseph Siry noted, "people listened to and read what Rachel Carson had to say and were led to defend what our ancestors had always taken for granted: the resiliency of our inland seas."[8] *The Edge of the Sea* focused on the Atlantic Coast and increased respect for nonhuman life thereby making Americans realize that they were loving their coasts and estuaries to death with metropolitan growth and pollution. In the preface Carson explained, "I have tried to interpret the shore in terms of that essential unity that binds life to the earth." Cutting to the heart of the matter, she stressed that marshes and coastal areas were

6. See Earl Arnett, "Probing the Bay's Ecology," *Maryland Magazine*, 3 (Winter, 1970): 2–5.

7. See Rachel Carson, *The Edge of the Sea* (New York: New American Library, 1955), 36–38.

8. Joseph Siry, *Marshes of the Ocean Shore* (College Station: Texas A and M Press,1984), 135. See also Donald Fleming, "The Roots of the New Conservation Movement," *Perspectives in American History*, 6 (1972): 11–14, 23–24.

valuable ecosystems worthy of survival apart from the hand of man.[9]

What Rachel Carson saw taking place everywhere around her in the United States was simple enough, the death of nature through pesticides and other toxins. In 1962 she published *Silent Spring,* documenting the degree to which the insecticide DDT (dichloro-diphenyl-trichloro-ethane) destroyed bird life in American forests, swamps, and wetlands. Heaps of dead birds in wetland areas revealed the danger of this dread poison to both man and animals. Her opening chapter, entitled "A Fable of Tomorrow," imagined in the future a terrible spring "without voices. On the mornings that had once throbbed with the dawn chorus of robins, catbirds, doves, jays, wrens and scores of other bird voices there was now no sound; only silence lay over the fields and woods and marsh. On the farms the hens brooded, but no chicks hatched. The apple trees were coming into blossom but no bees droned among the blossoms, so there was no pollination and there would be no fruit."[10] Sprays like DDT and chlordane, another chlorinated hydrocarbon, were popular farm and land management tools in the United States but so poisonous that they threatened everything living. "Can anyone believe it is possible to lay down such a barrage of poisons on the surface of the earth without making it unfit for all life? They should not be called 'insecticides' but biocides."

It was not Carson's contention that chemical insecticides never be used, but their indiscriminate use created the potential for great harm. The public, she wrote, was unaware of this danger, because scientific specialists and industry dominated discussion of pesticides, and, further, the right to make a dollar was seldom challenged. One of the most sinister features of DDT and other related chemicals was the way in which they passed from one organism to another through all the links of the food chain. Carson believed the poison could be passed on in humans from mother to offspring. Phosphorous insecticides like parathion were even more toxic. Parathion was popular with farmers and in the 1960s over seven million pounds of the chemical were applied to the fields and orchards of the United States. At the time Carson wrote *Silent Spring* the public knew little of the dangerous interactions among chemicals, which she called "elixirs of death."[11] *Silent*

---

9. Carson, *The Edge of the Sea,* viii, 11–12, 36–38.
10. Rachel Carson, *Silent Spring* (London: Hamish Hamilton, 1964), 4.

*Spring* launched a public uproar that forced the removal of many pesticides from the market. After reading her book, residents of the Chesapeake understood all too well what was happening to bird and animal life in the bay and its wetlands. For one, the bald eagle population, symbol of American greatness, had rapidly diminished. After Rachel Carson, attitudes toward Chesapeake Bay's environment would never be the same.

The new environmental thinking also offered citizens a chance for more autonomy in the face of a larger world of big government, big corporations, and a civic sphere that had lost its intimacy. Study of the Chesapeake Bay prompted complex questions about modern life. Could nature withstand the onslaught of human agency? In an imperiled environment, whose rights were paramount—man's or nature's? Could the bay coexist with modern industrial civilization? Arguments about the Chesapeake's future became increasingly impassioned and convoluted.[12]

By 1960 a growing number of ecologists interpreted nature in terms of ecosystems. Using terminology developed by Howard and Eugene Odum at the University of Georgia, scientists began to shift ecological metaphor, terming nature a machine susceptible to manipulation and "ecological engineering." A system as small as a pond or as large as the Chesapeake could be managed to ensure optimum efficiency and well-being. Eugene Odum's research on coastal salt marshes showed the value of regarding wetlands as ecosystems.[13] The Odum brothers and others called upon scientists to redefine their roles in terms of environmental affairs. One role was to anticipate emerging environmental problems rather than studying just those currently at hand. The other was to become involved in the political process.

11. Ibid., 11, 19, 27.

12. See especially Walter A Rosenbaum, *The Politics of Environmental Concern* (New York: Praeger Publishers, 1973), 1–27; Hazel Erskine, "The Polls, Pollution and Its Cost," *Public Opinion Quarterly,* (1972): 120–35; Harold Sprout, "The Environmental Crisis in the Context of American Politics," in Leslie L. Roos, Jr., *The Politics of Ecosuicide* (New York: Holt Rinehart, and Winston, 1971), 35–49; Arvin W. Murch, "The Public Concern for Environmental Pollution," *Public Opinion Quarterly* (1972): 94, 106.

13. Eugene P. Odum, "The Role of Tidal Marshes in Estuarine Production," *Conservationist* (June–July): 1961, 12–35. "The New Ecology," *Bioscience,* 16 (1964): 14–16. See also Howard Odum, *Environment, Power and Society* (New York: Wiley-Interscience, 1971).

The latter many Chesapeake scientists were loathe to embrace, because it placed them squarely in the middle of political firefights with grant-making agencies in state governments. But if individuals and communities were going to shoulder increased responsibility to find solutions to the problems of the bay caused by anthropogenic stresses, then scientists had to lead and support them.[14]

Environmental action grew by fits and starts after 1960. It often pursued conflicting agendas and suffered from weak leadership and funding. Yet in the 1960s and 1970s the words "ecology," "environment," and "pollution" became buzzwords that energized public opinion to "Save the Bay!" On Earth Day, April 22, 1970, the modern environmental movement leapt onto the national stage and demanded attention. More than twenty million people participated in Earth Day events, listening to speeches, holding seminars, and taking small but practical steps to clean up the environment. Infused by the spirit of Earth Day, many young environmental reformers converged on Richmond and Annapolis to demand a cleanup of Chesapeake Bay. In Washington D.C., a quarter of a million people voiced their support for decisive action in protecting the environment. To accommodate a flood of orders for information on conservation, the Sierra Club published more than four hundred thousand copies of its handbook, *Ecotactics*.[15] Behind Earth Day was the stark realization that American shorelines included fifteen of the twenty largest standard metropolitan statistical areas of the country. The seashore was a magnet for people who demanded service, accommodation—and ecological integrity of the coasts.[16]

The Chesapeake, like Earth Day celebrations, has always played well as melodrama. Its four-century public history has seen plenty of heroes and villains and has been riddled with a fair share of bullets and blood. Out of the contention arising in this recent period would come one key question: What balance should be struck between nature and the political economy of the region? Events were to prove that achieving balance and saving Chesapeake Bay would be no easy task.

14. Stephen Bocking, "Visions of Nature and Society: A History of the Ecosystem Concept," *Alternatives,* 20 (July–August, 1994): 12–15.

15. Christopher Manes, *Green Rage: Radical Environmentalism and the Unmaking of Civilization* (Boston: Little Brown and Company, 1990), 45–46.

16. Philip Nobile and John Deedy, eds. *The Complete Ecology Fact Book* (Garden City, New York: Doubleday, 1972), 22, 30, 41.

Melodramatic as they sometimes were, those who sought to save the bay raised important questions about environmental safety, the limits to growth, and corporate greed. A number of factors helped to bring about a politically and socially vigorous response to industrial pollution. As early as 1948 the Federal Water Pollution Control Act sought to regulate municipal sewage treatment facilities and called attention to the problem of industrial discharges in American waters. In 1948 smoke control laws for the steel industry and others in Pittsburgh demonstrated that people were willing to pay higher prices for environmental quality. In 1970 the U.S. Congress created the Environmental Protection Agency to enforce the statutes of the National Environmental Policy Act for a better environment. In terms of the Chesapeake, the EPA was charged to protect the bay against pesticide poisoning, safeguard coastal lands, and establish maximum standards for the emission of pollutants into the air and water.[17]

Chesapeake rivers became noticeable environmental sores widely covered by the press. Wastewater discharge and urban runoff, combined with heavy loads of lead, copper, and mercury around Hampton Roads made the Elizabeth one of the most highly polluted rivers in the Chesapeake watershed. Oil and chemical storage tanks along its banks routinely leaked their toxic contents into the river by the thousands of gallons. Generations of dredging to enhance navigation had deposited most of the "spoil" directly into the bay. In 1957 the Army Corps of Engineers estimated that since 1900 it had deposited as much as 40 million cubic yards of dredge spoil on the bottom.[18] The Elizabeth, a sluggish tidal river with poor flushing characteristics, suffered decades of misuse, which correlated strongly with fish with lesions, cataracts, and fin rot. Yet because of political confusion and business opposition in Richmond, little was done. As late as 1983 the Environmental Protection Agency still considered the Elizabeth a "toxic hot spot."[19] While the Hampton Roads business community liked to call the Elizabeth a "working river," sportsmen and conservationists voiced

17. See U.S. Government Reports, *Environmental Quality – 1979* (Washington, D.C.: U.S. Environmental Protection Agency, 1979); Joel Tarr, *The Search for the Ultimate Sink: Urban Air, Land and Water Pollution in Historical Perspective* (Akron, Ohio: University of Akron Press, 1996), 7–35.

18. Hoffman. "Who's Killing the Chesapeake Bay?" 33.

19. "The Elizabeth and the Chesapeake Bay," River Fact Sheet, Chesapeake Regional Information Service, Alliance for the Chesapeake Bay, Inc., August 9, 1994.

growing anger. The Elizabeth's headwaters were fed by the Great Dismal Swamp, and sportsmen feared that tidal surges and expanded industrial development would move toxic water up into unpolluted marshes and creeks.

Similarly, the Patapsco, a Maryland tidal waterway, showed signs of serious stress by the 1950s. To maintain Baltimore's viability as a port, the Patapsco was routinely dredged each year to protect the ship channel and the spoil dumped behind an extensive dike located at the mouth of the river. Years of industrial and shipping activity had left accumulations of toxic compounds on the river bottom. The problem was not new—factories like Allied Signal had long discharged chemical waste into the river. One report concluded that "Even back in 1910, Baltimoreans christened their harbor 'Hellbroth' in honor of the foul odor wafting from the water." Over time little changed on the noxious waterway, and the river was greatly feared by locals as a cause of typhoid, hepatitis, polio, and cholera. Concerns about the river's health grew even worse in the 1960s, as the Patapsco appeared to approach "the abyss of ecological disaster."[20] The Potomac was equally disgusting. President Lyndon Johnson highlighted its pollution problems in 1964, but a decade later federal officials were still warning citizens not to swim, bathe, or fish in its waters. The public came to view polluted waterways as a problem with dramatic local ramifications.[21]

Civic leaders and conservationists sensed that the Chesapeake was changing radically, because its tributaries carried nutrients and toxic chemicals, a condition for which Maryland, Virginia, and Pennsylvania had yet to develop viable alternatives. Scientists in the Environmental Protection Agency nevertheless were unwilling to conclude that the bay was dying. "We contend," said Tom DeMoss, deputy director of the agency's Chesapeake Bay Program, "that it's changing. It's up to the public to decide if it's for better or worse." Whether it was dying or evolving, the Chesapeake was certainly showing signs of stress, and responses took place on a variety of bureau-

20. "The Patapsco River and the Chesapeake Bay," River Fact Sheet, Chesapeake Bay Regional Information Service, Alliance for the Chesapeake Bay, Inc., August 1994.

21. See Alliance for the Chesapeake Bay, *Chesapeake Citizen Reports*, 1973–89. A good example of citizen monitoring of local waterways can be found in *Chesapeake Citizen Report*, November–December 1990, 6–7.

cratic and organizational levels. The problems were not essentially new, but their size and complexity now began to capture public attention as journalists increasingly reported them in the local and national press. Perception of the bay's ills took place on a personal level as well. Fishing guides and owners of duck and goose blinds saw their businesses diminish with dwindling numbers of fish and wildfowl. Recreational anglers bemoaned the loss of perch and rockfish, and beaches increasingly became unsafe from sewage contamination and the scum of algae blooms.[22]

## Bureaucrats, Polluters and Scientists

In response to the growing environmental awareness in America generally and the Chesapeake specifically, federal agencies carved threatened regions like the bay into administrative fiefdoms. State governments, in turn, developed their own regulatory bureaucracies in order to receive the tax revenue largesse that would come with federally sponsored conservation programs. The Army Corps of Engineers, long familiar with bay problems, led the way. Soon followed the Environmental Protection Agency, the Coast Guard, the National Oceanic and Atmospheric Administration, the Nuclear Regulatory Commission, and a host of state and interstate agencies, all designed to save the bay with new regulations, task force studies, compacts, commissions, and education campaigns. An inquiring reporter in the late 1970s who sought to understand the crusade to save Chesapeake Bay had to understand the working of twenty federal and six interstate agencies, twenty-eight academic institutions, a plethora of state agencies, and some 260 public interest environmental groups. James B. Coulter, head of Maryland's Department of Natural Resources and a respected civil servant, referred to bay management politics as "anarchy in its classic sense." Said Maryland Senator Charles McC. Mathias, "the Chesapeake is like a circus without a ringmaster."[23]

In 1972 the federal government passed the Clean Water Act, giving state

22. "Chesapeake Bay Altering Greatly," *Salisbury Daily Times,* August 7, 1982; Jay Taft, "Nutrient Processes in Chesapeake Bay," in *Chesapeake Bay Program Technical Studies,* 45–103.

23. David Hoffman, "Who's Killing the Chesapeake Bay," *Washington Post Magazine,* April 29, 1979.

officials in the Chesapeake region an important tool with which to enforce the law, a system of permits limiting the amount of pollutants that individual dischargers could dump into any body of water.[24] Specifically, the mission of the Clean Water Act was to "restore and maintain the chemical, physical, and biological integrity of the nation's waters." Virtually every city in the United States was required to build and operate a wastewater treatment plant with the Environmental Protection Agency providing most of the funding and technical assistance.[25] The law, however, was honored more in the breach than in the promise, as companies routinely violated their permits. A *Washington Post* study of two years of environmental records in 1986 revealed that all 124 companies with permits to discharge industrial waste in Maryland and Virginia sewage systems had exceeded the legal levels of discharge in one or more pollutants. Maryland and Virginia authorities rarely punished violators with heavy fines; those fines levied were often far less than the law allowed. Illustrating the enormity of the situation was the fact that each year industries and sewage plants in Maryland and Virginia discharged nearly four trillion gallons of wastewater into the bay, or about one-fifth of the total amount of water in the bay at any given time. Worse, environmental authorities routinely ignored illegal discharges. Such developments contradicted the rosy optimism of activists who believed that the bay could be rescued from its death throes.[26]

Although many industries in the watershed spent millions of dollars getting rid of pollutants in their waste water discharges, they also developed their own economic calculus of costs. Industries factored the costs of pollution controls against the fines and possible jail terms provided in the Clean

24. For analysis of the strengths and limitations of the Clean Water Act as a national strategy to reduce water pollution under the authority of the EPA, see Michael T. Olexa, "Agricultural Chemicals and Water Pollution: The Clean Water Act," Fact Sheet–FRE-77, Florida Co-Operative Extension Service, November 1991. The law specifically exempted farmers from its provisions with telling consequences for Chesapeake Bay.

25. National Resources Defense Council, "History of the Clean Water Act," Washington, D.C., October, 1999.

26. Victoria Churchill, "The Poisoning of Chesapeake Bay," *Washington Post*, June 1, 1986; James Smullen, Jay L. Taft, and Joseph Macknis, ""Nutrient and Sediment Loads to the Tidal Chesapeake System," in *Chesapeake Bay Program Technical Studies*, 158.

Water Act. Often it was easier for an industry to pay a fine than to purchase expensive pollution control equipment.

The Clean Water Act also spewed forth a flood of paperwork in the form of sewage permits and industrial records. File boxes of these records became so abundant at Baltimore's Department of Health and Mental Hygiene that workers piled them up as room dividers, separating those who wrote the permits from those who enforced them. Similar cascades of paper flowed out of state offices 145 miles away in Richmond. Originally intended to make it easier for state officials to monitor pollution, this paperwork swamped the offices and often made it difficult for officials to raise their heads and have a clear perspective of what was actually happening to the region.

Many industries simply circumvented the Clean Water Act by routinely sending their industrial waste to municipal sewage plants that lacked the equipment to remove toxic chemicals from the water. At a time when the permit system was geared toward conventional pollutants, unconventional pollutants like carcinogens and heavy metals found their way into local sewage treatment plants. Each year during the 1970s Bethlehem Steel at Baltimore dumped over a thousand tons of cyanide, toxic metals, and ammonia into the bay. Said James Thornton, an attorney for the National Resources Defense Council and a critic of the permit system: "It's an incredible national scandal . . . and nobody knows about it." At this point, reported the Environmental Protection Agency, one thing was certain. By 1980 the Chesapeake Bay floor was "a major sink for metals and organic compounds." What no one knew was how to determine "the relative capacity of different parts of the bay to assimilate toxicants." Scientists at Gloucester Point, Virginia, noted that the impact of toxicants on Chesapeake biota was exceedingly complex.[27] What was the overall impact on the ecosystem of a steady rain of contaminants? Scientists were not certain. Some areas like the Elizabeth and Anacostia Rivers were obvious toxic hot spots because of high chemical contaminant loads. Here the evidence was clear. But in other cases, contaminants flowed from non-point sources that were difficult to monitor or control. There was, however, "significant evidence" to indicate that

27. "Bethlehem Discharges Often Exceed Permit," *Washington Post,* June 1, 1986; *Chesapeake Bay Program Technical Studies,* 347, 350; M. A. Bender, E. A. Shearis, L. Murray, and R. J. Huggett, "Ecological Effects of Experimental Oil Spills in Eastern Coastal Plain Estuaries," *Environment International,* 3 (1980): 121–33.

contaminants had the potential to enter the food chain that thrives on riverbeds and the bay's bottom.[28]

The federal government's National Estuary Study of 1970 outlined the dilemma scientists and the public faced in estuarine protection, restoration, and development. Saving the Chesapeake would be of little avail if polluted river waters destroyed the biological integrity of marshes, mudflats, and coastal lands. Unless public responsibility for estuarine resource use was broadly distributed, and conservation laws were widely rather than narrowly interpreted, the Chesapeake system would continue to poison itself.[29]

One of the ironies of the Save the Bay campaign was that potentially helpful legislation was rendered ineffective by the permit-enforcement process. Between July 1985 and February 1986, for example, Maryland levied only fifty-five fines against industrial polluters. In the same period Virginia obtained but three consent orders to force polluters to adopt a cleanup schedule. Out of much legislation and optimism came few results.

Bureaucrats in state regulatory agencies actually developed a working familiarity with industrial polluters and their lawyers. With limited budgets and an awareness of how lobbyists for businessmen could hamper the effectiveness of a conservation agency, state officials pursued a go-slow policy, bringing only the most egregious polluters to justice. Despite the region's growing environmental awareness, politicians were reluctant to take the bay's problems seriously because to do so would mean unpopular legislation and a major commitment of money at a time when fiscal austerity was in vogue. Conservation bureaucrats got the politicians' message. Even a devoted civil servant like James B. Coulter, who was appointed secretary of the Maryland Department of Natural Resources in 1972, knew his limits.

The main problem with the Save the Bay effort was that it required a significant commitment of time on the part of individuals to learn the details and problems of the Chesapeake. The bay was such a large and complex ecosystem that not even environmental professionals, much less the

28. Jack Greer, "Spotlight on Research, The Trouble with Toxics in the Bay," *Marine Notes,* 14 (November–December, 1996).

29. U.S. Senate, *The National Estuarine Pollution Study,* Report of the Secretary of the Interior, Senate Document 91-58, 91st Congress, 2nd Session, March 25, 1970, 144–45, Appendix C, 9–11.

average voting public, understood all of what was wrong. For education to be effective, all parties had to be educated, a highly unlikely circumstance. Government regulation of the environment faced a different kind of pitfall. There, to be effective, government had to monitor the region constantly and enforce laws against environmental violators, an expensive proposition and one that raised into high relief questions about personal and property rights and the limits of freedom. Said Professor Richard Collins, Professor of Urban Planning at the University of Richmond: "We are faced with a problem of growth that has no technological solution."[30] It also raised the question as to whether governments had sufficient financial and legal resources to pursue their interests against those of large, well-financed groups in the private sector. Where money was involved, as in the case of hazardous waste management and toxic pollution, litigation stalled environmental controls and passed on the problem to future generations. In many cases scientists and bay managers neither knew nor could demonstrate the economic value to society of resources like rivers and wetlands, nor could they compute the social benefits of rescued marshlands and clean water.

That is not to say that enthusiasm for bureaucratic empire-building was lacking. After 1970 bureaucracies, research centers, and public interest groups with a responsibility or commitment to Chesapeake Bay sprang up like mushrooms after a summer rain. The Environmental Protection Agency launched a $27 million study of the bay's problems, and the Army Corps of Engineers spent over $10 million to construct a hydraulic model of the bay at Kent Island, Maryland, to research water flow. Some, like the Maryland Department of Natural Resources, performed important functions as vehicles of environmental education. Others like the Alliance for Chesapeake Bay grew into powerful lobbying and public interest groups. Often it was individuals from these organizations who highlighted important issues and galvanized public opinion.

Perhaps the most important individual was Dr. Eugene Cronin of the Chesapeake Bay Laboratory at Solomons Island. A rarity among scientists, Cronin wrote in clear, understandable prose for a lay audience. In 1967 his article, "The Condition of Chesapeake Bay," published by the National

---

30. Richard Collins, cited in William Hingst, "Bay Must Overcome Personal, Corporate Greed," *Cambridge Banner*, January 18, 1979.

Audubon Society, became a clarion call to address the bay because it was "still a magnificent, beautiful, and highly productive estuary." In twenty-six years as a researcher at Solomons, Cronin had seen a steady decline in the bay's health in areas of heavy use. For Cronin, the specter of things to come could be seen at Baltimore Harbor and Hampton Roads, both of which showed the effects of chemical pollution. "Almost nothing is known of the input of biocides from agricultural, metropolitan and domestic sources," he warned. Repeatedly, Cronin stressed the dangers of thermal pollution from power companies, a position that brought him into conflict with state officials and legislators who had a more benign view of the uses of nuclear energy in the Chesapeake. Cronin also wrote of increased nutrient loads entering the bay from sewage plants, and the dangers rapid population increases posed to the ecosystem. Patterns of bay use were changing in revolutionary ways. Until the 1960s the bay had been a commodity resource from which fish, clams, crabs, and oysters had been extracted. Now, Cronin observed, the bay was increasingly devoted to recreational use. "Boating, swimming, water-skiing, beaching, fishing, and hunting are all increasing rapidly, but reliable data are scarce," he said.

Viewed more than two decades later, "The Condition of the Chesapeake Bay" still remains a powerful analysis of the many changes that were and are coming to the estuary. In a quiet moment Cronin wondered if in the future Chesapeake waters would become nothing more than "waste lagoons."[31] Somehow despite his fears he remained optimistic that the scientific community, the general public, and politicians could recognize the fundamental unity of Chesapeake Bay and work to protect it.

Perhaps the most radical scientific proposal to save the bay in the 1970s came from Jerry R. Schubel, an estuarine oceanographer at the Johns Hopkins University. The task, said Schubel, was to save the bay from pollution and helter-skelter use while it was still in fairly decent condition. He emphasized a program he called "Bay zoning," which would be flexible and take into account that natural uses of the bay change with the seasons. Schubel argued, for example, that spawning grounds for fish should be undisturbed in spring but could be opened for fishing and recreational uses

---

31. Eugene Cronin, "The Condition of the Chesapeake Bay," *Transactions of the Thirty-Second North American Wildlife and Natural Resources Conference, March 13, 14, 15, 1976* (Washington, D.C.: Wildlife Management Institute, 1968), 139–50.

in summer. Other areas, such as deep channel lanes for ocean-going vessels, would be permanently zoned for that purpose. Other zones could be set aside for industrial uses. "Man zones his terrestrial environments into residential and industrial areas and sets aside areas for parks and forests. He does not make it official policy to spread his garbage and trash uniformly over the landscape." That, Schubel worried, was precisely what was happening to Chesapeake Bay. Zoning would bring limits to development, and "some people would have to suffer for the overall good, just as in land zoning."[32] This idea became part of environmentalists' discussion on the bay's future and raised questions about whether the democratic ethos of American political economy was compatible with rescuing the bay from destruction. Land developers were certainly quick to criticize Schubel and other "elitists" who suggested controls on business enterprise. Despite the wealth of evidence to support their cause, few scientists openly spoke out for saving the bay. Fewer still entered the political fray.[33]

Cronin, Schubel, and their scientific allies were not without supporters in the private sector. In 1967 a small group of environmentally concerned citizens founded the Chesapeake Bay Foundation with a single mission—to save the bay. The CBF, as it came to be known, had connections with wealthy businessmen, many of whom had recreation homes on or near the water. Lawyers and teachers donated their time, and the organization demonstrated considerable acumen in dramatizing the plight of an ecosystem that extended over a watershed of sixty-four thousand square miles. The Chesapeake Bay Foundation believed that a vast amount of habitat could be saved. The bay was nothing more than a "microcosm of the planet," and if it failed, the Earth itself might fail as well. Though many CBF members demonstrated country club manners, they could lobby and crusade like

32. Hal Willard, "Chesapeake Bay Zoning Plan Urged," *Washington Post*, December 31, 1972.

33. These scientists spoke out, often with risk to their professional careers: Eugene Cronin, Jerry Schubel, William Hargis, Joseph Mihursky, Robert Costanza, Clem Counts, and William Goldsborough. Hargis battled well and eloquently on behalf of the bay and angered corporate leaders and politicians in Virginia. His career as head of the Virginia Institute of Marine Science ended in forced retirement following the Kepone controversy and his acquittal in court of trumped up charges of misuse of state property. Cronin had to fight his own colleagues, who wanted him to lower his voice on the Calvert Cliffs nuclear power issue.

experienced politicians from Baltimore's wards. The CBF established head-quarters in Annapolis, Harrisburg, Richmond, and Norfolk and became a major conservation force of eighty thousand members nationwide with a staff of 120 and hundreds of local volunteers.

Responding to pressure from environmentalist groups, Governor Harry Hughes abandoned the earlier approach to the Chesapeake as something only to be dredged for ship commerce. At the 1983 Governor's Conference on the Chesapeake Bay, Hughes surprised many in the legislature by championing the bay and pioneering new legal territory. In 1983 the Hughes administration won passage for nearly every piece of a "Save the Bay" package that included hundreds of millions of dollars to be spent over the following decade. Since that time, noted Tom Horton, "Maryland's actions on the bay, accompanied on a lesser scale by Pennsylvania and Virginia, have . . . become nationally and internationally recognized models of environmental restoration." In 1984 Maryland spent $70 million on Chesapeake cleanup operations, while Virginia spent $6 million and Pennsylvania $2 million. Partnership on the bay transcended money. The most important aspect of the Governors Conference was that now three states were willing to work in concert as never before to restore the estuary. They created the Chesapeake Bay Commission with offices in Annapolis, Richmond, and Harrisburg.[34] The future would determine whether dollars and good will were sufficient for the task.

## From Thermal Pollution to Three Mile Island

The call to protect the bay and its huge drainage area prompted a tidal wave of questions. How much would the cleanup cost? Who would pay for it? And would citizens be willing to forego preferred lifestyles if it meant keeping the estuary healthy? Of all the denizens of the Chesapeake watershed, the most complex and nettlesome was man himself. During the decades after 1960, population exploded in the Chesapeake country, bringing the tremendous pressure of people seeking the good life to Maryland and Virginia shores and waterways. Among the first organizations to feel the effect were utility companies. In their quest to develop increased and inexpensive electrical capac-

34. Tom Horton, "Our Land, Our Water," *Baltimore Sun Magazine*, May 17, 1987, 121. Davison, et. al., *Chesapeake Waters*, 198–200.

ity, the power companies inadvertently entered the Chesapeake melodrama as one of its principal villains.

Perhaps the single most important issue forcing Marylanders to take stock of the condition of their bay was the construction of a controversial nuclear power plant at Calvert Cliffs by the Baltimore Gas and Electric Company. When plans were announced in 1966, a public outcry, sparked in large measure by faculty members at the Johns Hopkins University Medical School, grew up around the unknown menaces of radiation and thermal pollution. As controversy mounted, state regulatory agencies were strangely quiet. According to a recent environmental study, "When the Atomic Energy Commission refused to file an environmental impact statement dealing with the proposed Calvert Cliffs Nuclear Plant, no government agencies, despite their responsibility for protecting the public, opposed the position of the utility and the Atomic Energy Commission."[35] A citizens group, the Calvert Cliffs Coordinating Committee, had to sue the Atomic Energy Commission in court to get the agency to observe due process and file an environmental impact statement. Court orders, appeals, hearings, and reports mushroomed over Calvert Cliffs like an environmental thunderhead menacing the bay's future. Would Chesapeake fish become irradiated and inedible? Would atomic waste seep into the bay? Would a power plant discharging millions of gallons of hot water into the bay upset the ecological balance? In the end it became a contest of raw power and economic might. Electric utility lobbyists overwhelmed the legislature with arguments that assured nuclear safety, an increased tax base, and a better employment picture for economically distressed Calvert County. Baltimore Gas and Electric got its plant, a two-unit, $398 million facility that allowed the company to double its output of electricity in 1974. To show its commitment as a good citizen, the power company helped to build the Calvert Marine Museum to chronicle the history and lore of the bay.

Conservationists did win some battles during the controversy. Construction of the facility on the cliffs was delayed two years to give archaeologists time to explore the fossil-rich landscape that dated from the Miocene Age. A power line scheduled to run through a section of Anne Arundel County was diverted. Thermal pollution, however, was increasing rapidly in the mid-

35. John H. Cumberland, "Public Choice and the Improvement of Policy Instruments for Environmental Management," *Ecological Economics,* 2 (1990): 160.

Atlantic, warned Eugene Cronin. In the future, new generating stations around Baltimore would use about a million gallons of bay water a minute for condenser cooling, and that water, with a rise of ten to twelve degrees Fahrenheit, he said, would go straight back into the Chesapeake. Power companies, he insisted, had to be held accountable through strict controls. For once the Maryland legislature agreed with Cronin and his fellow scientists and passed a tough law that limited the company to thermal discharge only ten degrees hotter than bay water and never to exceed ninety degrees Fahrenheit. Militant conservationists, though, wondered why, if the plant was such a benign institution, so many alert sirens sat on poles that stretched in a network from Calvert Cliffs to Maryland's Dorchester County and the Eastern Shore?

The company currently operates from a comfortable economic position, despite its initial large capital costs. The alternative, say economists like Lewis Parl, vice-president of National Economic Research Associates, is to rely on coal power for electricity generation with all of its attendant pollution.[36] The nightmare of the future, however, is how to package and dispose of the plant's highly toxic wastes. Calvert Cliffs reflected a confusion of moral constraints for the safety of the bay and its inhabitants with the obligation to meet exponential demands for more electricity. The power plant debate also raised the issue of what obligation we currently have to future generations who will live in the bay country. For radical groups, Calvert Cliffs was nothing more than "a crime against the future."[37]

One thing was certain, claimed Dr. William Hargis, Director of the Virginia Institute for Marine Sciences at Gloucester Point. Neither the utilities nor the politicians had given serious attention to the "certain level of degradation that is inherent in population growth and industrial development. People have a great deal more faith that science and technology will bail us out of our problems than is warranted. We must understand that only a certain amount of human activity can be tolerated before conditions change in such a way that degradation can result."[38] A lot of factors, Hargis argued, had to be taken into account when thinking about the bay. Practically no

36. Julian McCaull, "The Cost of Nuclear Power," *Environment,* 18 (1976): 11.

37. R.and V. Routley, "Nuclear Energy and Obligations to the Future," *Inquiry,* 21 (1980): 165.

38. "Chesapeake Bay Fights for Its Life," *Business Week,* March 7, 1970, 44.

scientist or citizen was ready to accept the prospect of an atomic meltdown polluting the Chesapeake water supply, but precisely this specter came to haunt the bay during the Three Mile Island crisis.

On March 28, 1979, a near disaster of a nuclear meltdown occurred at the Three Mile Island Nuclear Station Unit 2, owned by the General Public Utilities Corporation of Pennsylvania. During a five-day period the unit had a serious malfunction that if unchecked could have led to the nuclear contamination of the Susquehanna River environment. Fortunately enough water flowed into the core to keep the reactor cool during the malfunction. Had the cooling system shut down, engineers would have had no choice but to pump water from the reactor outside the containment building, thereby creating a massive radiation leak.

What would have been the consequences had a nuclear meltdown at Three Mile Island occurred? Although there would have been no explosion, a lethal cloud of radioactive gases would have blown across the countryside endangering the lives of more than six hundred thousand people living within twenty-one miles of the reactor. "Molten fuel embedded in the ground under the plant could leach large quantities of radioactive contaminants into the groundwater and neighboring bodies of water for decades," concludes a recent Three Mile Island study by nuclear policy expert Daniel F. Ford.[39] Could any greater disaster befall the Chesapeake than having the Susquehanna, the principal source of the bay's fresh water, become a radioactive conduit? In addition to the near meltdown at Three Mile Island, grave deficiencies were reported in the operation of the Peach Bottom Plant near Philadelphia and the Calvert Cliffs plant. Both received fines for multiple safety violations, and the problem of nuclear power came under serious discussion in the national media.[40] Calvert Cliffs and Three Mile Island helped to refocus public attention on the environmental consequences of economic activity. Said Robert Costanza, an ecologist at the University of Maryland's Chesapeake Biological Laboratory, "A resource [like the Chesapeake] can be driven to extinction before the market even realizes it was there." The question to ask, added Costanza and others, was whether technology was developing rapidly enough to solve the problem of environ-

39. Daniel F. Ford, *Three Mile Island: Thirty Minutes to Meltdown* (New York: Penguin Books, 1981), 33, 253.

40. R. and V. Routley, "Nuclear Energy and Obligations to the Future," 133–79.

mental degradation. The answer was that technology might be more of a problem than a solution.[41]

## Sewage: The Wrong Kind of Bay Enrichment

Of all the problems confronting this estuary in the 1960s and 1970s, sewage was the major scourge of Chesapeake Bay. The long-standing sewage flow became a torrent of filth and chemical effluent from homes, factories, and farms. Sewage emanated from numerous and mostly inadequate treatment centers as well as from septic tanks not connected to municipal systems. The sheer magnitude of the debacle took the region by surprise. In 1979 the U.S. Geological Survey calculated that on an "average day" some forty-five billion gallons of fresh water flowed into the bay; according to the Johns Hopkins Chesapeake Bay Institute, each day a *bare minimum* of four hundred million gallons of sewage plant effluent were also pumped into the bay.[42]

Biologists had detected algae blooms as early as 1916, when sewage "scum" began to pollute the oyster beds of the Potomac River. Although the earliest public concerns focused on health and sanitation, untreated sewage was causing oxygen depletion in receiving waters that led to major fish die-offs.[43] Sewage enriches water with nitrogen, which feeds dark algae blooms that prevent the sunlight from reaching grasses on the bay bottom, where the food chain begins. Without light, photosynthesis cannot take place, and marine grasses starve. As filters of sediments and chemicals and producers of oxygen, grasses are paramount to the survival of the bay. By the 1960s, however, sewage in the Potomac was present in amounts sufficient to carpet the waters with blue-green algae.

In Maryland, the once clear Patuxent River had become a sewer duct, often in summer carrying as much raw sewage as clean water. Other rivers suffered from similar nutrient enrichment problems. Nitrogen again was

41. Robert Costanza, cited in "Pricing Environmental Health: The New Thinking," *Marine Notes* (June 1990): 1–3.

42. Cited in Hoffman, "Who's Killing Chesapeake Bay." By 1988 these figures had nearly tripled. See Tom Horton, William M. Eichbaum (contributor), *Turning the Tide: Saving the Chesapeake Bay* (Washington, D.C.: Island Press), 69.

43. H. S. Cummings, "Investigation of the Pollution of Tidal Waters of Maryland and Virginia," United States Public Health Service, Bulletin No. 75, 1916.

the culprit. On the Eastern Shore, change was noticeable on the Choptank River. In the 1940s and 1950s the water was so clear that a man walking up to his waist in the river could see his feet. Now the water had turned brown and turbid. Scientists by 1960 found the upper bay near Baltimore to be seriously polluted with sewage, and so, too, were Virginia's York and Rappahannock Rivers. The net result of the enrichment or algae blooms resulted in an oxygen imbalance uncharacteristic of the bay's natural system. Tourists and fishermen did not have to be scientists to discern what was happening in Chesapeake waters. They could see it and worse, smell it.[44]

While estuaries are complex mechanisms that respond to sewage in a variety of ways, increased loads of fecal matter can overload a system and result in what scientists call fantastic algae growth rates that can literally deny the estuary much of its oxygen supply. Using several decades of anecdotal and quantifiable data on sewage flows, scientists were able to discern several trends.[45] The upper bay and Western Shore tributaries of Maryland were the most seriously affected, areas whose enrichment problems in summer were a source of increasing alarm. As late as 1982, John Toyooka, a Naval Academy midshipman oceanography major who regularly scubadived in the bay, frequently saw human waste floating by in the water. "It disappoints you," he said. The main sewage pollution problems continued to come from the Patapsco (Baltimore), the Potomac (Washington, D.C. and Northern Virginia suburbs), and the James (Richmond metropolitan area). After 1960 these rivers would flow through regions affected by major development and population growth that threatened to overwhelm municipal sewage capacities. Oxygen supplies in Maryland's Patuxent River were seriously depleted, even in the stream's deeper parts. The middle part of the bay was still reasonably healthy, not yet showing too many signs of nutrient enrichment, and the lower bay was relatively free of the nutrient invasion characteristic of the upper portion.[46]

Flush toilets were not the Chesapeake's only source of unwanted nutrients.

44. This problem appeared to be outside the scope of the solutions science offered. See "Conclusions on Nutrient Enrichment," in *Chesapeake Bay Program Technical Studies,* 262–66.

45. Christopher F. D'Elia, "Nutrient Enrichment of Chesapeake Bay: An Historical Perspective," in *Chesapeake Bay Program Technical Studies,* 36–98.

46. Ibid., 94–97. See also J. H. Carpenter, D. W. Pritchard, and R. C. Whaley,

Farmers and lawn-conscious suburbanites used prodigious amounts of fertilizer to enhance their "crops," and nitrogen and phosphorous from "non-point" (non-discernable) pollution added greatly to the nutrient enrichment already taking place. In the Susquehanna River Valley alone, farmers and residents sent fifty-eight million pounds of nitrogen and three million pounds of phosphorus bayward annually, reported John Hartigan of the Northern Virginia Planning District Commission. In a wet year the amount often doubled. Small wonder that a massive blue-green carpet of algae blossomed.[47]

With submerged subaquatic vegetation dying rapidly, and the decline in oxygen content threatening fish and oyster populations, could state and local governments manage their sewage flows in terms of pollution per gallon? And could jurisdictions develop sewage plants for future generations who would reside in the Chesapeake Bay country?

Engineering problems could be solved with a technological fix. After 1980 Virginia, Maryland, and Pennsylvania each developed ambitious programs to eliminate phosphorus from Maryland waters and develop tools to remove nitrogen. The District of Columbia Blue Plains Sewage Treatment Plant became a model that was, according to Tom Horton, "a generation ahead of most other places." Ironically, as municipalities struggled to control their sewage outflows federal installations, including dozens of military bases, routinely violated sewage laws.[48] Environmentalists in the 1980s reported concerns about manufacture, transport, and storage of chemical and biological warfare agents on military installations. A recent study of military bases in the Chesapeake region cited five installations generating toxic contamination of receiving waters. The military owned more than 112,000 acres of Chesapeake waterfront land and was free to use that land insulated from control by state and local officials.[49]

One issue seemed to escape the great discussion over sewage and Chesapeake waters in the 1960s and 1970s: the massive proliferation of septic tank

---

"Observations of Eutrophication and Nutrient Cycles in Some Coastal Plain Estuaries," in *Eutrophication: Causes, Consequences, Correctives* (Washington, D.C.: National Academy of Sciences, 1969), 210–21.

47. Frank Allen, "Dying or Evolving? The Chesapeake Bay," *Wall Street Journal*, September 27, 1982.

48. Horton, *Turning the Tide*, 69, 71.

49. Tetra Tech Inc., "Water Quality Assessment of DOD Installations/Facilities

systems in the suburban and rural tidewater. By 1991 about 250,000 homes in Maryland had septic systems with 656,000 in Virginia and over a million in Pennsylvania. According to a recent study by the Environmental Protection Agency, septic tanks are notoriously ineffective as waste removal mechanisms. The average septic tank removes only 15–45 percent of the nitrogen in wastewater.[50] As suburbs blanketed the Chesapeake countryside, tax-starved rural counties and towns found it difficult to control the issuance of septic permits, because they wanted the revenue and jobs development would create. Building public sewers in rural areas and outlying suburban districts was financially impractical, argued municipal authorities. Rural counties like Accomack in Virginia and Calvert County in Maryland, complained that expensive sewage systems would stifle economic growth in their communities.[51] Moreover, septic systems were underground and people did not give them much thought.

After 1970 two out of every five new homes in Maryland and Virginia relied on septic systems, a number that would rise in the two states to about twenty-four thousand per year a decade later. With growth came septic tank problems, especially in Virginia subdivisions. In a typical septic system, solids and liquids flow from the home through the pipe to an underground tank. Solids settle in the tank, and over time liquids may leach into the soil and eventually into the ground water, which courses to the bay. Septic systems do not have a long life; they begin to deteriorate in less than twenty years. Yet suburbanites and rural dwellers continued to rely on septic systems because they feared that sewage systems would bring intensive development that would destroy their bucolic setting.

Recently the *Washington Post* reported that in Virginia "about 5 percent of the state's one million septic systems are failing a year, about the same percentage as among Maryland's 350,000 tanks, according to state regulators."[52] Throughout this period, too many county governments wasted money and

in the Chesapeake Region," Consulting Report for the U.S. Army Corps of Engineers, Baltimore District and the U.S. Secretary of Defense (Washington: 1980).

50. Cited in Horton, *Turning the Tide*, 73.

51. For a general overview of this sewage problem see, "Twenty Years Later, Water Still Polluted," *Civil Engineering*, 61 (1991): 30.

52. Stephen C. Fehr and Peter Pae, "Aging Septic Tanks Worry D.C. Suburbs," *Washington Post*, May 18, 1997.

reduced open space by allowing home construction in remote areas where septic tanks were the only option. As Maryland and Virginia geared up to spend millions to save the bay after 1970, a lot of their work would be undone by rural sprawl and the lowly septic tank.

## Kepone and other Toxics

Because of its proximity to large urban centers, the Chesapeake has not remained immune to sudden environmental disaster. While the Three Mile Island crisis was a near miss, the Kepone menace scored a direct hit, becoming arguably one of the most serious environmental misfortunes on Chesapeake Bay in recent times. In 1973, two former employees of the Allied Chemical Corporation, Virgil A. Hundtofte and William P. Moore, set up a company in Hopewell, Virginia, on the banks of the James River to make Kepone, a powerful pesticide akin to DDT. Allied owned the patent on the chemical, which carried the trade name chlordane, a powerful pesticide used in Europe to protect potato crops. Hundofte had an exclusive licensing arrangement to make and distribute Kepone for Allied Chemical and won over the city fathers with promises of an increasing tax base and jobs. Hopewell in turn was delighted to bill itself as the "Chemical Capital of the South" and supported Hundtofte's New Life Science Products Company despite widespread scientific information that Kepone caused cancer, liver damage, reproductive sterility, and other serious diseases in fish, birds, and mammals.

The trouble with Kepone was not how much it was used but how it was dumped into Chesapeake waters as waste. At their Life Science Products facility, Hundtofte, Moore, and their workers dumped two hundred thousand pounds of Kepone laden wastewater into the James River. The Hopewell facility had no environmental controls; it was in reality nothing more than a refurbished former gas station. Workers handled the chemical without protection from safety goggles, gloves, or other devices, and several employees were severely contaminated by the poison. After a medical inspection, Virginia state environmental and medical authorities found half of the company's work force to be suffering from memory loss, liver damage, sterility, and chest and joint pains. Fortunately the physicians who treated the men were able to use chlosetyramine, a drug used to lower blood cholesterol, to "flush" the Kepone from their systems.[53] But by then the pesticide was flowing into the James River and through sewage treatment plants that were powerless to halt the lethal chemical. Within a short time Kepone showed up in the air and on land as well.

Not until July 1975 did Virginia health authorities shut down the Kepone plant at Hopewell. Despite enormous political pressure to remain silent, Director of the Virginia Institute for Marine Science William Hargis sounded the Kepone alarm, and the crisis quickly captured national attention. Some in the legislature and in the Hopewell business community denounced Hargis for resorting to "scare tactics" on a chemical problem, and for a while state officials temporarily removed Hargis from his position on charges of mismanagement at the Gloucester facility. By that time Kepone had seriously contaminated the James River, and authorities in both Virginia and Maryland worried that it would spread throughout the bay with the tidal flow and then enter the lower reaches of the tributaries. Allied Chemical, driven to the wall, fought back with every legal and economic resource at its command. Shortly after the plant closing, scientists from the Maryland Department of Natural Resources discovered that bluefish were seriously contaminated with Kepone and other species in the lower bay were beginning to pick up the pesticide. Kepone was detected in crabs. Fish as far upriver as Richmond bore traces of the poison.

The Kepone scare had a disastrous impact on the Chesapeake's $50 million-a-year fishing industry as people began to avoid any fish from the bay. U.S. Food and Drug guidelines on permissible Kepone levels in finfish resulted in fish caught in the James River being kept from the market for two years. Governor Mills Godwin also used his emergency powers to ban recreational boating and fishing on the James River from Richmond to Hampton Roads, a distance of ninety-eight miles. Even though the Virginia Seafood Council reported that a 132-pound man would have to eat twenty-four thousand pounds of Kepone-tainted fish to suffer any appreciable harm, hysteria rapidly replaced common sense. Commercial bluefishing all but stopped. The Chesapeake crabbing industry was seriously affected as well,

53. Lewis Regenstein, *America the Poisoned* (Washington, D.C.: Acropolis Books, 1982), 147. The Virginia Kepone crisis was covered by the CBS News program, *60 Minutes* on December 14, 1975. "Spread of a Deadly Chemical—And the Ever-Widening Impact," *U.S. News and World Report,* September 6, 1976.

because it was known that crabs migrate northward from contaminated Virginia waters during the year. Seafood businesses like Family Fish Houses Inc., a chain of twenty-one seafood restaurants, assured their customers in expensive media advertisements that the fish they served had been taken in the Atlantic Ocean and not the bay.

In May 1976 the State of Virginia charged Allied Chemical and the owners of New Life Science Products Company with 940 counts of violating water pollution laws. Life Science Products Company and the town of Hopewell were charged with over a thousand counts. Hundtofte and Moore pleaded guilty to 153 counts of violating pollution laws. For a time, litigation replaced chemical manufacturing and fishing as the major growth industry in this area of Chesapeake Bay. Judges and the Environmental Protection Agency officials presided over a national melodrama that cast Allied Chemical as the villain. Yet federal courts were surprisingly lenient, allowing Allied a *nolo contendere* plea to help it solve its civil litigation. The U.S. District Court of Richmond imposed a criminal fine of $13.24 million on the company. The fine was later reduced to $5 million, which Allied was able to claim as a tax-deductible business expense. Allied agreed to establish the Virginia Environmental Endowment with a donation of $8 million. The endowment provides money for projects to help Virginia's environment.

Meanwhile, the Virginia fishing community, civic organizations, and generally injured parties launched a wave of legal suits against Allied Chemical. When fishermen, crabbers, workers, and other claimants were finally paid off, Allied had spent more that $200 million in fines, settlements, and legal fees. The $3.5 million fine against New Life Science Products Company was never collected because the company went bankrupt. Finally, despite this being the largest environmental crime ever perpetrated on the waters of Chesapeake Bay, not one Allied Chemical executive went to jail.[54]

Fortunately, Kepone did not spread as scientists had feared. It has, however, entered the sediment strata of bay bottom in the lower Chesapeake.

54. For a discussion of the Kepone pollution litigation, see Davison et. al., *Chesapeake Waters,* 172–76. See also the panel discussion, "Allied Chemical, the Kepone Incident and the Settlements: Twenty Years Later," *University of Richmond Law Review,* 29 (1995): 493, 508–9; "Allied's Fine Cut to $5 Million for Kepone Pollution," *Washington Post,* February 1, 1977; William Goldfarb, "Kepone: A Case Study," *Environmental Law,* 8 (1978): 645.

Waiting for time and tide to ease the problem, scientists have been unable to calculate what Kepone's final impact on the region will be.

The Kepone crisis, oil spills, and other pollution problems in the 1970s reflected a serious deficiency on the part of both Maryland and Virginia governments to prevent environmental hazards from entering Chesapeake waters. Dr. Max Eisenberg, a scientist for Maryland's Kepone Task Force, believes that Kepone, like mercury, which still turns up in fish, may come to be accepted as inevitable. "As far as we know, we can live with Kepone as the problem exists now," he said. "But our lifestyle has become one where we are bombarded with one chemical after another—and unfortunately the cumulative effects of them are not known."[55] Since the 1970s tougher environmental laws have made the James River cleaner, but the river's bottom is laced with Kepone. Because scientists linked Kepone to cancer in laboratory rats, the James River was closed to fishermen for thirteen years. State officials estimated the cost to the public, including revenue lost to watermen, at tens of millions of dollars.

Nearly lost in the controversy surrounding Kepone were the long-term effects of water pollution by Smithfield Foods, the smoked-ham giant. It would take nearly two decades for this Virginia tidewater company to be punished for its enormous misdeeds. From 1970 onward conservation authorities in Virginia documented that Smithfield Foods flushed fecal matter and other bodily waste from slaughtered hogs directly into the Pagan River, a tributary of the James. Phosphorus in the waste created enormous algae prints that depleted the river's oxygen and created dead zones that imperiled Chesapeake aquatic life. Smithfield Foods was active in Virginia state politics, and Democratic Party leaders who controlled the state were reluctant to punish an important ally for pollution crimes. As late as 1995 environmentalists who spoke out against Smithfield Foods were denounced as fanatics who used environmental scare tactics to kill off jobs. Finally in 1997 the Environmental Protection Agency intervened, citing the company for seven thousand violations of the Clean Water Act. Federal courts levied a fine of $12.6 million against Smithfield Foods and chastised Virginia for being exceptionally lax in its enforcement of water pollution laws.[56]

55. *Baltimore Sun,* August 29, 1976.
56. "Smithfield's Dirty Deeds," *Washington Post,* July 13, 1997.

Oil pollution also lurked as a growing menace. As a commercial lane, the Chesapeake is an exceedingly busy estuary. In the 1970s more than five thousand ocean-going craft visited the port of Baltimore. Oil and bilge droppings from motor boats and tankers for the most part became part of the bay's untreated effluent. Bulk oil tankers dominated Chesapeake waterborne traffic, worrying reformers about the consequences of a massive oil spill in the bay. Said Secretary of the Interior Stewart Udall in 1967, "a massive oil spill akin to that of the *Torrey Canyon* could effectively eliminate most of the marine resources of the whole region."[57]

Throughout the 1970s and 1980s environmentalists pointed out that pollution was Chesapeake Bay's second enemy. Politics was its first. Those persons with the most interest in the bay were oil shipping companies, lobbyists and representatives of chemical conglomerates, bayside developers, electric utilities, and municipalities with sewage problems. In most cases, watermen, sportsmen, environmental reformers, and professional ecologists were usually outmuscled in Richmond and Annapolis.

## Contention's Cradle

Early in 1978 the Chesapeake Bay Consortium, a federation of environmental and scientific study groups, compiled a directory of organizations manifesting an interest in Chesapeake Bay affairs. Just listing the organizations required 108 pages. Most tax money spent on saving the Bay was directed toward "Chesapeake Bay studies," a hydra-headed program that became a more significant industry than the Chesapeake Bay fishery itself. For example, the Army Corps of Engineers ultimately spent $23 million on its bay study, which included the construction of the bay hydraulic model. Its final expensive summary, *Chesapeake Bay Future Conditions Report,* relied on data already collected by other agencies. The Corps of Engineers thus was

57. On March 18, 1967 the *Torrey Canyon* struck a reef off Land's End, England. She was the first of the big supertankers, carrying a cargo of 120,000 tons of oil. Thirty-one million gallons of oil leaked from the ship and spread along the sea between England and France, killing most of the marine life it touched along the whole of the south coast of Britain and the Normandy shores of France, and blighting the region for many years thereafter. For oil pollution, see also Hoffman, "Who's Killing the Chesapeake Bay."

little more than a very high-paid librarian for bay studies. The Environmental Protection Agency's study of the bay cost more than $25 million, and its recommendations did little that resulted in direct political and economic action to effect long-term solutions. Small wonder that both politicians and civic groups complained that the Chesapeake was being studied to death. Senator Charles McC. Mathias, himself a proponent of the EPA's bay study, by 1979 had become fond of quoting an unnamed waterman who said, "There are lots of studies made of the bay, but *we* never see many answers." Senator Mathias and others were fond of quoting the simple fact that in the 1970s the federal government spent over $21 million of American tax revenue with little to show save row upon row of environmental studies on library shelves.[58]

For environmental journalists who routinely covered Chesapeake Bay affairs, scientific problems paled in comparison to the larger problem of demographic change in the region. The construction of two large bridges from Sandy Point to Kent Island transformed what was once a sleepy area of farms and fishing villages called the Eastern Shore of Maryland. Long-distance commuters regularly crossed those bridges, and during the 1980s the Eastern Shore counties close to the bridges grew at a steady pace, spurred by highway improvements that made a trip from Easton to Washington, D.C., an easy ninety-minute jaunt. The population of Queen Anne's County, 18,500 in 1970, skyrocketed to 33,953 in 1990. Similar developments occurred elsewhere. Between 1952 and 1986, the region's population increased by 50 percent. Outside Baltimore and Washington, new "Edge Cities" sprang up, and Michael Lettre, the assistant director of the Maryland Office of Planning, noted that most of the change took place "outside the historically suburban counties."[59] By the 1990s, demographers believed population growth was the "single most important factor underlying the various stresses on the Bay ecosystem." In 1950 the Chesapeake Bay watershed contained 8.4 million residents. By 1990 that had grown to 14.7 million.[60]

58. David Hoffman, "The Suffering Chesapeake," *Washington Post Sunday Magazine,* April 29, 1979, 37.

59. Sue Anne Pressley, "Struggling to Keep Suburbia at Bay," *Washington Post,* April 3, 1991.

60. "Bay Challenged by Growth in Population, Wastewater," *Bay Journal,* 4 (February 1995).

The roots of the Chesapeake's problems lay in the rush to settle in rural areas and enjoy the bucolic life. Metropolitan sprawl and its effects have been the major ecological phenomena of recent times. Writer Tom Horton minced few words. "For those who wonder how many more people can ultimately live around Chesapeake Bay without degrading it, the answer is this: Too many are here already." The only solution, Horton believed, was "channeling growth" into more settled areas with infrastructures like public transportation and municipal sewage systems.[61]

The future looked anything but good. Demographers predicted that by 2020 at least 2.6 million more people would move into the bay country.[62] Limiting growth would take "a new kind of economics" that would place controls on property ownership, specifically American exponential land hunger. In 1950, each resident accounted for .18 acres of developed land. By 1980, each resident accounted for .65 acres of development.[63] Increasingly, environmental concerns were largely pegged on land-use issues. Even the most casual review of the state of the Chesapeake Bay revealed disturbing population and land use trends that overtook attempts to protect the region's environmental quality. The only thing certain about the future was that the Chesapeake would be contention's cradle on the East Coast.

## The Passing of the Chesapeake Waterman

In the modern age the oystermen and fisherfolk of Chesapeake Bay are becoming extinct. Soon their unique maritime culture and independent ways of living will pass into folklore and history, much like that of the whaling communities of New England. The men and women who have pursued their craft of oystering, crabbing, and fishing for nearly three centuries have fallen victim to diminishing harvests, pollution, political indifference, and bureaucratic harassment. No one can withstand the onslaught of economic realities. Fish and oyster harvests have dropped precipitously. Oysters, for

---

61. Horton, *Turning the Tide*, 189–200.

62. For population projections, see *Population Projections for Maryland Subdivisions, 1970–2010* (Baltimore: Maryland Office of Planning, Planning Data Services, 1990).

63. 2020 Panel, *Population Growth and Development in the Chesapeake Bay Watershed to the Year 2020* (Annapolis: Maryland State Government, 1988.)

example, have dropped from 125 million pounds of meat in 1880 to twenty-five million in 1978. Each year fewer men choose to follow the water. Out of 4,729 oystermen who applied to Annapolis for licenses in the 1978–79 season, only about 1,500 were engaged full-time in the business. Of the much publicized skipjacks, that romantic flotilla of sailing oyster dredge boats that numbered nearly one thousand at the turn of the century, only thirty-one worked in the 1978–79 season. Most of the skipjacks were old and water-logged; captains turned a better dollar using their boats for tourism than for hunting oysters. Skipjacks in the 1990s were more often seen in museums than on the water.

As late as 1979 the Chesapeake was still wondrously productive, providing nearly one-fourth the total U.S. oyster catch and nearly half the blue crab catch, while spawning 90 percent of the rockfish caught along the entire northeast coast. In 1978 William Warner, a writer based at the Smithsonian Institution, published a warm-hearted tribute to Chesapeake watermen that netted him a Pulitzer prize and cast those who harvested the bay as America's last honest rugged individualists.[64] But even those watermen whose families had worked on the bay for generations sensed that something was wrong. Beyond slumping harvests in the late 1970s were discouraging spat set trends for oysters, ongoing declines in underwater grasses, and increasing counts of chlorine and herbicides and heavy metals in the water. According to George Krantz and Donald Merritt, scientists at the Horn Point Environmental Laboratory of the University of Maryland, the slump in spat sets indicated a long-range oyster crisis, not a short-term slump.[65] Over the next two decades watermen relied more on harvesting crabs for their livelihood, and under the increased harvesting pressure, crab yields declined. Toward century's end, oysters and crabs, once two of the most abundant resources, were sorely diminished. Beginning in 1988, Maryland scientists conducted a six-year study of the Chesapeake Bay crab harvest. From 1988 to 1992 crab numbers fell from an estimated population of 1.7 billion to 440 million, a 50 percent decline. By 1994 crab stocks had not returned to earlier levels. Scientists worried that with harvest pressure high

64. William W. Warner, *Beautiful Swimmers: Watermen, Crabs and the Chesapeake Bay* (Boston: Little, Brown, 1976).

65. Michael Fincham, "An Uncertain Season for Watermen," *University of Maryland Magazine*, (Winter 1979): 7–8.

and crab populations low, the species could be hard hit, especially if the weather was bad during spawning seasons.[66]

Watermen were more concerned about government regulatory agencies than bad harvests, They had experienced their share of bad times on the bay, but they saw in Maryland's Department of Natural Resources the chief villain in many of their struggles. The DNR, complained Larry Simms, president of the Maryland Watermen's Association, nearly taxed, supervised, and regulated them out of business. "They treated us as a nuisance to be gotten rid of," rumbled Simms. Highly individualistic by nature, watermen lacked organization and political clout in Richmond and Annapolis. They had neither the money nor the resources to struggle against chemical companies, bayside developers, power companies, and sports fishing groups. Rebuilding the Chesapeake fishery in modern times requires major changes in maritime industries. With new management of the bay's resources will come an end to the Chesapeake as a "commons" and the advent of a scientifically managed fishery. "What they want," Simms laments, "is to have us punching time clocks on the Chesapeake."[67] Watermen opposed fishing bans and limitations on crab and oyster harvests, often blaming tourists and sportsfishermen for the declining yield. By the 1990s, bay country watermen were overwhelmed by government regulation, sewage, pollution, and disease in the fishery, like MSX, caused by a protozoan parasite that kills oysters before they reach market size. Aside from travel writers who saw the watermen as quaint museum pieces from a bygone era, their passing was scarcely noticed.

## Saving Chesapeake Wetlands

Although a kind of rough conservation consensus has recently prevailed concerning the Chesapeake's recreational potential, the use of wetlands—salt marshes, swamps, tidelands, and sloughs that border estuaries—has divided farmers, developers, and environmentalists. Environmentalists value wetlands as natural environment areas, whereas farmers and developers view them as potentially profitable real estate. Over the years Maryland and

66. "Blue Crab Survey Raises Questions About Stock's Health," *Bay Journal*, 5 (March, 1995).
67. Interview with Larry Simms, January 15, 1980.

Virginia farmers had established local county drainage commissions to dig ditches and use eminent domain to reclaim farm land from the marsh, but more recently what was once accepted community practice has been challenged in the courts, and political battles rage over the assumptions concerning the use of natural resources. From 1870 to 1970 Virginia lost 42 percent of its nontidal and tidal wetlands and Maryland lost 73 percent. A decade ago, Tom Horton reported that until the 1970s Maryland had lost more than a thousand acres of tidal wetlands annually to real-estate development. The battle over the tidal marshes, wrote Joseph Siry, involves one of "the least understood sections of the coast."[68]

A major cause of wetland loss in Maryland and Virginia derives from the efforts of property owners, primarily developers and farmers, trying to halt shoreline erosion through the use of bulkheads and stone piles known as riprap. By hardening the shoreline these man-made constructions prevent the formation of marshland and turn wetlands into open water. At issue in the 1970s was whether tidal wetlands would remain marshes where the bay's productivity begins or become condominium communities, marinas, power plants, and sewage treatment facilities. Maryland passed a law in 1970 to protect tidal wetlands, and Virginia followed suit in 1972. The federal government also joined the effort with the Water Pollution Control Act of 1972, which closely regulates the filling of wetlands.[69] Maryland's interest in the law stemmed from developers creating new land out of the public domain by draining marshes and enriching themselves in the process.

At first the laws went largely untested while developers relentlessly pursued their demands to use wetlands as their private property. Then the debate reached an emotional peak in 1976 when the Army Corps of Engineers proposed to cut a 150-mile channel through the Eastern Shore coastal wetlands of Delaware, Maryland, and Virginia to the mouth of Chesapeake

68. Horton, *Turning the Tide*, 149. See also John Teal and Mildred Teal, *Life and Death of the Salt Marsh* (New York: Ballantine Publishers, 1975), 1–35. V. Siry, *Marshes of the Ocean Shore*, 6. Wetlands are low-lying areas where the land merges with salt or fresh water. In the Chesapeake, wetlands are where the food chain begins.

69. See *Maryland Annotated Code*, Environment Article, Title 16, Maryland Wetlands Act, 1970. Virginia Submerged Lands Act, *Code of Virginia*, Section 28.2 1200–1213. *United States Code Public Law 92–500*, Sec. 2, 1977, Section 401 of the Clean Water Act.

Bay, south of the fishing village of Wachaprague, Virginia. Supported by marina, restaurant, and hotel owners and commercial fishermen who expected to improve their livelihood on the mid-Atlantic coast, the waterway was viewed as an important tool of economic growth. The prospect horrified environmental groups. Wetlands were the heart of the region's ecosystem, they claimed, and served as buffers against erosion and tidal flooding. Not only would such a "canal" upset the ecological balance of the Atlantic wetlands and coastal barrier islands, it would damage valuable breeding and spawning grounds for hundreds of species of fish and shellfish that eventually make their way into Chesapeake Bay. Environmentalists feared that once the waterway was constructed, wetland developers would have a green light to dredge and fill in their property for hotels, shopping centers, and condominiums.

Under fire from conservation groups, the corps retreated and required all participants in the waterway scheme and, virtually anyone else planning to dredge and fill Chesapeake or Atlantic waters, to first secure a wetlands permit. The permit process slowed the pace of development and gave citizens, community organizations, and environmental groups a chance to discuss the future of wetlands. Developers complained that the permit process was dictatorial. Said Cambridge seafood dealer Calvin Tolley: "We work and live here. Why should the muskrat, the heron and the egret suddenly become more important than humans?"[70] But groups like the Chesapeake Bay Foundation saw the Chesapeake Waterway fight as a breakthrough in the battle to save the wetlands. Since 1990 strict federal and state laws have been in force, and developers who break them have received multimillion dollar fines and prison sentences. In 1996 Virginia developer James J. Wilson was sentenced to twenty-one months in jail and fined a million dollars for filling in seventy acres of wetlands for a real-estate development in Charles County, Maryland. The issue of wetlands as private property remained unresolved, however, and business groups like the Cambridge-based Fairness to Land Owners Committee complained that the laws denied their rights to private property.[71] Meanwhile, it was often difficult for state and

---

70. For background, see Karl Blankenship "CBF Permit Process Slows Wetland Losses," *Bay Journal*, 4 (December, 1994): 1, 10; Calvert B. Tolley, cited in "Saving U.S. Wetlands," *U.S. News and World Report*, July 12, 1976, 37–38.

71. Timothy B. Wheeler, "Builder May Face Jail for Filling in Wetlands: Stiff

federal authorities to monitor compliance with wetland regulations in remote rural areas with hostile landowners. Wetlands in the Chesapeake continued to disappear at the alarming rate of 4,500 acres a year.

By the late 1970s, the Chesapeake was beginning to show signs of serious stress. Fear of fecal contamination shut down oyster beds. Rivers were closed to swimming. Shad, rockfish, and other freshwater spawners appeared in greatly reduced in numbers or disappeared altogether. Data released by the Environmental Protection Agency Bay Study confirmed naturalists' worst fears. Farm fertilizers and other sources of nitrogen were causing massive blooms of algae that blocked sunlight and smothered underwater grasses. Herbicides and chemicals entered the bay in record amounts, contaminating the water and accumulating in river and bay sediment. When the EPA issued its final report in 1983 there was little cause for celebration. "I used to be guardedly optimistic, but now I'm a little pessimistic," remarked estuary expert Eugene Cronin. "The Bay's problems are growing faster than our ability to react to them. The Bay is a signal system. If we can't save it, we can't save any of our estuaries."[72]

By 1990 the Chesapeake Bay was clearly in trouble, despite curbs on industrial polluters and sewage plant discharges in its watershed and recent limits on development along its shoreline. Toxins, sediment, and trash clouded its once clear waters. And the bay's most potent image—the Chesapeake skipjack—had virtually disappeared. The region clearly had reached a crisis, and experts had come to believe that restoring the Chesapeake meant major growth limits. Between 1970 and 1980 Maryland's population grew 7.5 percent, but the amount of developed land grew by 16.5 percent.

The crusade to save the bay, which really began with the Clean Water Act of 1970, initially attacked pollution from sewage plants and factories. Only much later did officials take a look at non-point pollution, the harder to control runoff contamination from the daily lives of city dwellers, suburbanites, and farmers. By 1990 states and localities were waging campaigns against dumping toxins into storm drains that emptied into the bay, urging

Fines Could Make Company Go Bankrupt," *Baltimore Sun,* June 17, 1996; Dianne Dumanoski, "Maryland Wetlands Convict: Victim or Villain," *Boston Globe,* December 7, 1992, 6.

72. Quoted in Richard Wright, "The Changing Chesapeake," *New York Times Magazine,* July 10, 1983, 27

homeowners to use less fertilizer, and tightening sediment-control rules at construction sites.

Maryland's 1984 Critical Areas Act and Virginia's Chesapeake Bay Preservation Act of 1988 were aimed at controlling the effect of shoreline development on water quality and did not address the broad issue of growth throughout the watershed. Maryland's law was by far the more comprehensive and controversial. The Critical Area Act was a sweeping rezoning of land one thousand feet back from the edge of the bay and its tidal rivers. Essentially it stripped land use power from property owners and local jurisdictions in order to protect the Chesapeake's tidal shorelines. Opponents of the Critical Area Act denounced it as nothing less than land theft by the state and argued that it would end economic growth in the bay country. In fact few dire results ensued, and economic growth continued along the shoreline albeit in the form of more expensive $200,000-housing units on two-acre lots. Virginia's law had enough legal loopholes to keep property owners reasonably content.

As the century ended, the problem of growth dominated the region as farms disappeared and demands for increased land use and economic development created a highly charged political and environmental debate. It was much harder to "fix" the problem of growth than to solve other problems affecting the bay. People don't like to be fixed; they want the right to control their destiny even if it means despoiling a mighty estuary in the process. Further, as the need for managed growth became more apparent in the Chesapeake, the issue became one of well-off suburban elites seeking to stifle development in more rural and less prosperous counties.

## The Chesapeake at Century's End

In 1990 nature writer Tom Horton looked out on the great estuary and saw what he called "muddled" progress. Since the first Earth Day celebration in 1970 there had been an increase in environmental regulation of the bay and a few successes with rivers, he said, "but no clear trend towards a systemwide rebound."[73] Thus by 1990 in many enviro-reform circles the initial optimism that had sustained the Save the Bay campaign of the 1970s and 1980s had given way to a wary sense that the trouble with the Chesapeake was

73. Tom Horton, "State of the Bay," *Mid-Atlantic Country* (October 1990): 94.

awesomely complex. At its core lay a soaring regional population growth that neither politicians nor scientists could control. Critics remarked that it was easier to herd cats than to get compliance from all the businesses, localities, and governments who used Chesapeake waters. And all of the millions of dollars spent on research, conservation, interstate cooperation, and task forces could not return the Chesapeake to its pristine state.

Chesapeake problems stemmed from critical developments scarcely noticed by the media. At the end of the twentieth century the rate of deforestation in the region rivaled the rapaciousness of the colonial era. According to a recent satellite photo study by the conservation group, American Forests, in the 1980s and 1990s trees fell throughout the watershed at a surprising rate. This time it was not the logger's saw but the developer's bulldozer at work. Tree cover in the area closest to the bay declined from 51 percent in 1973 to 39 percent in 1997. "The dominant ecological feature here just 30 years ago was heavy forests," said Gary Moll, vice-president of American Forests Urban Forest Center. "Today it is development and lands scarcely covered with trees. These changes are so large they threaten to undermine many important natural functions performed by forest ecosystems." Unlike the forest losses of the colonial period which were short-term, these losses are permanent. While foresters expected to see continued loss in urban areas like Baltimore and Washington, they were surprised by the loss in agricultural areas. Analysis performed by the U.S. Forest Service found that forests lost ground in Virginia, Maryland, and Delaware. During the fourteen years from 1978 to 1992, the amount of forest-covered land in the watershed fell by 1.5 million acres. Said Richard Cooksey, U.S. Forest Service liaison to the Chesapeake Bay area, "We're losing the war, in fact, we have already taken major damage."[74] Trees are highly effective at intercepting and storing rainfall. The cost of lost tree cover was estimated at $1.08 billion, the amount the American Forest Service estimated it took to build a stormwater control capacity equal to that provided by the trees. The vanished trees had reduced pollutants, including nitrogen dioxide and carbon dioxide, in the air, and supplied a habitat for animals and plants. Ultimately, the loss to the Chesapeake Bay itself was extreme, as massive amounts of previously contained fresh water poured into the bay, further disturbing an

74. Quoted in Karl Blankenship, "Forests Closest to Bay Losing Ground to Development," *Bay Journal*, 9 (May 1999): 1, 6–7.

already disturbed ecosystem. Nitrogen not absorbed by forest cover ultimately contributed to the death of underwater sea grasses.

As Pennsylvania entered the twenty-first century it arguably took on one of the most critical roles in the Chesapeake Bay country. In the past two decades the lower Susquehanna, the area closest to the bay, continued to lose forests. Three Pennsylvania counties, York, Lancaster, and Adams, experienced an 11 percent decline. Foresters warned that "rapidly developing Harrisburg already lost 6.2 percent of its forests during the same time."[75] According to one study, "vast acreages of hardwood trees [oak, cherry and maple] came of age for cutting. The forestry activity may rival anything seen there since the early years of this century."[76] In the 1990s the Potomac and Susquehanna Rivers produced several post-winter freshets that poured nutrients and sediments into Chesapeake Bay in amounts greater than anything seen since Hurricane Agnes in 1972.[77] Continued deforestation along the Susquehanna guaranteed that similar freshets would continue into the next century.

As roads and buildings displaced undeveloped forest lands, polluted runoff to streams increased, threatening the ability of bay waters to maintain reduced nutrient levels. Demographers predicted that the number of people living in Virginia, Maryland, the District of Columbia, and Virginia would grow from 23.5 million in 1990 to 27.5 million in 2020, with the most rapid growth taking place in Virginia. In the last twenty years of the century, Maryland's population grew by eight hundred thousand people, 425,000 of whom moved out into the countryside from urban areas. In central Maryland, which includes Baltimore and eleven counties, a projected 39.6 percent growth in population threatened to consume 104 percent more land than is currently used for housing.[78] With gasoline prices at a record twenty-year low in the last decade of the century, people commuted ever-longer distances from their new homes in rural developments. Fueled by the auto-

75. Karl Blankenship, "Study Finds 4.5% Loss in Forest Lands," *Bay Journal,* 5 (August 1995): 1–4.

76. Horton, *Turning the Tide,* 139.

77. Karl Blankenship, "Meltdown '96 floods the Bay," *Bay Journal,* 6 (March 1996): 6–7.

78. "Chewing Up the Landscape: Is Our Appetite for Sprawl Killing the Chesapeake?" *Bay Journal,* 5 (December 1995): 8–9.

mobile and low mortgage rates, metropolitan sprawl across the countryside was beyond the control of local governments.

The loss of forest cover underscored two salient facts: the Chesapeake's environmental problems at century's end were more serious than generally regarded, and there were limits to the solutions that science and technology could provide. The current philosophy of democracy in America is almost an ideology of continuous economic growth that in the long run will produce ecological scarcity through environmental degradation. How well property and wealth will be sustained in a time of ecological scarcity is an issue with which we are only now coming to grapple.

Science has offered a parable for modern times. Atlantic sturgeon were abundant in Chesapeake Bay in the colonial period. Growing up to eight hundred pounds and living as long as sixty years, the sturgeon was prized for its meat and roe. Without sturgeon, John Rolfe's generation in Virginia would have suffered even greater privations than they experienced. Catches of Atlantic sturgeon in the bay peaked at more than 722,000 pounds in 1890. In 1996 the fish had become so rare that when two were caught, one in the Severn River and one in the Potomac, it was a major news event.[79] If man can push a fish as tough as the Atlantic sturgeon, which harkens back to the age of dinosaurs, to near extinction in so short a time, does a similar fate lie in store for other species, including man himself?

At the end of the twentieth century Chesapeake Bay was an estuary of profoundly altered states: alive in some areas, wounded but sustainable in others, and in places dead. Was it a fishery, a recreational paradise, a real-estate market, a sewage lagoon, or a toxic dump? What Americans had to discover is exactly what they already knew. Reality was in the eyes of the beholder.

79. "Two Atlantic Sturgeon Caught Within One Week, Tagged for Research," *Bay Journal,* 6 (March 1996): 7.

## CHAPTER SEVEN

# Epilogue
## The Changing Chesapeake

"Our age characteristically tries to solve all its irrationalities with a gimmick."
— Murray Bookchin, *Post-Scarcity Anarchism*

"The Chesapeake Bay is a body of water and like the human body, its health depends on what goes into it."
— *Chesapeake Regional Information Service*

## A Region Under Pressure

The Chesapeake Bay on any given day is fecund and beautiful, but historically it has been a place of overwhelming contention. Since aboriginal times, the transforming agency of man has been a constant presence in the Chesapeake. The early Americans exerted many influences on their land, using fire, exploiting the regional habitat for agriculture, hunting, and fishing, and effectively changing it. Even our limited archaeological studies suggest that in terms of human activity the Chesapeake was a far busier place than we have imagined. Nature has always been under pressure from human populations; the only thing that has really changed over time is the size and complexity of those pressures. The Chesapeake Bay country was never Edenic, and nature in the Chesapeake has never been as balanced and as pretty as we think.

Over the centuries the Chesapeake has become an invented place, a region both humanly created and socially constructed. This is not to deny the existence of the Chesapeake as a natural place, rather, it is to assert that the Chesapeake is more than a physiographic designation. It has been invented by journalists, scientists, tourists, politicians, and the people who "follow the water" and harvest its resources. Long before the bay country succumbed to the automobile and became enmeshed in a complex net of highways, it was "invented" by tobacco planters, steamboat companies, and the seafood packing industry as a machine for producing money. Certain practices and cultural ideologies reinforced this symbol and kept it foremost in local imagination, even when it was undergoing change and decline. If place is part of the cultural process, then anything that changes "place" has important cultural implications, something we are just beginning to understand about the bay country.

The Chesapeake first became a social and cultural entity during the colonial period, and the term "Tobacco Coast" defined the spirit and function of the region. American slavery was nurtured in the cradle of the Chesapeake over three centuries ago to serve the tobacco colossus, and slavery conditioned everything from land use to sexual relations. Later the technology of waterpower—steamboats, ship-building, gristmills, and small factories—helped usher in the industrial revolution, which became the centerpiece for the unified development of the entire watershed. As a result of national affluence and changing consumer tastes, the nineteenth century witnessed the massive extraction of fish, oysters, and crabs from Chesapeake Bay. Oyster wars and general mayhem became a frequent occurrence. The nineteenth century was also the great age of lumbering and coal mining, two key industries that did so much to change the environment of the watershed. Urban and industrial development brought pollution to Chesapeake waters, and in the twentieth century proliferating highways, metropolitan growth, and tourism accelerated the problems affecting the bay country. Over the course of four centuries, man wrought incredible change in the Chesapeake, changes that affected everything from the chemistry of the environment to the quality of the water we drink and the fish and food we eat. Certain symbolic reference points of the Chesapeake as a place no longer apply. The region will have to be reinvented.

Part of the problem in dealing with public perceptions about Chesapeake Bay is that people think it will last forever. This obviously is not true. As oceanographer Jerry Schubel has noted, twenty thousand years ago there was no Chesapeake Bay. Since that time, "There have been other beginnings and endings of other Chesapeake Bays."[1] As we look to the future, however, we can see that increasingly the transformation of the Chesapeake will be more a human phenomenon than a work of nature. We live in times when momentous technological change can alter the face of the planet;

1. J. R. Schubel, *The Living Chesapeake* (Baltimore: Johns Hopkins University Press, 1981), 5.

and in the depressing words of Bill McKibben, we have already stepped across the threshold of such a change; we are at the end of nature.[2] In the years since the Civil War and most recently since World War II, we have brought about great and unwelcome changes on the Chesapeake, literally altering and killing a good deal of the bay's ecosystem. Wars and ideological controversies have not wrought these changes; they have accompanied our habits and economies, our desire for a lifestyle of enhanced luxury. They have come out of our pursuit of profit and our selfish delusions that we should control nature for man's benefit. We also learned in this process that the natural resources of the Chesapeake are not limitless. Environmental rhetoric and calls for more research and more money are not enough to repair an increasingly dysfunctional estuary. Clearly "technological fixes" like coal scrubbers, nitrogen reduction equipment, or auto emission controls can only address small parts of the total problem. As theologians tell us, we cannot have cheap grace. Neither can the bay have a future worthy of its name as an overused, polluted and derelict seascape.

Most of us, unfortunately, refuse to see in the present the lineaments of times to come. One day our industrial civilization will end. Scientists like Richard C. Duncan of the Institute on Energy and Man predict that the life-expectancy of our industrial civilization is less than one hundred years and call for a new social and economic paradigm for the future.[3] By 2030, in terms of energy use, we will not be able to sustain current rates of economic growth. With the exhaustion of fossil fuels, we may contemplate reversions to elementary, civilized ways of life or to farming and fishing villages. Localism with its spiritual, social, and environmental connections currently enjoys increased popularity.

In recent times the problems of Chesapeake Bay have simply increased faster than our ability to solve them. Meanwhile, growth and change give certain segments of American society attacks of anxiety, and many of us spend much of our time trying to defend ourselves from change's onslaught. The material standard of living, so enshrined in our capitalist folklore, no longer has the driving force that it once had. What kind of satisfaction, Americans might well ask, comes from living at a high consumption level

2. Bill McKibben, *The End of Nature* (New York: Anchor Books, 1989), 47–91.
3. Richard C. Duncan, "The Life-Expectancy of Industrial Civilization: The Decline to Global Equilibrium," *Population and Environment*, 14 (1993): 325–57.

in an unhealthy, derelict landscape? Progress in the modern age, we want to believe, does not necessarily mean living in degraded surroundings. While we are not quite ready to go so far as to accept the Deep Ecologists' doctrine of bioregional egalitarianism, which asserts the equal and intrinsic worth of all living things, most of us are willing to admit that a rich and complex natural world enriches our lives.[4] The problem is largely that people in the Chesapeake region do not sense any connection between their own actions and what ultimately happens to the bay. Furthermore, it is very hard to develop justifications for people not to pursue affluence. Why should any-one downsize his life for the sake of an estuary that hardly enters his consciousness? Ultimately we are possessed of the naive assumption that "science" and "progress" will prevail and find us a way out of our environmental problems. Such assumptions may or may not be tenable; certainly we have yet to develop a "technological fix" for Chesapeake Bay. As Bill McKibben notes, a lot could be accomplished in saving our environment just with the voluntary simplification of our lifestyles. This simplification, he writes, "is not beyond our abilities, but it is probably outside our desires."[5]

In the final pages of *Silent Spring*, Rachel Carson wrote that this is an era dominated by industry, in which the right to make money, at whatever cost to others, is seldom challenged.[6] When her book came out the chemical industry and other industries launched a fierce attack, and in many quarters Carson was roundly denounced for frightening and arousing people. Today most people remember her for pointing out the dangers of DDT, which was banned by the fledgling Environmental Protection Agency in 1974. Her warning at that time was already ten years old, but in the same work she also pointed out the dangers of chlordane (Kepone), which was not banned at the time and which eventually caused a major environmental crisis in the Chesapeake. Despite Carson's warnings, the use of toxic chemicals is still widely tolerated in the United States, and disturbingly large amounts of hazardous chemicals continue to enter the Chesapeake. From 1954 to 1987 pesticide use tripled in the watershed from 3,500 tons to 13,000

4. For a discussion of the pros and cons of Deep Ecology, see Warwick Fox, "Deep Ecology: A New Philosophy of Our Time?" *The Ecologist*, 14 (1984): 194–200.

5. McKibben, *The End of Nature*, 193.

6. Rachel Carson, *Silent Spring*, 227–43.

tons. Mercury and dioxin, a powerful solvent used by paper mills, continue to be found in alarmingly large amounts.

These days it is hard to be alone in the Chesapeake. The din of motorboats, bulldozers, automobiles, and trucks is always close at hand. Increasingly the Chesapeake country is becoming a conquered province. We shape and alter the bay to suit our own needs and desires rather than in conformance to the natural flow of the estuary. Dams and locks on Chesapeake rivers like the Susquehanna control water flows into the bay, and great sewage plants determine the amount of waste and chlorine that will flow into the bay to poison the biomass. Given the size of the populations that now inhabit the Chesapeake region and the enormous industrial and agricultural forces that impact on the bay itself, making even simple remedial changes at saving the landscape and the estuary can prove exceedingly difficult.

It is not enough, however, to blame our environmental troubles on the obsessions of an affluent society. The market system in this country and abroad generates its own need for growth and has obliterated from most people's memory another world that once placed limits on expansion, stressed cooperation over competition, and valued human solidarity. Once there was an agricultural society which, though subsistence-oriented, showed through the power of historical example that there are alternatives. We do not have to reduce all our personal values to entrepreneurial ones. Once such vision is offered us by Wendell Berry, novelist, professor, farmer, and advocate of country living. Berry lives in Henry County, Kentucky, a far cry from Chesapeake Bay but a region that has been plundered and abused in much the same way as our estuary. In his classic work, *The Unsettling of America,* Berry calls for "land stewardship" that opposes chemical agriculture and seeks to redevelop rural culture in terms of an ethic and way of life based upon love of place and devotion to the land.[7] It was the small farm, writes Berry, that sustained the local landscape, for the farmer was essentially a peasant who had to care about the land because it was all he had to sustain him. A good farm contained woodlands and orchards that were necessary to the farm's health. It contained lovingly cultivated fields, and farmers who were proud of their independence. Now, says Berry,

7. Wendell Berry, *The Unsettling of America: Culture and Agriculture* (San Francisco: Sierra Club Books, 1977), 27–38.

"we have attempted to substitute the concepts of land use, agribusiness, and development, for the *culture* of stewardship and husbandry." This change comes not only from the business community but from the educational system and the universities as well.[8]

Long ago in the Chesapeake, agricultural reformers like John Beale Bordley preached the virtues of a fifty-six-acre farm with a small timber plot. Today in order to find anything that approximates Bordley's vision of the independent Chesapeake yeoman, we have to look to the Amish. The Amish do not abandon children, cast off old people, or abide criminals and vagrants. They have a community instead. Surely the Amish have their problems, but they are motivated by two simple ideas: God gave them the land to love and to use; and it is sinful to destroy what you do not make. Now giant corporations make colonies out of rural America, and the small family farm blows away as dust in the wind. A way of life dies, says Wendell Berry, when there is a change in cultural values. Land and sea can die "for want of people with the motivation, the skill, the character and the culture to keep them alive." All land cannot be wilderness, and all the seas cannot be pure. But we can proceed in the future with what Berry calls "kindly use" of the resources we have rather than hastening their destruction.[9]

From an historic viewpoint, what made the Chesapeake Bay country both comfortable and comforting? Simply put, it was the balance of the natural and the human in the region. Enterprises were limited to scale, and farming and fishing were in the best of times perceived by people to be both practical arts and spiritual disciplines. Even today watermen on the Chesapeake shore are the most religious of working groups, whose faith ties them to a union of soil and sea that today is broken in most other places. In the past, people practiced thrift and were not enamored of waste-making as we are today.

## Traffic: The Problem of Problem-Solving

In 1960 Great Britain had yet to build a system of freeways, but with the increased ownership of cars, the problem of automobile congestion in cities was becoming paramount. A study prepared by the British government

8. Wendell Berry, "An Argument for Diversity," *Hudson Review*, 42 (1990): 542.
9. Berry, *The Unsettling of America*, 183–223.

showed that construction of a highway system to satisfy the demands of vehicle ownership was beyond the government's engineering and financial means. Since the full potential of highway construction could not be realized, it had to be curtailed.[10] Put bluntly, the government forced Englishmen to either find other ways of transportation or face growing inconvenience on a highway system originally designed for the horse and wagon. Faced with a problem, the British government said: "Too many cars." Americans faced with a similar problem would say: "Insufficient roads."

The insufficient roads view, as it came to be implemented in the Chesapeake, put an entire region under the control of highway industries who could claim that they were doing what people wanted. Before World War II much of the Chesapeake Bay country was remote and fairly inaccessible by car. An automobile trip from Baltimore to the resort of Ocean City, Maryland, in the 1930s, required either a car ferry from Annapolis to the Eastern Shore or a long and uncomfortable ride over country roads north through the town of Elkton and then south and east through dozens of sleepy towns and villages busy with weekend market congestion. A railroad line out of Baltimore offered a much easier and potentially more exciting alternative form of transportation to seaside resorts.

After the war, the Federal Aid Highway Act of 1944 brought highways to the cities of the Chesapeake. Highway building really accelerated, however, during the 1950s, when President Dwight D. Eisenhower launched a major highway construction program by using taxes on gasoline to pay for road construction. The underpinning rationale for highway construction was "national defense," and Washington, Baltimore, and Norfolk benefited tremendously from the new highway largesse. The effect of this policy was to make transportation in the Chesapeake a highway policy only. The Eisenhower administration scarcely considered other forms of transport in the region. The automobile's assault on the Chesapeake countryside intensified after 1956 with the construction of the thirty-one-mile Baltimore County Beltway. Envisioned originally as a means of connecting the towns of Baltimore County with one another, the beltway offered a major stimulus to already booming suburban growth. Almost overnight Baltimore County became a residential and workplace dream for commuting white-

10. Colin D. Buchanan, et al., *Traffic in Towns, Shortened Edition of the Buchanan Report* (Harmondsworth, England: Ministry of Transport, 1964), 140.

collar workers. Joining the new suburban bandwagon to Baltimore County, the United States Social Security Administration moved its national head-quarters to an eighty-acre site at Woodlawn on the western side of the county. According to one highway historian, the "federal agency moved seven thou-sand workers to the new office complex and left behind some 600,000 square feet of space in eleven buildings in downtown."[11] Meanwhile state highway planners toyed with the idea of demolishing Fells Point, Federal Hill, and other historic areas of Baltimore to allow the construction of an express-way to the suburbs. The unspoken assumption was that the region would be able to accept volumes of traffic that the highways brought. Such an assumption quickly proved to be wrong.

One example will suffice. From the late 1950s, the backup of resort-bound traffic on Route 50 in the summer showed the inadequacy of the region's highways and bridges. Building two spans across the bay for car traffic and additional lanes of highway across the Eastern Shore did relatively little to ease summer congestion. In fact it increased it, as many areas of the Chesa-peake were now settled by long-distance commuters who worked in Balti-more and Washington and clogged the highways every day at rush hour.

An arithmetic increase in supply of highways and beltways in the Chesa-peake led to a geometric increase in demand and use. Prior to World War II most of the Chesapeake Bay country was served by rail passenger systems. In the 1930s it was possible to board a train at the Maryland tidewater vil-lage of Princess Anne in the morning and arrive in New York City in time to get refreshed and see a Broadway show. Passenger trains offered a density of ridership that reduced traffic congestion in the region. After the war the federal government's highways-only policy increased congestion and con-tributed to urban sprawl as people rushed from the city to new suburban tracts and country retreats.

Today the physical effects of traffic and urban sprawl are everywhere evident from Baltimore City to the Eastern Shore, from the Washington suburbs to the mountains of western Maryland. The traffic solution of the 1940s and 1950s has become today's monumental problem as new genera-tions flee the older suburbs for new sprawling developments in the coun-tryside. The problem has become so big, editorialized Maryland's Gover-

11. Michael P. McCarthy, "Baltimore's Highway Wars Revisited," *Maryland His-torical Magazine*, 93 (1998): 139.

nor Parris Glendening in the *Chesapeake Bay Journal,* that in the next twenty-five years Maryland could lose another half-million acres of farm and forest land."[12] Advocates of another by-pass around Washington point to the area's congestion, which has slowed *average* traffic on the D.C. Beltway from 53.6 mph in 1981 to 45.8 mph in 1987. Another artery is needed, say the by-pass promoters, because of a projected 30 percent increase in population. Increased travel needs will accompany population growth as employment continues to soar in the region. To live in the Chesapeake region is increasingly a matter of learning to cope with traffic congestion. Sprawl is built into the zoning codes of most communities and the lending policies of virtually every bank. Few think about sprawl in terms of social, technical, and aesthetic issues. The presence of sprawl indicates that we have lost our ability to think complexly.

Although there have been changes in national transportation policy in recent times, the damage has been done in the Chesapeake. To make the automobile work, the region had to be transformed to suit the needs of the car. Today's Chesapeake landscape of beltways, national roads, defense highways, and recreation arterial systems demonstrates how a region can be made to acquiesce to a solution that may kill it. As Anthony Downs, a transportation expert for the Brookings Institution, has recently put it, "we may be able to learn to live with the added sprawl, congestion, and pollution, the Bay may not."[13] Solutions are available and largely unwelcome because they are inconvenient. They are also as close as a stout pair of walking shoes and a good bicycle.

At century's end Maryland began to take a hard look at suburban sprawl in terms of the allocation of taxpayer resources and residential development. The General Assembly under the leadership of Governor Parris Glendening passed the "Smart Growth and Neighborhood Conservation" initiative. According to Glendening, this program "is premised on a simple but profound principle: that taxpayers' dollars should not be spent on programs that either promote sprawl or damage the environment."[14] Smart

12. Parris N. Glendening, "Sprawl: The more you run from it, the faster it spreads," *Bay Journal,* 6 (January–February, 1997).

13. Quoted in Karl Blankenship, "Gridlock and the Bay: Can we love our cars and the Chesapeake?" *Chesapeake Citizen Report,* May–June, 1990, 5.

14. Parris N. Glendening, *Conserving Neighborhoods—Maryland's Approach to*

Growth encourages development and economic expansion in the Chesapeake but only in locations where it makes the most sense and where the infrastructure is in place or planned to support it. While Smart Growth initiatives multiplied around the nation, there was a special sense of urgency in Maryland. In the first six months of 1998 nearly ten thousand acres of forest and farmlands were lost. Applications for septic system permits for countryside development soared. Expressing his hopes for the future on the eve of the millennium, Governor Glendening said, "what I dream of is a change in the way we think about how we use the land. I am talking about a fundamental, almost cultural change in our approach to land use development."[15]

## An Impaired Estuary

The best way to look at the Chesapeake is to consider that over time the bay has become an "impaired" estuary. Impaired is now a popular word in bay analysis. In the 1970s the Environmental Protection Agency used the term "impaired water" a lot to refer to water that we cannot fully utilize as we want. Some water is unhealthy to drink, some unhealthy to swim in, some too unhealthy even to fish in. We now know, for example, that the Chesapeake drinking water that comes from wells has a high fertilizer or nitrate concentration. On occasion health authorities warn parents not to give tap water to their babies. As developments sprawl across the countryside, septic systems contaminate wells. In the not-too-distant future people will have problems with fecal matter in their drinking water. The day may well come when impaired water will impair people.

Most of our Chesapeake rivers are impaired in one way or another, but there are pleasant surprises given the pressures of growth on the bay country. The Nanticoke River on Maryland's Eastern Shore still has good water quality though it is threatened by potential non-point sources of pollution, and certain creeks and rivers like the Annemessex and Sassafras still can be fished and swum. How long they will remain clean is anyone's guess. Today only the reckless would drink the untreated waters of the Potomac, the James, and the Susquehanna.

---

*Controlling Suburban Sprawl* (Annapolis: Maryland Office of Planning, 1998).
15. Ibid.

Impairment takes many forms. When you fly across the Chesapeake country in a small plane, it is easy to spot the runoff from growth and to see the bright emerald checkerboard lawns of the region's affluent suburbs. The suburbs now use as much fertilizer as farmers do, and the water from lawn sprinkler systems flows bayward to feed plant-killing algae blooms.

The trouble with water is that it generally looks good even when it carries toxins. Once I sailed on an old oyster buy-boat up the Pocomoke River with my wife and a company of friends. It was a crystal clear, sky-blue day, the osprey were circling off the river from the cypress trees, and the sun-dappled forest offered a romantic counterpoint to the dark, slow Pocomoke. I yearned to dive off the boat and swim a few lengths, but I did not have a swim suit. In 1997 that same river was the source of great public alarm. Pfiesteria contamination in the Pocomoke caused dizziness in fishermen, skin sores on watermen, and lesions on turtles and fish.

The Pfiesteria problem was first documented in North Carolina, where scientists noticed that nutrients and organic material in the Neuse River promoted the growth of Pfiesterian-like organisms. Called "the cell from Hell," Pfiesteria induced a bay-wide, media fed panic about the safety of Chesapeake waters. In Maryland waters Pfiesteria piscicida, a normally placid microbe, seemed to be morphing into a single-celled, fish-eating predator and anti-human toxin. Some scientists argued that nutrient runoff like that from chicken manure from large poultry operations caused the Pfiesteria outbreak, news that sent a cold shudder of apprehension throughout the community of six thousand poultry growers on the Delmarva Peninsula. The rogue microbe paralyzed the tourism industry; politicians and voters alike wanted a quick scientific fix to eliminate the problem. Pfiesteria, however, was a tough customer. The microbe that killed thousands of fish in the Pocomoke River was not easily controlled. "The estuary's soup of pollutants might have made it more aggressive," cautioned the *Baltimore Sun*.[16] People cancelled fishing trips. Seafood restaurants and supermarket fish counters were deserted. In a replay of the Kepone hysteria of 1975, the Pfiesteria epidemic caused massive layoffs and losses for Maryland's $400 million-a-year fishing industry. Dr. Sandra Shumway, a scientist from Long Island University who studied the problem, complained that the public had

16. Douglas M. Birch, "Scientists Find No Easy Way to Control Fish-Killing Bacteria," *Baltimore Sun*, August 29, 1997.

been "whipped into a frenzy by the press."[17] To counter press reports, Governor Glendening committed $500,000 in state money to promote the safety of the Maryland fishery. With the arrival of cold weather the fish kills abated. On November 2, Eugene Meyer, a reporter for the *Washington Post*, wrote that "the pfiesteria scare that cast a dark cloud over the local seafood economy has lifted."[18]

In the aftermath of the scare, scientists like Roger Newell at the University of Maryland's Center for Environmental Science at Horn Point, suggested that decimation of the Chesapeake's once abundant oyster population may have removed one of the bay's natural mechanisms for controlling organisms such as Pfiesteria. Oysters remove algae and other microscopic phytoplankton such as Pfiesteria from the water. "They're the equivalent of sewage-treatment plants," said Newell.[19] Increased inflows of nutrients from chicken manure and human waste might be part of the Pfiestieria equation. But the large-scale disappearance of oysters in the bay was the other part.

Ironically the twentieth century ended in the Chesapeake much like the nineteenth had, with people talking and arguing over oysters. Scientists hoped for a day when the oysters would return to the bay to build gigantic "oyster reefs" like those that had tormented early colonial mariners. Some like Roger Newell thought that a new disease-resistant oyster could be imported to return the Chesapeake to the time when oysters filtered the entire bay in three to five days. Others counseled against the introduction of alien species into Chesapeake waters. At least this much was true. Restore the oyster population, argued Roger Newell, "and you will have restored a critical natural buffer against excess nutrients in the bay."[20] The bay's gimmick or silver bullet against disease was the lowly oyster.

17. Frank D. Roylance, "Media, Public Panic, Not Pfiesteria Seen as Damaging Bay," *Baltimore Sun,* September 26, 1997.

18. Eugene L. Meyer, "Calm After Storm Over Pfiesteria," *Washington Post,* November 2, 1997.

19. Frank D. Roylance, "Fish Woes Linked to Oysters' Decline," *Baltimore Sun,* September 27, 1997.

20. Tim Zimmermann, "Filter It with Billions and Billions of Oysters," *U.S. News and World Report,* December 29, 1997.

## Backwards into the Future

The basic problems of the Chesapeake are political in nature, and scientists too often have been prone to act as if politics and ecological research inhabited different spheres in the region. Everyone knows what the bay's ecological problems are—too many people and too much pollution. The Chesapeake is one of the most closely studied estuaries in the world. Public policy for the region, however, has lagged behind with weakly enforced laws, zoning nightmares, and commissions, compacts, and task forces worthy of Macbeth's discourse on sound and fury. In the past whenever conservation measures undertaken by concerned publics and environmentalists led to unpopular management actions, political leaders intervened to either cancel or modify those conservation measures.[21] Bay scientists Christopher D'Elia and James Sanders summed up the problem from the viewpoint of their profession. Many decisions about the bay were made by "an adversarial legal system that discounts scientific evidence," they argued. Most scientists were "generally in low-level advisory capacities" when it came to making decisions and were not in the power loop. Decisions made on the basis of legal technicalities allowed the legal system to get in the way of "knowledge-gathering activities needed to determine the public policy."[22] Too often what looks good as policy in the short run is behavior that is really inconsistent with the long-term best interests of citizens and their society. Scientists are usually much more cautious than politicians and are reluctant to say that they have a "fix" for the bay's problems. They, like Maryland biologist Joseph A. Mihursky, worry that wasting millions on bad programs and bad science "will garner bad press, negative headlines, and ultimately negative Chesapeake legislative votes and loss of public confidence."[23] Unless saving the Chesapeake can be perceived as having a direct social and

21. Victor S. Kennedy and Linda L. Brisk, "Sixteen Decades of Political Management of the Oyster Fishery in Maryland's Chesapeake Bay," *Journal of Environmental Management,* 16 (1983): 153–71.

22. Christopher F. D'Elia and James G. Sanders, "Scientists Don't Make Management Decisions and Why We Wish that Sometimes We Did," *Marine Pollution Bulletin,* 18 (1987): 430, 434.

23. Joseph A. Mihursky, "Overview of Political Science and Management Issues in the Chesapeake Bay Region," undated, Contribution No. 1641, Center for Environmental and Estuarine Studies of the University of Maryland. See also John H.

economic payoff to the citizens of the region, it is doubtful that state legislatures and the federal government will take the issue seriously.

In 1999 the Chesapeake Bay Program, the tri-state conservation consortium, was committed by law to a major reduction in nutrients in Chesapeake waters by the year 2010. If it did not succeed, the U.S. Environmental Protection Agency could legally enforce nutrient cutbacks throughout the watershed. Questions about 2010 were more numerous than answers. In terms of nutrients, how clean was a clean Chesapeake? Could a program that forced detailed plans to be spelled out and implemented to clean up the bay and its tributaries survive lawsuits and a loss of political will?[24]

From 1955 to 1980 about 1.4 million new residents moved into Maryland. During that time we lost unspoiled land in the Chesapeake country at the rate of one acre for each new Chesapeake resident, which is perhaps the greatest waste of all. In one of the few blunt assessments on the future of the Chesapeake by a public official, Royce Hanson, Montgomery County, Maryland's planning chief, wrote: "The character of the Bay, in fifty years . . . may be determined more by what happens to agriculture and flood plains and its tributaries now than by immediate programs aimed at the Bay itself. Current laws are going to do damned little toward remedying the troublesome trends."[25] So long as social groups can get away with exporting their problems elsewhere, whether downstream or to a distant land, there appears to be no reason to make any effort to solve them. The Susquehanna affords an arresting example. Despite a significant body of environmental knowledge on acid mine drainage, it continues to be "a principal contributor to pollution in the Susquehanna River." Even after decades of good intentions, "the river is a net sink for mine water" that eventually makes its way to the Chesapeake. But since it is a low threshold problem, very little is being done about it.[26]

---

Cumberland, "Public Choice and the Improvement of Policy Instruments for Environmental Management," *Ecological Economics,* 2 (1990): 149–62. To understand why environmental problems persist when technical solutions are possible, see Robert Costanza, "Social Traps and Environmental Policy," *BioScience,* 37 (1987): 407–12.

24. Karl Blankenship, "Bay Program Must Clean Chesapeake by 2010—Or Else," *Bay Journal,* 9 (September, 1999).

25. *Baltimore Sun,* June 15, 1980.

26. T. Walski, M. Curry, and K. Klemow, "Is the Susquehanna River a Source or

The current trend toward devolution of power from the federal to state levels does not auger well for the Chesapeake. According to John D. Donahoe of Harvard's Kennedy School of Government, "A state contemplating tough antipollution rules might calculate that not only will its citizens pay the full cost for environmental improvements that will be enjoyed, in part, by others [but they also will be] . . . losing jobs and tax revenues to states with weak environmental laws." In the future in the mid-Atlantic we might well see a "race for the bottom," competitive loosening of environmental laws in order to lure business.[27]

In the fall of 1988 the University of Maryland School of Law at Baltimore sponsored a National Environmental Symposium on the Chesapeake Bay and invited some of the most important legal, environmental, and policy management scholars in Maryland to attend and give papers. The authors were "profoundly pessimistic" about the future of the bay and agreed that very little could be done to reverse generations of environmental damage to the region. While these experts agreed that much more could be done to use existing regulatory authority in the bay states to protect Chesapeake waters, the major problem was that people expected laws and regulations to do too much by themselves. Professor Robert Percival of the University of Maryland law school summed up the matter succinctly when he noted that "competing interests involved in environmental policy issues sometimes seem so difficult to resolve that they appear to be antimonies—intractable conflicts or choices seemingly insoluble in light of existing knowledge."[28] Despite the fact that under the critical area legislation Maryland has effectively rezoned 10 percent of its land surface to improve water quality and preserve wildlife habitat, problems of relentless growth continue to plague the region. Growth was so hydra-headed that writer Tom Horton exhorted the audience "to think of the *whole state* as a critical area."[29] Ulti-

a Sink for Acid Mine Drainage in the Wyoming Valley of Eastern Pennsylvania," *Journal of the Pennsylvania Academy of Science,* 68 (1995): 197.

27. John D. Donahue, *Disunited States* (New York: Basic Books, 1997), 63.

28. Robert Percival, "Protecting Coastal and Estuarine Resources—Confronting the Gulf Between the Promise and the Product of Environmental Regulation," *Maryland Law Review,* 47 (1988): 415.

29. Tom Horton, "Protection of the Chesapeake Bay: Environmentally Legal, Eminently Uninhabitable," *Maryland Law Review,* 47 (1988): 424.

mately the issue of the bay becomes the largest issue of all, the issue of human freedom. The only way that the bay can be protected at all is through the kind of political and legal coercion that may make the region a far less pleasant place in which to live. But dramatic solutions were needed, said Professor Oliver Houck of Tulane Law School. "There is no place here for faint hearts or the ideologues of laizzez-faire," he exclaimed. "This is the place to take a stand."[30]

An invasion of alien species has complemented the human invasion of Chesapeake Bay. According to Dr. Greg Ruiz, a scientist at the Smithsonian Environmental Research Center, more than a hundred alien species have entered the bay in the last two decades. Once introduced, they tend to run rampant. Reports the *Bay Journal*, "They can spread diseases that native species have no immunity to or, without predators, they can rapidly overwhelm an area crowding out the natives." The diseases MSX and dermo, which have devastated oyster populations, are thought to have been accidentally introduced. Most alien species currently find their way to the Chesapeake in the discharged ballast water of ships from foreign ports, in Korea and the Baltic, for example. Some, like the mute swan, came by human invitation and are now overgrazing Chesapeake sea grasses. Some scientists fear it is just a matter of time before the dreaded zebra mussel, which has infested the Great Lakes, reaches the bay. Foreign species like phragmites are already overwhelming and degrading wetlands. Rapa whelks introduced from Japan threaten to overwhelm native whelk populations.

The invasion of alien species into estuaries like the Chesapeake may bring serious economic consequences, and may seriously disturb the ecological balance.[31] For this reason, scientists have been reluctant to introduce the Pacific oyster into the bay. When a species moves out of its natural ecological fabric, it may end up reproducing unchecked. At the root of the matter is the simple fact that neither scientists nor conservationists want to "play God" by introducing alien species into the bay. According to Hannibal Holton of the U.S. Fish and Wildlife Service, "the threat of invasive species

30. Oliver A. Houck, "Ending the War: A Strategy to Save America's Coastal Zone," *Maryland Law Review,* 47 (1988): 405.

31. See Harold A, Mooney and James Drake, eds. *Ecology of Biological Invasions of North America and Hawaii* (New York: Springer-Verlag, 1986), and Beth Baker, "Botcher of the Bay or Economic Boon?" *Bioscience,* 42 (November, 1992).

may be the largest cause of species becoming endangered after habitat loss." Meanwhile invasive aliens seem to be finding their own way to the Chesapeake. The greatest irony of the alien species issue, however, may very well be contained in this simple observation: Americans zealously protect indigenous species as part of pristine nature while they continue to degrade the "natural" areas of the bay country with industrial agriculture, urban pollution, and suburban sprawl.[32]

At century's end the Clean Water Act and a host of federal and state laws controlled the "bad guy polluters," noted Chesapeake Bay Alliance writer Michael McCabe.[33] There was no doubt that the estuary and its tributaries benefited from these laws. But the battle for the Chesapeake was far from over. There was some optimism in the Chesapeake scientific community at Maryland's Center for Estuarine Science that the bay was demonstrating a new resiliency. More sea grass was growing and some fish species had rebounded. The water held more life-giving oxygen. William Goldsborough, chief scientist for the Chesapeake Bay Foundation was skeptical. The bay's healthy appearance "may reflect natural fluctuations rather than human efforts to stem pollution," he said. Most Chesapeake Bay action groups saw the bay in poor health and doubted that it will ever be pristine again. At the dawn of the millennium, hope was the cheap popular currency of public thinking on the bay's future.[34] Pessimists believed though that only some great biological tragedy would ultimately bring people to their senses.

Decisions about environmental problems in the Chesapeake Bay country are inseparable from decisions concerning the kind of society we will have in the future. Human endeavor rarely results in a world we want. One man's utopia is another's dystopia. T. S. Eliot summed up our dilemma well: "Between the idea and the reality, Between the motion and the act, falls the shadow." On autumn nights the shadows fall early in the Chesapeake Bay country. We see the shadows and wonder what is coming to us in the way of

32. Aliens in the form of barnacles, crustaceans, clams, fish, centepods, diatoms, dinoflagellates, flatworms, xanthid crabs and others are now well established and rapidly expanding along the Atlantic coast from Chesapeake Bay to Cape Cod. "Alien Ocean," *Bay Journal*, 7 (November 1997).

33. Michael McCabe, "It's Not Who's Polluting the Bay, But Who's Willing to Clean It Up," *Bay Journal*, 6 (January–February, 1997).

34. Peter Goodman and Todd Shields, "Not-So-Sick Bay," *Washington Post*, October 27, 1997.

change. The bay country is the last major green space of consequence on the Eastern seaboard between Richmond and Boston. It is the last great gift of land and sea that Captain John Smith said was the beneficence of heaven and earth. And if the Chesapeake ceases to exist as a force of nature and becomes a kind of channel or bulkheaded waterway or cesspool fit only for ship traffic and human effluvia, we will know at least how it came to pass. We cannot claim innocence.

# Bibliographical Note

Ironically, as the Chesapeake Bay has declined since the 1970s, the region has entered the realms of scholarship and popular thinking with a rich literature. It is not my intention to describe all of these articles, reports, and books. Rather, I wish to identify those recent available works that have been particularly useful to me in the writing of this book and offer insight on the transformation of the Chesapeake Bay country over time.

## Physiography

Readers interested in the physical structure of the region should consult Charles S. Hunt, *Natural Regions of the United States and Canada* (San Francisco: W. H. Freeman, 1974), James E. Dilisio, *Maryland, A Geography* (Boulder: Westview Press, 1983), and *Maryland Geological Survey Reports*. The Survey maintains a web site at www.mgs.dnr.md.gov. Alice Jane Lippson, ed., *The Chesapeake Bay: An Atlas of Natural Resources* (Baltimore: Johns Hopkins University Press, 1973) offers the historian an important overview of the resources of the Chesapeake during a critical period in the bay's recent past. J. R. Schubel's *The Living Chesapeake* (Baltimore: Johns Hopkins University Press, 1981) and Arthur Sherwood's *Understanding the Chesapeake* (Cambridge, Md.: Tidewater Publishers, 1973) are excellent one-volume introductions to understanding the Chesapeake's natural environment.

## Environmental Change and Bay Affairs

For contemporary problems caused by man's interaction with the Chesapeake Bay environment one should consult Tom's Horton's delightfully informative and passionately written books, *Turning the Tide: Saving the Chesapeake Bay* (Washington, D.C.: Island Press, 1991) and *Bay Country* (Baltimore: Johns Hopkins University Press, 1987). For understanding the institutional environment of legislation concerning the conservation of Chesapeake Bay resources, see the useful study by Steven G. Davison, Jay G. Merwin, Jr., Garrett Power, and Frank R. Shivers Jr., *Chesapeake Waters: Four Centuries of Controversy, Concern and Legislation* (Centreville, Md.: Tidewater Publishers, 1997).

Excellent models for understanding the historical process of environmental change in the Atlantic region are offered by Carolyn Merchant, *Ecological Revolutions, Nature, Gender, and Science in New England* (Chapel Hill: University of North Carolina Press, 1989), William Cronin, *Changes in the Land: Indians, Colonists and the Ecology of New England* (New York: Hill and Wang, 1983), Timothy Silver, *A New Face on the Countryside: Indians, Colonists, and Slaves in the South Atlantic Forests, 1500–1800* (Cambridge: Cambridge University Press, 1990), Mart A. Stewart, *"What Nature Suffers to Groe"* (Athens: University of Georgia Press, 1996) and Jack Temple Kirby, *Poquosin, A Study of Rural Landscape and Society* (Chapel Hill: University of North, Carolina Press, 1995).

## Indians, Slavery, and Disease

Recently Indians of the Atlantic seaboard have received much scholarly attention from anthropologists and historians. Among the most illuminating have been Francis Jennings, *The Invasion of America: Indians, Colonization and the Cant of Conquest* (Chapel Hill: University of North Carolina Press, 1975), Helen C. Rountree and Thomas E. Davidson, *Eastern Shore Indians of Virginia and Maryland* (Charlottesville: University Press of Virginia, 1997), and Peter H. Wood, Gregory Waselkov, and Thomas Hatley, eds., *Powhatan's Mantle: Indians in the Colonial Southeast* (Lincoln: University of Nebraska Press, 1989). An excellent introduction to mid-Atlantic Indian culture can be found in William C. Sturtevant, ed., *Handbook of North American Indians,* Volume 15, *Northeast* (Washington, D.C.: Smithsonian Institution, 1978). Also of value is J. Frederick Fausz, "Profits, Pelts, and Power: English Culture in the Early Chesapeake, 1620–1652," *The Maryland Historian,* 14 (Fall/Winter 1983). The thesis of this essay is that Anglo-Indian relations "Americanized" the environment of the English Chesapeake.

The literature on slavery in the Chesapeake has been stunning in its extent and richly documented. Most, however, do not focus on the impact of racial slavery on the environment. Two studies are now classics in the field and deserve the reader's serious attention: Allan Kulikoff, *Tobacco and Slaves: The Development of Southern Cultures in the Chesapeake, 1680–1800* (Chapel Hill: University of North Carolina Press, 1986), and T. H. Breen, *Tobacco*

*Culture: The Mentality of the Great Tidewater Planters on the Eve of the Revolution* (Princeton: Princeton University Press, 1985).

Research on disease in the Chesapeake currently stresses its impact upon culture. Readers on this subject should consult Alfred Crosby's seminal work, *Ecological Imperialism: The Biological Expansion of Europe* (Cambridge: Cambridge University Press, 1986). Also of value are Darrett B. Rutman and Anita H. Rutman, "Of Agues and Fevers in the Early Chesapeake," *William and Mary Quarterly*, 33 (1976), and Carville Earle, "Environment, Disease, and Mortality in Early Virginia," in Thad W. Tate and David Ammerman, eds. *The Chesapeake in the Seventeenth Century: Essays on Anglo-American Society and Politics* (New York: W. W. Norton & Co., 1979).

## Chesapeake Watershed

Students of the sixty-four-thousand-square-mile Chesapeake watershed should consult these works: Michael Williams, *Americans and Their Forests, A Historical Geography* (Cambridge: Cambridge University Press, 1989), Susan Stranahan, *Susquehanna, River of Dreams* (Baltimore: Johns Hopkins University Press, 1989), Richard L. Stanton, *Potomac Journey: From Fairfax Stone to Tidewater* (Washington, D.C.: Smithsonian Institution Press, 1993), Ann Woodlief, *In River Time: The Way of the James* (Chapel Hill: Algonquin, 1985), John Seelye, *Beautiful Machine: Rivers and the Republican Plan, 1775–1825* (New York: Oxford University Press, 1991), 2020 Panel, *Population Growth and Development in the Chesapeake Bay Watershed to the Year 2020* (Annapolis: Maryland State Government, 1988), Harold K. Kanarek, *The Mid-Atlantic Engineers: A History of the Baltimore District United States Corps of Engineers, 1774–1974* (Washington, D.C.: Government Printing Office, 1978).

## Urban Pollution and Agriculture

A study of the environmental health of Chesapeake cities in the nineteenth and early twentieth centuries is long overdue. Readers looking for background material on the bay in relation to urban pollution should consult, Joel A. Tarr, *The Search for the Ultimate Sink: Urban Pollution in Historical Perspective* (Akron, Ohio: University of Akron Press, 1996). Also much-needed is a general history of agriculture in the Chesapeake. In this latter regard, readers can consult older studies like Lewis C. Gray, *History of Agriculture in the Southern United States to 1860,* 2 vols. (Gloucester, Mass.: Peter Smith, 1958) and Avery O. Craven, *Soil Exhaustion as a Factor in the Agricultural History of Virginia and Maryland, 1606–1860* (Gloucester, Mass.: Peter Smith, 1965). A rich corpus of scholarship exists on agricultural practice in the colonial Chesapeake. Among the more interesting are Paul Clemens, *The Atlantic Economy and Colonial Maryland's Eastern Shore: From Tobacco to Grain* (Ithaca: Cornell University Press, 1980) and Lois Green Carr, Russell Menard, and Lorena S. Walsh, *Robert Cole's World: Agriculture and Society in Early Maryland* (Chapel Hill: University of North Carolina Press, 1991). The best single book on early Chesapeake society, soil, and sea that I have read is Arthur Pierce Middleton's *Tobacco Coast: A Maritime History of Chesapeake Bay* (Newport News: The Mariner's Museum, 1953). See also, E. L. Jones, "Creative Disruptions In American Agriculture, 1620–1820," *Agricultural History,* 48 (1974). A primer on contemporary agricultural problems in the Chesapeake is Samuel N. Stokes, Elizabeth Watson and Shelley Mastran, *Saving America's Countryside: A Guide to Rural Conservation* (Baltimore: Johns Hopkins University Press, 1997). Also of value is Maryland Department of State Planning, *Maryland's Land: A Portrait of Changing Uses, 1973–1985* (Baltimore: Department of State Planning, 1985).

## The Watermen's Culture

Over the centuries Chesapeake Bay has produced a unique culture of men and women who "follow the water" and harvest the resources of the estuary. Their work and culture has been chronicled in several fine books: John R. Wennersten, *The Oyster Wars of Chesapeake Bay* (Centreville, Md.: Tidewater Publishers, 1981), Varley Lang, *Follow the Water* (Winston-Salem, N.C.: John Blair, 1961), Randall S. Peffer, *Watermen* (Baltimore: Johns Hopkins University Press, 1979) and William W. Warner, *Beautiful Swimmers: Watermen, Crabs and the Chesapeake Bay* (Boston: Little Brown & Co., 1976).

Interest in the bay has also spawned an overflow of books dealing with contemporary culture in the tidewater. Of special interest are Richard Harwood, ed., *Talking Tidewater: Writers on the Chesapeake* (Chestertown,

Md.: Literary House Press, 1996), Boyd Gibbons, *Wye Island: The True Story of an American Community's Struggle to Preserve Its Way of Life* (Baltimore: Johns Hopkins University Press, 1977), John R. Wennersten, *Maryland's Eastern Shore: A Journey in Time and Place* (Centreville, Md.: Tidewater Publishers, 1992), and Eugene R. Meyer, *Chesapeake Country* (New York: Abbeville Publishers, 1990).

## Maryland Historical Magazine

The *Maryland Historical Magazine* has many articles that shed light on the environmental history of the Chesapeake Bay country. Among the more noteworthy are: Michael P. McCarthy, "Baltimore's Highway Wars Revisited," 93 (1998); Cynthia Ott, "A Sportsman's Paradise: The Woodmont Rod and Gun Club," 92 (1997); Geoffrey L. Buckley and Betsey Burstein, "When Coal Was King: The Consolidation Coal Company's Maryland Division Photographs," 91 (1996); John R. Wennersten, "Soil Miners Redux: The Chesapeake Environment, 1680–1810," 91 (1996); Bayly Ellen Marks, "Rakes, Nippers, and Tongs: Oystermen in Antebellum St.Mary's County," 90 (1995); John G. Kester, "Charles Polk: Indian Trader of the Potomac, 1703–1753," 90 (1995); Gregory Feldman and M. Stephen Ailstock, "Greenbury Point: The Interplay of History and Ecology," 90 (1995); Todd H. Barnett, "Tobacco, Planters, Tenants, and Slaves: A Portrait of Montgomery County in 1783," 89 (1994); Charles C. Euchner, "The Politics of Urban Expansion: Baltimore and the Sewerage Question, 1859–1905," 86 (1991); William M. Franklin, "The Tidewater End of the Chesapeake and Ohio Canal," 81 (1986); Basil L. Crapster, "Hampton Furnace in Colonial Frederick County," 80 (1985); Bayly Ellen Marks, "Clifton Factory, 1810–1860: An Experiment in Rural Industrialization," 80 (1985); Carl Everstine, "The Potomac River and Maryland's Boundaries," 80 (1985); J. Frederick Fausz, "Present at the Creation: The Chesapeake World that Greeted the Maryland Colonists," 79 (1984); Wayne Clark, "The Origins of the Piscataway and Related Indian Cultures," 75 (1980); John W. McGrain, "Historical Aspects of Lake Roland," 74 (1979); Douglas F. Stickle, "Death and Class in Baltimore: The Yellow Fever Epidemic of 1800," 74 (1979); Harold Kanarek, "The U.S. Army Corps of Engineers and Early Internal Improvements in Maryland," 72 (1977); John W. McGrain, "The Development and Decline of Dorsey's Forge," 72

(1977); George B. Scriven, "The Susquehanna and Tidewater Canal," 71 (1976); Frank W. Porter III, "From Backcountry to County: The Delayed Settlement of Western Maryland," 70 (1975); Lorena S. Walsh and Russell R. Menard, "Death in the Chesapeake: Two Life Tables for Men in Early Colonial Maryland," 69 (1974).

## Science and Legal Affairs

The continuing problems of the bay have prompted many cynics to remark that there have been more scientific studies of the Chesapeake than there are watermen and oysters. Some of the more noteworthy studies of bay ecology are as follows: U.S. Environmental Protection Agency, *Chesapeake Bay Program Technical Studies, A Synthesis* (Washington, D.C.: Government Printing Office, 1982), Chesapeake Research Consortium, *Perspectives on the Chesapeake Bay, 1990* (Gloucester Point, Va.: Virginia Institute of Marine Science, 1990), U.S. Environmental Protection Agency, *Chesapeake Bay: Introduction to an Ecosystem* (Washington, D.C.: Government Printing Office, 1989). Maryland and Virginia need official histories of their state conservation bureaucracies. Currently all that is available to shed light on their historical development are Commissioners of Fisheries of Virginia, *Annual Reports,* Maryland Commissioners of Fisheries, *Annual Reports,* and Maryland Conservation Department, *Annual Reports.* The latter two are excellent sources for the development of bay conservation policy in the 1920s and 1930s. Because the fate of the oyster is inextricably tied up with the fate of the bay, readers should consult Victor S. Kennedy and Linda L. Breisch, *Maryland's Oysters: Research and Management* (College Park: University of Maryland Sea Grant Publication, UM-SG-TS-81-04, 1978) This last study has what the Chesapeake desperately needs—scientific vigor, historical perspective and a wry sense of human possibility. Joseph V. Siry, *Marshes of the Ocean Shore: Development of an Ecological Ethic* (College Station: Texas A&M University Press, 1984) is essential to understanding why an estuary is ecologically and morally necessary. Rachel Carson is perhaps the single most important scientific writer of her time in matters relating to the health and future of our estuaries and oceans. *Silent Spring* (Boston: Houghton Mifflin Co., 1962), *The Edge of the Sea* (New York: New American Library, 1955 ) and *The Sea Around Us* (New York: Oxford University Press, 1950) still constitute important reading. *The Bay Journal,* the official publication of the Alliance for the Chesapeake Bay, has the last several years of its magazine on its web site at www.bayjournal.com. It contains a wealth of articles on the ecological health of the bay. Also, *Marine Notes,* published by the Maryland Sea Grant of the University of Maryland, contains valuable articles on Chesapeake science addressed to both the professional and lay communities of the region. The web site for *Marine Notes* is www.mdsg.umd.edu/ Marine Notes. One of the best of these *Marine Notes* is Jack Greer, "The Trouble with Toxics in the Bay, 14 (November–December, 1996). The web site, www.vims.edu, of the Virginia Institute of Marine Science is a valuable electronic library of bay data. Lastly, American Rivers, a national conservation organization, regularly issues reports and press releases on the condition of Chesapeake tributaries. Its web site is www.amrivers.org. The Chesapeake Regional Information Service, James Madison University, should not be overlooked. Its web site, www.gmu.edu/bios/bay, carries fact sheets on all the major tributaries of the bay. Its material on the James and Elizabeth rivers is particularly informative.

Ultimately all problems of Chesapeake Bay become grist for the lawyer's mill. Fortunately scholars and general readers can benefit from the enormously insightful work of Professor Garrett Power of the University of Maryland School of Law, *The Chesapeake Bay in Legal Perspective* (Washington, D.C.: United States Department of the Interior, 1970). This work touches upon nearly every aspect of Chesapeake law from the colonial period to the present. Its case studies survey everything from water quality to fish and shellfish management. No single article encompasses so much bay conservation law as Garrett Power's, "More About Oysters Than You Wanted to Know," *Maryland Law Review,* 30 (1970). Also for legal approaches to Chesapeake problems see the special issue on "National Environmental Symposium on the Chesapeake Bay," *Maryland Law Review,* 47 (1988).

# Index

Jenkins-Black Award (1877), 126–27
Jesuits, 18, 24
Johns Hopkins University, The, 129, 170, 190, 193, 196
Johnson, Pres. Lyndon B., 184
Jones, E. L., 16
Jones, Gordon, 28
Jones, Rev. Hugh, 4, 11, 45
Jones Falls, 99, 102
Joppa Town, Md., 54

Kanarek, Harold, 145
Kanawha River, 83
Kennedy, John Pendleton, 107
Kent County, Maryland, 123
Kent Island, Md., 24, 31, 157, 189, 205
Kepone, 200–203, 226
Kepone Task Force, Maryland, 203
Kirby, Jack Temple, 168
Krantz, George, 207
Kulikoff, Allan, 42

Lake Otsego, N.Y.
    as wellspring of Chesapeake, xiv, 92
Lake Roland, 147
Lancashire Works, 56
Land, Aubrey, 44, 56
Land Grant Act, Morrill, 63
Lane, Sir Ralph, 19
Lemon, James T., 68
Lettre, Michael, 205
Lewis, Fielding, 77
Lillard, Richard, 50
lime trade, 107
Lindsey, Judge Ben, 165
*Lippincott's Magazine,* 117
Lloyd family, 44
lobbyists, 150, 163
Lock Haven, Pa.
    and Chesapeake timber trade, 94
Locke, John, 63
loggers. *See* timbering
London, England
    and Chesapeake trade, 7
Loudoun County, Va., 85, 107
lumber. *See* timbering
Lynchburg, Va., 87
McCabe, 232

McCay, Bonnie, 138–39
MacCleery, Douglas, 57
McCready, Capt. Robert H., 120
McEvoy, Arthur, 138
McKibben, Bill, 218
MCusker, John, 47
Madison, James, 90
Magothy River, 21
Main, Gloria, 61
Makemie, Francis, 24–25
malaria, 29–30, 102
Maltby, Caleb S., 111
Mancall, Peter, 93
Mann, Gov. William Hodges, 131
Manokin River, 54, 144
Marks, Bayly Ellen, 110, 112
Martin, Calvin, 13
Marx, Leo, xviii–xix
Maryland Board of Health, 104
Maryland Conservation Commission, 152. 156
    and fish hatcheries, 155
    support from oyster tax, 154
*Maryland Gazette,* 100
"Maryland Plan," 168–69
Mason, George, 90
Mason-Dixon Line, 93
Mathias, Sen. Charles McC., 185, 205
Maxwell, Hu, 14–15
Menard, Russell, 41, 43, 47, 66
Mercer, Charles Fenton, 85
Merchant, Carolyn, ix, xvi, 13, 36
Merritt, Donald, 207
Meyer, Eugene, 227
Michener, James A., xv
Middleton, Arthur, 54
Mihursky, Joseph A., 228
Miles River, 7
militias, 13
Miller, Henry M., 59–60
missionaries, 18
Mobius, Karl, 136–37
Moll, Gary, 213
Monocacy River, 107
Montgomery County, Md., 80, 229
Moore, William P., 200
Morris, Ian, ix
Morriss, Margaret, 31–32